Business and Social Reform in the Thirties

Business and Social Reform in the Thirties

ALVIN FINKEL

James Lorimer & Company, Publishers
Toronto 1979

ISBN 0-88862-235-X paper
ISBN 0-88862-236-8 cloth

Design: Don Fernley

6 5 4 3 2 1 79 80 81 82 83 84 85

Canadian Cataloguing in Publication Data

Finkel, Alvin, 1949-
Business and social reform in the Thirties

Bibliography.
Includes index.

ISBN 0-88862-236-8 bd. ISBN 0-88862-235-X pa.

1. Industry and state – Canada. 2. Canada – Economic policy. 3. Canada – Social policy. I. Title.

HD3616.C22F56 322'.3'0971 C79-094232-1

The publisher gratefully acknowledges the financial assistance of the Social Science Federation of Canada.

James Lorimer & Company, Publishers
Egerton Ryerson Memorial Building
35 Britain Street
Toronto M5A 1R7, Ontario

Printed and bound in Canada

CONTENTS

I

INTRODUCTION

It has become commonplace to describe Canada and other western countries as welfare states, in which the state apparatus is said to act as an umpire among competing economic interest groups, regulating and overtaxing the once-mighty capitalists.[1] Who created the welfare state and in whose interests does it operate? The groundwork for the Canadian transition to the welfare state was laid in the 1930s and the country's major business interests either initiated or approved of all the reforms of the decade. Businessmen pressed for reforms not because they wished to remove injustices that existed within the capitalist system but because they recognized that the system could not survive without some structural reforms. Both the tendency of the uninterrupted business cycle to slide towards depression and the tendency of working people and farmers to respond by sliding towards radicalism spurred the businessmen to modify the rules of capitalism.

Popular pressure also demanded changes in the system. But the government programs that were established mainly reflected the business point of view, even when in some cases they also satisfied the demands of other social classes. Despite the vast number of new programs that have been established and the tremendous growth in government spending that has occurred since the 1930s, little redistribution of wealth and power has taken place. Wealth redistribution, the promise of the interventionist state, has been negligible while economic power has become less democratically distributed. The concentration of economic power in Canada is growing and the corporations still exert the dominant influence upon both government and the major political parties.[2]

Unfortunately, it seems that Canadian scholars have too readily accepted that these changes in legislation and the broadening of areas of government responsibility are synonymous with fundamental reform. They have assumed too easily that the postwar period with its proliferation of new government agencies and programs has produced a peaceful revolution in which private ownership of the means of production has been protected but significantly enough modified to place our economic system somewhere between capitalism and socialism. The CCF threat, the influence of academics, the bleeding hearts of Depression and wartime politicians, and the collective national spirit that characterized the war and the postwar reconstruction period are all invoked to explain the expansion of the government's role in the economy.[3]

This kind of interpretation suggests that everyone favoured reform except the business community, the ruling class that had the most to lose from changes aimed at redistributing wealth and power. And it is no doubt true that businessmen did oppose reforms that threatened to undermine their profits and prestige. It is not true, however, that the business community opposed an expansion of the role of the state. In fact, most businessmen wanted reform—the kind of reform that would have the conservative effect of preserving intact both the existing social system and the power and privileges of its economic leaders.

It was during the Depression that the business community was forced to re-evaluate the role of the state. From their pre-Depression experience with government intervention, businessmen already knew that the state could be more than a thorn in the side of entrepreneurs. The state had provided much of the capital that had built the railways; it had erected high tariffs to limit competition for manufacturers; it had protected property and scabs during strikes.[4] But during this time the state had played a minor role as a regulator of either internal competition or the business cycle.

In the Dirty Thirties the economic system that had most benefited businessmen reached its lowest point. Despite the magnificent technological breakthroughs of the 1920s and the heady economic expansion of the 1924-1929 period, the 1930s was a period of stagnation during which people's lives wasted away while machinery sat idle. Profits, which had eaten away most of the surplus value created by the productivity advances in the late 1920s, fell far less than overall incomes in the Depression.[5] But if businessmen were not exactly suffering, many saw the writing on the wall (see Table 1).

During the Depression the business community faced two particularly threatening problems. Over a million unemployed people, mainly young and concentrated in urban areas, constituted something more than the reserve army of labour that textbook economics recommends to force down wages. They were also a potential army of opposition to the existing economic system. The

Table I: Canada's Economy During the Depression

A. BREAKDOWN OF EARNINGS

	1928 or 1929	1932 or 1933
National Income	$4,823 million (1928)	$2,452 million (1933)
Exports	$1,364 million (1928)	$ 498 million (1932)
Construction	$ 475 million (1929)	$ 97 million (1933)
Imports	$1,300 million (1929)	$ 400 million (1933)

From: J. Harvey Perry, *Taxes, Tariffs and Subsidies: A History of Canadian Fiscal Development*, Volume One (Toronto: University of Toronto Press, 1955), p. 253.

B. GROSS NATIONAL PRODUCT, 1929-1939

1929	$6.2 billion	1935	$4.3 billion
1930	$5.5 billion	1936	$4.7 billion
1932	$3.7 billion	1937	$5.3 billion
1933	$3.5 billion	1938	$5.2 billion
1934	$4.0 billion	1939	$5.7 billion

C. CAPITAL INVESTMENT AND INDEX OF EMPLOYMENT

	Capital Investment	Index of Employment (1928 = 100)
1929	$1,391 million	119
1933	$ 157 million	83.4
1935	$ 425 million	99.4
1938	$ 595 million	111.8

B. and C. from: Irving Brecher, *Monetary and Fiscal Thought and Policy in Canada, 1929-1939* (Toronto: University of Toronto Press, 1957), p. 11.

threat of the unemployed was not all that concerned the business leaders. By 1930 a tremendous concentration of capital had occurred in Canadian industry. The big monopoly and oligopoly capitalists had made a large investment in machinery and were concerned that the economic system be adjusted to prevent a cyclical idling of this expensive machinery. Private mechanisms could not solve the dilemma since even big industrialists distrusted their collaborators in private collective decisions about prices, output and wages. Without the enforcement that only state agencies could provide, businessmen found themselves hopelessly caught in a contradiction between their aims of maximizing the profits of their individual firms and of stabilizing the workings of the economy as a whole.

More and more they saw the state as a means of reconciling these ends. Those who saw the state as the means of stabilizing the economy and strengthening the position of the biggest companies recognized dangers inherent in this approach. Expanded state intervention meant greater state expenditures, and there was no absolute guarantee that much of the required state revenue would not come from the businessmen's pockets. There was also no way of knowing what expectations might be raised among the people as a whole once it was admitted that the state should be an active participant in the economy. The state could be almost an arm of the private economic sector. But what would happen if it should fall into the hands of a group dedicated to crushing the private sector? The agencies created to strengthen the business community could be used as weapons to destroy it.

For some businessmen of the old school such considerations were more pressing than the threat of the unemployed and losses from idle machinery. But by the mid-to-late 1930s these businessmen were a minority—though a vocal minority—within the business community, and the concern of businessmen as a whole was how to control, rather than prevent, the process of reform.

Business and Government to 1930

Close ties between business and government did not develop suddenly during the Depression. The relationship dates back to the period before the rebellions of 1837 in Upper Canada (Ontario) and Lower Canada (Quebec). In this period the ruling classes, derisively called the Family Compact in Upper Canada and the Château Clique in Lower Canada, developed with the support and encouragement of Britain's colonial office. British governors, through their control over appointments at all levels of government and over the granting of land, encouraged the development of a political economy in which the small group of people that monopolized the appointed positions in government also dominated merchant activities, banking and land-holding. In Britain's Constitutional Act of 1791 the governors and their appointed councillors were granted executive power. The act provided for each province an elected assembly and an appointed upper house (called the legislative council) with both sharing equal veto power. Popular assent to the policies of the ruling classes was restricted to a small minority in Lower Canada and generally to less than a majority of the population in Upper Canada.[6] Since formal democracy had not yet been established, the merchants spent little time attempting to convince the population that their proposed legislative schemes were in the general interest. Nor did they make much attempt to win elections to the assembly, concentrating instead on either getting themselves appointed or influencing the executive and legislative councils from the outside.

The popular will, expressed in the democratically-elected assembly, was particularly at odds with the ruling class in Lower Canada. As Donald Creighton eloquently demonstrates, the ruling class of Lower Canada sought to turn the province into a commercial empire to act as the major intermediary for Britain's trade with both British North America and the rapidly-expanding American midwest. Capital for such a venture came partly from the exorbitant rents that the merchants who had bought the seigniories charged the habitants. It came also from the profits made by speculating in lands not yet developed for agriculture, which were usually bought by English-speaking immigrants. In both cases business interests relied on their control of the executive council to insure their profits: laws freezing habitant rents that dated back to the French regime were not enforced; undeveloped land, which was controlled by the government, was sold cheaply to large land companies controlled by the merchants. Deprived of capital to buy land and squeezed by the land speculators of the Clique into a small corner of the province, the habitants rebelled.[7] Meanwhile, the land issue headed the grievances that precipitated the equally ill-fated rebellion in Upper Canada. Britain followed the suppression of the rebellions with a forced union of the two colonies.

But if the Quebecois habitants were not happy with the turn of events before 1837 neither were the merchants. Despite the profits that they had made because of their control of the executive, their overall scheme was frustrated by the continual veto of the assembly. This scheme required a transportation infrastructure of canals and roads, and unwilling to marshall and risk the capital required for such an undertaking, the merchants demanded that the transportation facilities be built with public money. The assembly, powerless to control rents and land speculation, could and did refuse to vote for new taxes, thereby denying the merchants access to the public purse for their transportation plan.

After the rebellions the ruling classes, anxious to implement their transportation scheme (which soon expanded to include railroads), approached politics with greater sophistication. They sought election to the Canadian assembly and formed an alliance of convenience with the Roman Catholic Church. The Church delivered a near-bloc vote of Quebec assembly members in favour of the program of state-subsidized railways and canals proposed by the merchants; in return the Church received the merchants' support for increased public aid for the Roman Catholic separate school system, particularly in Protestant Ontario.[8] The merchants had learned even before Confederation to manipulate formal democratic structures to achieve a program of positive government intervention.[9] Significantly, as early as the 1840s Canadian businessmen preferred a positive interventionist state to a laissez-faire capitalism, in which the state played a minor role in economic development. A century later businessmen would support more extensive programs than a transportation infrastructure for industry, building on a long tradition of business support for government intervention on their behalf.

Quebec and Ontario merchants and railway-builders, anxious to develop the West and the Maritimes as markets and as resource colonies of central Canada, were largely responsible for the Confederation project of 1867 and the subsequent National Policy of 1879. The National Policy, established by the Conservative government in 1879 after considerable pressure, provided generous subsidies to railway-builders and gave industry a protective tariff.[10] It enhanced businessmen's tendencies to look to the state to save the capitalist system from difficulties they could not get rid of on their own. This attitude, long established by the 1930s, would lead the businessmen of that period to expand the number of areas for which they sought state intervention in the economy. As early as the period of the National Policy, economic and polical power was concentrated and interlocked extensively, as indicated by the sharing of personnel among the Hudson's Bay Company, the Grand Trunk Railway, the Bank of Montreal and the Canadian government.[11]

The election of the Liberals under Wilfrid Laurier in 1896 removed the CPR, the Bank of Montreal and other large interests from the position of having their board members in direct control of the state. But the new government did not greatly alter the design of Macdonald's policies. The Quebec wing of the government, aware that the Roman Catholic Church was not yet resigned to the breakup of Conservative party rule, was particularly anxious to accommodate the interests of capital. Laurier's chief Quebec lieutenant, Israel Tarte, wrote the Prime Minister in 1897:

> Il faut attacher le plus solidement possible à notre char les influences terrestres, la puissance du capital.... Avec ces deux grands compagnies de chemins de fer [CPR and Grand Trunk] derrière nous, nous pouvons faire face à l'orage clérical.[12]

Tarte's views were shared by the leading westerner in the Laurier Cabinet, Clifford Sifton, who as attorney-general of Manitoba had been "one of the great defenders of Capital in the Manitoba government and a leader in resisting the popular demands of the farmer." Sifton, who had bought the *Manitoba Free Press* from the CPR while Minister of the Interior, played a major role in getting the Laurier cabinet to grant the railway company $2.5 million to build the Crow's Nest Pass line.[13]

Before 1911 the Liberals could count on the solid support of many bankers, manufacturers, department store owners and resource industrialists. Laurier's attempt that year to negotiate a reciprocity agreement with the Americans produced a temporary defection of much of his business support, leaving only exporters and importers—traditional Liberals—behind the party. The costly failure of two new, largely government-sponsored but privately-owned transcontinental railways, the end of new immigration and an economic recession had cast some doubt on the premises of the National Policy.[14] But the forces in favour of that policy were too strong.

The National Policy produced a working class engaged both in manufacturing and extractive industries. Before World War I the state, while conceding some minimal trade union rights, in practice used extensive repression to break organizing drives, particularly by radical unions. Though labour shortages during the war gave unionism a major shot in the arm, the political power of the labour movement within the old parties was negligible. And while independent labour parties enjoyed regional power bases, they had slight national impact. Links between labour and the organized farmers' movement were weak.[15]

The domination of the two major parties by business interests produced a powerful but ephemeral farmers' movement in the postwar period. The disintegration of the National Progressive party from the second largest political bloc in the 1921 federal election to a spent force by 1926 indicated the incoherence of the first major attack on ruling-class hegemony. United at first by a desire to install a new National Policy that would replace the old big-business National Policy with reciprocity and nationalization of utilities, including railways, the farmers proved unable to maintain their organization. Factionalism, Liberal promises and a return to prosperity by the mid-1920s destroyed the farmers' attempt to organize themselves as an economic class with interests different from those of other social classes.[16] When the Depression struck, the two-party system and bourgeois hegemony had been re-established.

Business and Reform in the 1930s

What is of particular interest in the following analysis of the role the business community played in the adoption of economic reforms during the Depression is the ability of business leaders to channel the debate on reform and to minimize the effectiveness of other groups proposing more fundamental changes. At stake ultimately is the question of what conservative political scientists have referred to as consensus politics. Consensus theory argues that the dominant views in society result from the interactions and compromises of many groups. Italian Marxist Antonio Gramsci has more correctly called this phenomenon the operation of hegemony, which refers to the ability of one group to impose its views on society as a whole.[17] One group imposes its views on others by making it appear that its rule benefits everyone and that it is willing to share its power and to redistribute its wealth. While the few benefit, the many are made to believe that they benefit as well; or that if they do not, it is their own fault and not the fault of a political and economic system. They are also led to believe that the system is amenable to piecemeal reforms. When legislative changes occur they are inevitably presented as changes for the good of society as a whole regardless of how blatantly pro-government the changes are. The educational system and the media, according to Gramsci, present the existing social structure as if it were eternal and often convince even the most oppressed people to accept their fate passively. Resistance to the hegemonic ideology exists within the working class particularly. But a combination of repression and apparent concessions—concessions that are meaningless in terms of changing the power structure—deters radicals and convinces many that fundamental change is impossible and perhaps undesirable.

In the Canadian case, one must take note of the willingness of the ruling class to make apparent concessions before the industrial working class and the farmers had lost all faith in the existing economic system. The focus on the business debate during the Depression will also reveal that the groundwork for the process of reform, usually thought to be found in the late war years, had already been laid a decade earlier.

II

BUSINESS AND GOVERNMENT LEADERS IN THE THIRTIES

It is misleading to discuss business and government as two completely separate spheres, even though business rhetoric often makes it appear as if capitalists lack direct political representation. But is this the case in Canada? An examination of the structure of business-government relations in Canada in the 1930s indicates that there was extensive direct involvement of businessmen in government both in elected and appointed positions; that businessmen played a major role in political party fund-raising; and that businessmen had powerful organizations to back their reform proposals. The organizations of farmers and workers were comparatively weak, a fact which significantly reduced their effectiveness in influencing state policy. Businessmen had another advantage to fall back on as well: the extensive interlocking of corporations in the Canadian business community meant that businessmen formed a cohesive social class that could exert considerable influence on the state apparatus.

A study of government personnel will also indicate the validity of the Marxist theory of the role the state plays in capitalist societies and the failure of pluralist and élite theory models to explain the operations of the Canadian state.

Government-Business Relations

An analysis of the governments of the 1930s indicates that at both the federal and provincial levels—in the industrial provinces at least—a majority of the cabinets consisted of businessmen and lawyers (see Appendix).[1] Of twenty-one men who served in the

Bennett cabinet (1930-35) ten members, including four lawyers, had had direct business connections in the past, several with leading national business interests and others with smaller local concerns. The cabinet included five more lawyers, three physicians, one journalist, a civil engineer, a farmer and one labour representative (see Appendix).

Prime Minister R.B. Bennett was the leading businessman of the group. Bennett and Lord Beaverbrook were partners in the financial manoeuvering that brought about many of the company consolidations of the early twentieth century. Bennett acted as Beaverbrook's agent in merging grain elevators and hydroelectric stations in the West, and together they controlled the Alberta Pacific Grain Company, which operated over 400 grain elevators. Many of the firms with which Bennett was involved in his business career were either monopolies or oligopolies. As part of the syndicate that formed the Canada Cement Company, a thirteen-company merger that created a near-monopoly of the cement industry in Canada, Bennett made a substantial profit.[2] In the 1920s he was a large shareholder in Imperial Oil, the company's lawyer and head of the company's Turner Valley department. The Conservative prime minister also held the majority of shares in the E.B. Eddy Newsprint and E.B. Eddy Match Company, a monopoly in the industry. Bennett had also been a director of Imperial Tobacco and Canada Packers, two firms labelled as oligopolistic by the Royal Commission on Price Spreads in 1935. He served for many years as chief western Canadian solicitor of the Canadian Pacific Railway and was a leading shareholder in the Royal Bank, an institution which he served as director after his defeat as prime minister. The complete list of Bennett holdings included large blocks of shares in companies in most sectors of the economy.[3]

The Tory caucus was as unrepresentative of the social structure of Canada as the cabinet. About 90 percent of working Canadians in the 1930s were either wage earners (about 67 percent) or farmers (about 23 percent).[4] Of 116 caucus members (including the cabinet) for whom occupations of any type were listed in the *Canadian Parliamentary Guide*,[5] one was a wage earner, and six were farmers. The professions were well represented in the caucus with eleven doctors, two dentists and a druggist. Lawyers, a group comprising less than .5 percent of the general population, made up 30 percent of the government caucus. Over one-half of the caucus reported business connections. Together businessmen and lawyers accounted for 70 percent of the caucus.

A similar story can be written for the Liberal government elected in 1935. Mackenzie King's cabinet included a number of the country's most powerful corporate presidents and directors. In 1955 *Maclean's* published a list of Canada's leading businessmen, using as a yardstick the total assets each controlled while holding directorships. King's Minister of Finance, Charles Dunning, topped the list at $10.8 million.[6] The greatest proportion of cabinet ministers in the King government were lawyers. Only two positions were held by men outside the business and legal communities—a farmer and a university professor. Labour had no representation in King's cabinet.

Of 173 Liberal caucus members reporting occupations in the 1936 *Canadian Parliamentary Guide*, 111 were either businessmen or lawyers. Only three wage earners and twelve farmers had been elected as Liberals. Though there were proportionately more manufacturers in the Tory government caucus, manufacturers were not unrepresented in the Liberal caucus and lumber companies were especially well represented.

The provincial governments of Ontario and Quebec each had a large component of businessmen and lawyers. About half of George Henry's twelve-man Conservative government in Ontario consisted of businessmen. Premier Henry was president of the Acme Farmers Dairy Company of Toronto and director of Toronto Mortgage Company and North American Life Assurance. In 1935 Premier Taschereau of Quebec held directorships in Sun Life, North American Life, Metropolitan Life, Barclay's Bank, Royal Trust, Caisse d'Economie (a savings bank), three fire and casualty companies (London and Liverpool and Globe, Liverpool-Manitoba and Globe Indemnity), Credit Foncier Franco-Canadien, Canadian Investment Fund and the Seigniory Club.[7]

The revolving door between the private business world and government did not exist only at the elected level. The men appointed to head the new government agencies and royal commissions were more often than not recruited from the business community.

Graham Towers, the first governor of the Bank of Canada, was assistant general manager of the Royal Bank of Canada[8] at the time of his appointment. John I. McFarland, the first chairman of the Canadian Wheat Board, had had a long business association with Bennett and owned 45 of the 113 grain elevators that eventually formed the Alberta Pacific Grain Company. King later replaced the controversial McFarland with J.R. Murray, then vice president of Alberta Pacific Grain Company and former secretary of the Winnipeg Grain Exchange.[9] In 1936 King appointed Arthur Purvis, president of the multimillion-dollar Canadian Industries Ltd, as chairman of the National Employment Commission.[10] Newton Rowell, the first chairman of the Royal Commission on Dominion-Provincial Relations, had served as a corporation lawyer during the twenties and thirties and as general counsel for the Canadian Life Insurance Officers Association, an organization representing 99.8 percent of life insurance policies in force in Canada.[11] At the time of his appointment Rowell was Chief Justice of Ontario. Rowell's successor as chairman was Joseph Sirois, a director of Quebec's Provincial Bank of Canada, Catelli Macaroni Products Corporation Ltd and the Administration and Trust Society in Montreal.[12]

Many other leading businessmen of the 1930s were simply the leading politicians of previous decades. Sir Robert Borden, Conservative prime minister from 1911 to 1920, was president of Crown Life from 1920 to 1937 and director of many corporations. G. Howard Ferguson, Ontario premier from 1923 to 1930 and Canadian High Commissioner in London from 1930 to 1935, succeeded Borden as president of Crown Life.[13] Borden's Finance Minister, Sir Thomas White, was vice-president of the Canadian Bank of Commerce and was appointed by Bennett to the Royal Commission on Banking and Commerce in 1933. White, with Arthur Meighen, was the keynote speaker of the 1938 federal Conservative party convention.[14]

In the hierarchies of the two old party organizations, businessmen played influential roles. The Liberal finance committee for the 1935 federal election, recruited by Vincent Massey and Senator Norman Lambert, comprised Frank O'Connor, E.G. Long and Albert Matthews. All three had been "men of large interests," as King recorded in his diary.[15] The Conservative party's election campaign organizer in 1930 was prominent businessman Major-General (and later Senator) Alexander Duncan McCrae. His fund-raisers included Brigadier-General George Eric McCuaig, Montreal stockbroker and investment dealer. Half a million dollars had been donated by about fifty corporations and individuals in Montreal alone. These donors included Sir Herbert Holt, president of the Royal Bank and the nation's leading capitalist (as measured by assets of companies in which he held directorships), and Lord Atholstan, publisher of the *Montreal Star*. Ward Pitfield, president of the Montreal Conservative party and Bennett confidant, was head of a large brokerage firm and officer of a long string of corporations.[16]

The National Interest

With such influential businessmen so securely in possession of the reins of political power in the 1930s, who was looking after the national interest? British political scientist Ralph Miliband notes that the world view of the businessman-politician precluded his acting in the national interest when it conflicted with business interests:

> It may readily be granted that businessmen who enter the state system, in whatever capacity, may not think of themselves as representatives of business in general or even less of their own industries or firms in particular. But even though the will to think in "national" terms may well be strong, businessmen involved in government and administration are not very likely, all the same, to find much merit in policies which appear to run counter to what they conceive to be the interests of business, much less to make themselves the advocates of such policies, since they are almost inimical to the "national interest." It is much easier for businessmen, where required, to divest themselves of stocks and shares as a kind of rite de passage into government service than to divest themselves of a particular view of the world and of the place of business in it.[17]

Confirmation of the views of Ralph Miliband comes from some of the politicians of the 1930s. Harry Stevens, the bête noire of the Conservative cabinet of 1930-35, remembered his colleague, National Revenue Minister E.B. Ryckman, as a "very typical big interest man" whose "whole approach to public affairs was the approach of a wealthy, big corporation official." To Stevens, Secretary of State C.H. Cahan was "a typical legal friend of the big interests." After resigning from the cabinet, Stevens called Bennett a "champion" of the big interests.[18]

Among the politicians of the 1930s it is Mackenzie King who best corroborates Miliband's thesis. Though fundamentally conservative, King felt that businessmen played too strong a role in government and that many industrialists and corporation lawyers remained friends of the big interests while in office. With C.H. Cahan in mind, King told his diary that "the financial interests are an invisible government, believing in money power and able to control and employing the best brains of the world to that end, while government is left a prey to these very concerns."

That King might feel that Tories could not rise above self or class interest is perhaps understandable. But at times he was no more generous in his assessment of Liberals. Chubby Power was once said to be "in reality, a CPR agent", and Charles Stewart "a CPR man." Charles Dunning, his Finance Minister, was "an agent for Beatty and the CPR," and his "reliance upon the big interests in the last analysis will...see him along his way from now to the end of his days." Taschereau and company were described as a "gang" that was enmeshed with the CPR; Ontario Premier Mitchell Hepburn was "in the hands" of *Globe and Mail* editor George McCullagh, a man "in the hands" of financial mining interests.

King's view of the industrialists he had chosen for his cabinets is best summed up in his observation about one minister's ability to make a public-minded decision about exporting power. King believed the minister held shares in a hydroelectric power company and commented:

> How few men there are however who will move in any of these industrial undertakings without some motive of self-interest or who are prepared to defend public rights in the face of demands by vested interests.[19]

Party Financing

Business donations to party coffers further restricted the ability of politicians to act in the national interest. Both major parties were dependent upon business contributions, and it was generally understood that these contributions carried an implicit demand for a certain thrust in government policies. Business-supported parties were reluctant to even consider adopting policies that would alter the existing distribution of wealth and power.

Often companies gave money in expectation of direct benefits in the form of government contracts. The Beauharnois power scandal is the most famous example from the 1930s of the continued use of political bribery to achieve private profits. Seven hundred and fifty thousand dollars found its way into federal Liberal coffers before the 1930 election after a high-level agreement between party officials and private hydro promoters. Senator Andrew Haydon, chief organizer for the 1930 campaign, acted for the Liberal party. King always insisted that he had known nothing of these arrangements at the time and that the government's decision in 1929 to allow the Beauharnois Power Company to divert waters from the St. Lawrence River was unrelated.[20] There may also have been an involvement of members of the Ontario Conservative provincial government in the Beauharnois scandal. The Ontario Tories went down to defeat in 1934 under the shadow of a hydro-power scandal that involved the premier and Arthur Meighen, chairman of the provincial Hydro Commission.[21]

One study of the financing of the federal Liberals from 1935 to 1945 concludes:

> For there to have been no abuses in this system would have required a major miracle. Clearly there were offices available for sale. Clearly companies were virtually forced to contribute to party coffers out of fear of losing their government contracts. Clearly cabinet ministers were involved in collecting from firms with which their departments did business. And clearly abuses of a serious kind did exist.[22]

Concentration of Business

By the 1930s there was a remarkable concentration of power in Canadian business. Using as its source the *Financial Post's* "Directory of Canadian Directors" and "Survey of Corporate Securities," the League for Social Reconstruction claimed in 1938 that "some hundred and thirty names appear over and over again in the directorates of the two hundred and sixty corporations which dominate practically the whole of large scale industry in Canada." Assets of the leading 67 financial corporations were said to be $7 billion, and the assets of the leading 196 industrial and trading corporations over $6 billion.[23] CCF member of Parliament Angus McInnis, also using *Financial Post* publications as his source, claimed that the 325 leading non-banking corporations accounted for $8.8 billion of the $10.6 billion in assets represented by all of Canada's transportation systems, utilities, mines, construction companies, industries of all kinds, and wholesale and retail stores.[24]

The banks appeared to be the locus of power in the Canadian business community. In an article published in the October 1933 issue of *Canadian Forum*, Professor E.A. Forsey of McGill University indicated that of the ten banks operating in Canada the Bank of Montreal, the Royal Bank and the Canadian Bank of Commerce controlled 70 percent of all banking business. Four of 47 trust companies did 77 percent of the business, while three of 36 loan companies accounted for 82 percent of the money loaned.[25]

In 1934 the Parliamentary Select Committee on Banking and Commerce revealed the extent of interlocking directorships between the banks and the leading financial and industrial corporations in the nation, including subsidiaries of American firms. The three largest trust companies, for example, recruited between 30 and 60 percent of their directors from the board of one of the largest of the three banks: Montreal Trust interlocking with the Royal Bank; Royal Trust with the Bank of Montreal; and Canada Trust with the Canadian Bank of Commerce. Other major interlockings among financial institutions included the Bank of Toronto with Manufacturers Life and the Bank of Nova Scotia with Eastern Trust.[26]

In his article Forsey also claimed that three groups—Holt, Nesbitt-Thomson-Killam, and International Power and Paper—controlled the privately-owned section of the electrical power industry, and the League for Social Reconstruction maintained that these groups owned 80 percent of the industry.[27] Three companies controlled the steel industry; Canada Cement held a virtual monopoly in the cement industry; and International Nickel held a similar position in nickel production. While fifteen companies operated in the pulp and paper industry, seven interlocked with the Canadian subsidiary of International Power and Paper.[28]

The report of the Royal Commission on Price Spreads and Mass Buying indicated that Canada Packers controlled 59 percent of the sales of the meat-packing business and Swift Canadian another 26 percent. Imperial Tobacco bought over 70 percent of all tobacco grown. Four companies controlled 75 percent of all sales of agricultural implements, and three firms accounted for 71 percent of the capital invested and 51 percent of the wages paid in the fertilizer industry.[29] McInnis claimed that Sir Herbert Holt held directorships in 56 companies with combined assets of $4.76 million, but Peter C. Newman maintains that Holt had been president of 27 major business enterprises and a director of about 300 others.[30] His holdings touched almost every type of economic activity in Canada. Holt was followed by Sir Charles Gordon, who was among other things president of both the Bank of Montreal and Dominion Textiles.

From this evidence it is clear that the leading private economic institutions were not separate entities; the degree of interlocking directorships among the comparatively small number of major companies suggests a small and powerful economic élite.[31] That such a small and closely-linked group would share similar views about the government's role in the economy is not unlikely.

There were, however, antagonisms within the élite. Robert Graham, commenting on the rocky relations between Arthur Meighen and the Montreal tycoons, claims that the Montreal financial group believed that the party under both Borden and Meighen was allowed to be influenced too much by the Toronto financial interests, in particular by the Canadian Bank of Commerce and National Trust. The Montreal group felt the government takeover of the Canadian Northern in 1917 was motivated by a desire to save the Canadian Bank of Commerce from disaster.[32] Apart from intercity rivalry, Graham suggests that at a later period intracity rivalry may have hurt Meighen. Speaking of the "ruthless financial warfare of the city," Graham notes (though he admits to having no direct proof) that economic rivals of Meighen's "unofficial representatives" among English-speaking Montreal Conservatives—Lorne Webster and C.C. Ballantyne—may have opposed Meighen because of his association with these men.[33]

An interesting facet of the Canadian corporate community in this period is the degree to which its "Canadianness" is in doubt. Subsidiaries of foreign, and particularly American, companies were very important to the Canadian economy. A memorandum prepared for Bennett in 1932 indicated that "practically one-quarter" of all goods manufactured in Canada and about one-sixth of jobs in manufacturing were provided by American branch plants operating in Canada.[34] American investors owned over 86 percent of the capital employed in American branch plants; Canadians owned less than 12 percent of the capital employed in these plants.[35]

There appears to have been a great deal of integration between the American firms and dominant Canadian firms, particularly between the banks. For example, Colonel R.S. McLaughlin, president of General Motors of Canada Ltd, was a director of such Canadian concerns as the Dominion Bank, the Canadian Pacific Railway, Consolidated Mining and Smelting, Royal Trust and McIntyre-Porcupine Mines, as well as a director of the Canadian subsidiary of General Electric.[36]

Among those economic sectors in which firms accounting for a majority of output were subsidiaries of American firms were non-ferrous metal products, electrical products, oil, rubber and automobiles. These were capital-intensive sectors, which would account for a larger and larger share of total production in the post-Depression period. Although basic steel production was largely in the control of Canadian firms, it would appear that American firms played a larger role than Canadian-owned firms in developing these new capital-intensive sectors. In the more traditional labour-intensive industries established in Canada before the twentieth century (such as textiles and the processing of food products) Canadian firms continued to account for most of the output.[37]

Business Organizations

The business community did not rely either on a majority representation in government caucuses and boards or on social and economic ties with government and party officials to insure that government decisions would be made with the economic élite in mind. Organizations of businessmen in the same industry, as well as supra-industry organizations of various types, had existed before the Depression. Most served the double purpose of providing both a means of industrial cooperation—or, from another point of view, collusion—and an instrument of institutional pressure. Such organizations had multiplied in the postwar period, and even during the Depression new organizations were added.

The leading organization was the Canadian Chamber of Commerce, incorporated in 1929 as the national organization of 200 boards of trade spread throughout the country. Consistently led by businessmen with long lists of directorates, it acted theoretically on behalf of all business interests in its many representations to the federal government. Local boards of trade, particularly those in the larger centres, and provincial and regional boards of trade also made constant representations to federal and provincial governments on matters where several, if not all, industries agreed on the need for or against government action.[38]

The Canadian Manufacturers Association, dating from the 1870s, was the largest organization representing manufacturers in Canada. With 3311 members, it represented 75 to 80 percent of the industrial firms eligible for membership. Each divisional office had various departments (industrial relations, tariffs, transportation, etc.) that studied and proposed legislation on behalf of the membership.[39] Unlike the Canadian Chamber of Commerce and the boards of trade of Montreal and Toronto, during the 1930s the Canadian Manufacturers Association was not run by men who were corporation heads and directors. While its officers were successful manufacturers, they were not usually members of the economic élite of interlocking directorates.[40]

Most manufacturing industries had their own organization as well as membership in the Canadian Manufacturers Association. There were, for example, four organizations in the primary textile industry, despite the dominance of a few firms in all branches of the industry. The Primary Textile Institute, organized in 1934, was a confederation of the three other organizations, all of which continued to operate. The chief work of the general manager of the Canadian Woolen and Knit Goods Manufacturers Association, as reported by the Royal Commission on the Textile Industry, was promoting protective tariff legislation for the industry.[41]

After the Chamber of Commerce and the Canadian Manufacturers Association, the National Construction Council of Canada was the organization with a membership drawn from the largest number of individual firms in Canada. It was in fact a federation of the organizations of construction contractors (Canadian Construction Association), building materials manufacturing firms (a division of the Canadian Manufacturers Association) and lumbermen (Canadian Lumbermen's Association). The Council had very specific ideas about the proper relationship between the construction industry and government.

Very powerful business organizations protected the interests of the country's financial institutions. The Canadian Bankers Association dated back to 1893 and was followed by the Canadian Life Insurance Officers Association. In 1916 two other organizations came into being—the Investment Bankers Association of Canada and the Dominion Mortgage and Investments Association.

Few industries of consequence lacked a trade association. The mining companies were organized federally and provincially. Wholesalers belonged to organizations like the Canadian Importers and Traders Association and the Canadian Fruit and Vegetable Jobbers Association. Independent retailers had the Retail Merchants Association, and their chain-store competitors formed the Canadian Chain Stores Association to combat attempts of the Retail Merchants Association to have legislation introduced to curb the growth of the chain-store movement.

Many boards of trade and trade associations published their own journals and still others essentially had house organs in national business publications. Overall, most industries enjoyed a large measure of communication both among their members and between their members and governments.

Workers' and Farmers' Organizations

The extensive organization of industry contrasted sharply with the weak organization of workers and farmers during the thirties. By the end of the Depression the trade union movement had organized only 10 percent of the non-agricultural work force and was struggling to keep itself alive as more and more paying members became unemployed.[42] The unions had reached their peak in membership and militancy during and immediately after World War I. During the period of virtual full employment that had been created by the war, a state apparatus that was hostile to labour's desire for collective organization had been unable to dam the tide of unionism. But during the 1920s the most anti-capitalist unions had been decisively defeated by a combination of state and employer resistance and by the conservative unions' collaboration with the state and employers. The union movement as a whole, both conservative and radical factions, lost members during the 1920s as employers, backed by the state, made effective use of company unionism, blacklisting and "yellow-dog" contracts (contracts in which an employee "freely" agrees not to join a union as a condition of employment). Such losses were not recouped in the 1930s.[43]

The unions' ability to influence governments dominated by businessmen was restricted by their failure not only to enroll more than a small percentage of Canadian workers but also to achieve any internal cohesion. No labour equivalent of the Canadian Chamber of Commerce existed. The largest national trade union organization was the Trades and Labour Congress, based largely in the skilled craft unions affiliated with American unions. At no point in the 1930s did this central organization have as much as half of the organized labour movement enrolled in its ranks. It suffered large membership losses during the first half of the decade, and only slowly regained its totals of the late 1920s during the second half of the Depression decade. Rivalling this ideologically conservative Congress was the All-Canadian Congress of Labour, which was nationalist and social democratic in its orientation. But with less than half the members of the Trades and Labour Congress, it was unable to incorporate either the confessional unions in Quebec or the more radical national labour centre, the Communist-led Workers Unity League (which disbanded in 1935 and urged its constituent locals to join the Trades and Labour Congress), although the remnants of the syndicalist One Big Union did join the All-Canadian Congress of Labour. The success of the Workers Unity League and the One Big Union was limited by tremendous state repression.[44]

State action ensured not only that few workers would have unions to speak for them but also that the labour unions that did exist were fundamentally conservative. It was not accidental that the attitudes of the majority of trade union leaders were compatible with those of businessmen and state leaders. Consensus was achieved partly by repressing the potential radical leaders and strengthening the hand of the conservatives.[45] The extreme right of the labour movement, for example, included the dubious labour supporters who published the *Labour Leader* in Toronto. The newspaper carried two telling inscriptions to the right and left of its logo: "Canadian labour men should not tolerate the IWW and the One Big Union nor Bolshevism;" and "Canadian Labour men and Canadian employers should cooperate in the interests of Canadian Industry."[46]

The farmers, whose numbers dwindled dramatically from the Depression onwards, were in even worse organizational shape than labour. The Canadian Council of Agriculture, which had spawned the National Progressive party in the 1920s, fell apart in 1932, leaving farmers without a national organization for much of the decade. The three prairie wheat pools were under an effective state trusteeship.[47]

The Role of the State

There are a number of theory models that attempt to explain the role of the state in democratic societies dominated by a capitalist class, as Canada clearly was in the 1930s. In the pluralist model the state acts as a neutral arbiter balancing the interests of various groups within society. Studies done within the pluralist framework, however, admit that in formal democracies all is not equal, especially in the political arena—some interest groups exert more political influence than others.

Anthony Downs has provided a pluralist explanation of why the economic élite generally have more legislative influence than other groups. Applying traditional marketplace theory to political involvement, Downs has observed that only the wealthy and well-organized groups have the time and the ability to gather the data required to influence government policy. Just as unequal power in the marketplace creates a situation where oligopolies subvert the textbook operations of supply and demand, inequalities in access to political data and to the time and money required to use this data create a situation where formal voting equality gives way to élite control.[48]

But it is not enough simply to observe that there are élites within society and to present the economic divisions within society as those between producers and consumers, between rich and poor. Elite theorists ignore the question of the ownership of the means of production: the power that accompanies ownership and the lack of power that accompanies non-ownership, having only one's labour power to sell and suffering the exploitation that accompanies such a social status. Elite theorists regard the struggle between the owners and non-owners of the means of production as one of a variety of conflicts possible in a larger capitalist-democratic consensus.

Marxist theorists differ from the pluralists in asserting that the state in capitalist societies, as in class-divided pre-capitalist societies, is an instrument of class rule. Barry Hindess and Paul Q. Hirst define state power as the "organized set of state apparatuses" that a social class uses to establish and maintain—whether by coercion or persuasion—a certain set of productive relations. Social relations of production are created and maintained not by naturally-operating economic forces but by a political struggle for control of the state apparatus.[49] Marxists do not agree, however, on how the capitalist class maintains its control of state power and to what extent the state as the instrument of the whole bourgeoisie acts autonomously from its constituent elements.

Nicos Poulantzas argues most strongly that the state apparatuses need not be controlled by the same people who control the economy.[50] Because the capitalist state exists to maintain the capitalist mode of production, it functions in the long-term interests of capitalism. Its options for action are structurally limited by the extensive power of the private sector over investment and therefore jobs. It cannot ignore the desires of individual capitalists, but it can act as the agent of the capitalist class as a whole and choose the options that serve the long-term interests of stability for the system to compensate for the options favouring short-term profits for individual capitalists. Until state power is assumed by a social class that seeks to abolish the class rule of the bourgeoisie by socializing the means of production, the capitalist class can continue to exercise its political power through its economic power whether or not it has direct control of the state apparatus. Thus a social-democratic government, whose members are not capitalists but who accept the capitalist mode of production, is forced by the logic of the structure of capitalist relations of production to act largely in the interests of the capitalist class.

While the Poulantzian argument is useful in explaining the inability of both reformists and reactionaries to produce substantial changes in relations of power and distribution of wealth, it tells us little of the evolution of the capitalist state and of the direct political activity of the capitalist class. It is neither logical nor historically valid that the capitalist class depended solely on its economic control to keep the political apparatuses in line. In Canadian history, for example, the economic élite both sought and achieved the position of the political élite. It was because it attained this position that it was able to create the Canadian confederation, to use the state to build an expensive infrastructure for industry, and to achieve a tariff to protect local industries.[51] Several authors have convincingly argued that the Canadian government supported the American takeovers of much of the Canadian economy because of pressures from commercial leaders anxious to cultivate mutually profitable relationships with American capitalists.

Ralph Miliband, observing that a small number of oligopolistic corporations control the economies of advanced capitalism, agrees that such concentrations of economic power also give their owners and managers great political power. But he argues that the economic élite have taken as many command positions in the state system as possible so as to insure that the state will not try to discipline them. Both at the cabinet level and the level of the bureaucracy, members of the business community have successfully captured top positions of power in the state.[52] Miliband, however, underestimates the role of the state when he argues that differences among businessmen are tactical and that the capitalist class presents a "reasonably united front" on "most of the larger issues of economic policy and over other large national issues as well."[53] This implies that the job of the state is easy. In fact, there is much disagreement in the business community about when to inflate the money supply and when to deflate, when to go to war and when to end a war, when to tax and when to spend.[54] The state must take all these disagreements into account. The relative power of the different factions of the ruling class will be important in the final decisions.[55] Of equal importance is the role of class struggle since it is the state, on behalf of the ruling class as a whole, that must mollify or repress the demands of the workers and others outside the ruling group.

In the Canadian case various sectors of the capitalist class were less hesitant than others to move in the direction of reform. On a given reform issue, the banks and manufacturers might be found to be more progressive than the resource companies. Although not united on a program of reform and often presenting one demand at a time, during the 1930s Canadian businessmen as a group became actively involved in lobbying for government-sponsored reforms that would preserve the private-enterprise system and the economic power of the leading corporations. What businessmen wanted generally was a combination of restrictive measures to eliminate competition and positive state intervention to bring some measure of stability to the Canadian economy.

III

COMBINES LEGISLATION

Canadian businessmen in the 1930s were especially concerned with reducing competition among themselves and with stabilizing their particular economic sector. When their own attempts to make the market more predictable and stable had failed, businessmen looked to the state to create regulatory agencies that would protect the interests of their monopolies and oligopolies.[1]

Although monopolies and oligopolies in Canada have developed in most sectors of industry, at least nominally governments have been dedicated to maintaining competition. Defenders of the capitalist system traditionally emphasize that economic competition maintains efficiency and a measure of justice in a system in which private profit is the main dynamic. But even before the turn of the century, the Canadian state did not wish to oppose economc consolidation or to restore the forces of the free market.

Combines Investigations

Combines are formed by collusion between a number of corporations engaged in the same economic activity in order to fix prices, production quotas and quality standards. Instead of acting as separate, competing units, these corporations "combine" to act as one effective economic unit. If these companies control between them a significant portion of the market, their cooperation can create a monopoly in a particular economic activity.

The Combines Investigation Act of 1910, ostensibly introduced to protect public interest against consolidation of business, effectively limited the scope of government action. Minister of Labour Mackenzie King argued that bigness was not the issue behind the legislation and that the act sought instead "to afford the means of conserving to the public some of the benefits which arise from large organizations of capital for the purpose of business and commerce." In the following decade there was only one investigation and no prosecutions, despite over two hundred business consolidations, including the establishment of such monopolies and oligopolies as Canada Cement, Amalgamated Asbestos, Canadian Car and Foundry, Dominion Steel and Steel Company of Canada.

The legislation was revised in 1923 to make the complaint process easier and cheaper and to provide for a permanent official to undertake investigations. But the rate of consolidations tripled in the 1920s. There were only three prosecutions, and two were directed at small businesses. One prosecution dissolved the Proprietary Articles Trade Association, an organization of over 2700 retail druggists, 157 manufacturers of proprietary medicines and toilet articles and 28 wholesale druggists, united to maintain fixed minimum wholesale and retail prices. The claim against this combination was made by George Tamblyn Limited, a drugstore chain owned by Imperial Tobacco, a company involved in a price maintenance policy within the tobacco trade. The court ruling against the Proprietary Articles Trade Association indicates that, while it was legal for a chain to set common prices for all its stores, it was apparently illegal for non-chain companies to combine to set common prices. The Amalgamated Builders Council, an organization established to distribute contracts and set prices in the heating and plumbing industry, was the second organization dissolved by the courts after investigations of the Combines Registrar. In both of these rulings small business emerged as the underdog.

The one corporate conglomerate ordered broken up by the courts involved the common ownership of the largest shipping and wholesale companies in the fruits and vegetables industry of western Canada. The court-ordered restoration of competition was unsuccessful. A combines investigation in 1939 showed that the retail end of the industry had since fallen in part under the control of the still-thriving shipping and wholesale combine. Sales of stock and the setting up of new "dummy" companies had been the result of the prosecution, but the extent of competition in the industry had effectively been reduced.

As the Royal Commission on Price Spreads revealed, horizontal integration of industry was followed by vertical integration. The formation of larger and larger consolidations of companies was often accompanied by a watering down of the stock.[2] Governments were interested more in having competitions legislation on the books to appease the demands of farmers and small businessmen than in preserving competition. The ascent to power in 1930 of a man who had played no small role in the conglomerate movement was not likely to reverse this trend.

Industrial Self-Government

The government's stand on combines and tariffs, while clearly benefiting businessmen, was not sufficient to preserve the power of combines in Canadian industry. In the 1930s businessmen began to pressure the government to establish state agencies that would play a role in pricing, production and marketing practices. What the business community ultimately wanted was self-government—to control the state agencies established to enforce a set of rules businessmen evolved for themselves. The Natural Products Marketing Act of 1934 and the Dominion Trades and Industry Commission Act of 1935, two important components of Bennett's so-called "New Deal" legislation, were in large part the result of business pressure for industrial self-government.

The pulp and paper industry was one of the loudest and most persistent voices calling for state enforcement agencies and self-government. It exceeded all other industries in size, in capital investment and in the value added by manufacturing,[3] and the depression in the industry during the thirties reverberated throughout the economy. Joined by bankers and a rhetorically free-enterprise financial press,[4] the industry demanded throughout the thirties that the federal, Ontario and Quebec governments force members of the industry to honour price and production arrangements.

Annual profits ranging from 15 to 27 percent on capital in the 1920s had drawn new investors to the newsprint industry in the latter part of the decade. The result was overexpansion of capacity and collapse in the price of newsprint. Leading the industry's expansion and subsequent demoralization was Sir Herbert Holt.

Holt had been a key figure in earlier mergers that had produced Dominion Textiles in 1905 and the Steel Company of Canada in 1910. In the late 1920s Holt attempted to merge all the paper companies in Canada outside of the vast American-owned International Paper group. Canada Power and Pulp, Holt's new company, acquired four companies in 1928 and 1929 with assets of about $60 million, as well as first option to buy R.B. Bennett's controlling interest in E.B. Eddy Newsprint. Expecting to acquire the remaining newsprint outfits, the company issued debentures of $160 million, almost three times the value of assets actually held. But the plan fell through when the remaining companies did not sell out and in fact increased their newsprint tonnage and reduced prices. In a buyers' market created by the impact of both this overproduction and the depression in the industry, the price of newsprint fell from $79 per ton, a price established in the late 1920s, to $40 per ton in 1932, a price below the cost of production. Canada Power and Pulp and several other large companies, including Abitibi and Price Brothers, went into bankruptcy. The companies involved attempted to arrive at private collective agreements on price and output, but each firm, expecting its competitors to break the agreement, decided to break it first. Only government interference could stop competition, force cooperation for stable profits and save the day.

Holt, who often spoke about the need to keep government out of business, told a government committee:

> Holt:...The only solution I have is for the governments in the six provinces to get together and agree on a quota for each mill, so that one mill cannot run 100 per cent. As long as the present system exists, people will go out and try to get tonnage at cut rates. If the provinces would establish a quota, controlled by their pulpwood licenses, there would be no inducement to cut rates.
>
> Chubby Power, M.P.: And would it not be difficult for governments to come to an arrangement about quotas when the businessmen themselves have come together time and again and failed to come to any agreement?
>
> Holt: They couldn't agree, because each was for himself

and we *had no police power* [emphasis mine]. That is why we couldn't force them.
Power: If these men had come to some agreement as to the basis of re-organization, would it not have been easy to go to the respective governments and ask for a sanction?
Holt: They could not do it and nobody else would.
Power: Then why ask the government to do it? Why blame the politicians?
Holt: *It was the means by which the government could ask these people to behave. That is all I ask* [emphasis mine].
Power: Would you have compulsory cooperation in the paper business?
Holt: I should.[5]

As a whole the newsprint industry agreed with Holt.

Between October 1933 and spring 1934 all Canadian firms had joined an American price-fixing plan arranged under the terms of the National Recovery Administration (NRA). The NRA had been established by President Roosevelt in 1933 to urge industries to draw up codes for self-government. Pressure from American publishers, however, forced NRA director Hugh Johnson to exclude the Canadians from the price-fixing arrangements after May 1934.[6] With 80 percent of their market to the south, the Canadian firms immediately clamoured for the Canadian government to establish a body similar to the NRA for the newsprint industry. Indeed it was thought by Harold Crabtree, president of Howard Smith Paper Mills and the industry-wide Canadian Pulp and Paper Association, that an agency like NRA might be useful for Canadian industry in general. He told the association's annual general meeting in early 1934:

> ...Our government might do well to consider some such scheme for the stabilization of Canadian industry, which could be brought about by the vesting in industry of certain powers and authority which would enable it through trade associations to control itself in all its main phases, working hours, wages, manufacturing and

> marketing. I would very strongly urge upon the government that the setting up of such a position in the country is for the common good and greatly to be desired.[7]

When the Saint Lawrence Paper Company agreed several months later to sell newsprint to the Scripps-Howard and Hearst American publishing empires at a price below the one privately agreed upon by the companies, the demand for state enforcement of privately-reached agreements attained new heights. L.J. Belnap, president of the large Consolidated Paper Corporation of Montreal, wrote Agriculture Minister Robert Weir that all but a few manufacturers in the industry favoured a government-enforced marketing plan for the industry in order to discipline the "recalcitrant minority."[8] In 1935 the federal government passed legislation to implement such a plan. But the attack on federal jurisdiction over marketing caused the companies to turn to the provinces for aid. Ontario and Quebec cooperated with the industry to create a policing power sufficient to prevent overproduction and underpricing without incurring the wrath of the American buyers. An association of the major companies, with former Liberal Cabinet Minister J.L. Ralston acting as trouble-shooter, was able to win government intervention on several occasions against recalcitrant smaller companies.

Perhaps the most consistent business advocate of government intervention on behalf of the big companies was C.H. Carlisle, president of Canadian Goodyear Rubber Company and the Dominion Bank of Canada, and director of such companies as Montreal Trust, Dominion Bridge and Canada Bread. A few giants dominated the rubber industry and through their trade association maintained informal price and production agreements. But there were always new companies entering the industry and undermining the agreement. In 1934 Carlisle lashed out at Canadian Tire Corporation, a company on the make, accusing the corporation of buying cheap tires at a small percentage over cost and advertising them as first-grade. Carlisle wrote to Meighen:

> My contention is and has been that it is the duty of the Government to immediately enact a law, giving the Government full power to regulate the abuses existing in trade. The law should not specify any industry or any

> conditions but simply give the Government full power of regulation.[9]

Appearing before the Special House Committee on Price Spreads, Carlisle elaborated the views that won him the editorial support of the financial press. Organization and cooperation were better promoters of "the minimum of cost and the maximum of efficiency" in an era when it was possible for a few manufacturers to supply a large market. Price competition meant wage cuts, shoddy products, wasteful expenditures for competitive ends, loss of profits and lack of sufficient accumulation of capital for investments in product improvement. Carlisle suggested that the Combines Act be cancelled and that trade associations representing the majority of employers in an industry be allowed to set fair rules by which all members of the industry must abide. The government would police the agreement.

Like most Canadian businessmen, Carlisle believed the NRA had been subverted by American bureaucrats and insisted that governments must interfere only when business requested state intervention. The British government-business plan was a model for Carlisle. Trade associations in Britain set price, wage and marketing policies, which were enforced by government when trade associations could not coerce a member. The trade associations themselves, rather than an outside body like the American codes authority, decided when a practice violated an industry's agreement.[10] In support of adopting the British plan in Canada, industrialist Arthur Purvis argued that British industry was

> ...encouraged to formulate for itself—a most vital point—plans for rationalization and reorganization with the aid of the truly excellent civil service organization built up over many years with men of the highest calibre, and would then decide where it could support these plans by Government action, thereafter encouraging industry to put them in effect.[11]

The point of such rationalization, as Carlisle admitted, was to limit competition. To restrict the entry of new competitors into well-established industries, Carlisle went so far as to call for government licensing of only a small number of companies in each industry.[12] Organized business echoed the views of Carlisle and Purvis. The Canadian Manufacturers Association, speaking for the medium-sized manufacturers who dominated the organization, petitioned Bennett and Trade and Commerce Minister Stevens to adopt the British plan. Bennett responded positively.[13]

Supermarket chains also supported state compulsion. A half dozen chains controlled over 40 percent of the nation's food retailing by the 1930s, but price wars in Montreal and Toronto led to a desire for government regulation. George Berkstresser, general manager of Great Atlantic and Pacific Tea (operators of A and P), arguing that private companies could not on their own carry out standardization of wages, hours and loss leader practices, stated: "It will be necessary to have the whole matter under government supervision and control." This opinion was shared by the management of Dominion Stores.[14]

Even the securities industry wanted government regulation. Both the 1933 and 1934 conventions of the Investment Bankers Association heard presidential calls for government sanction of an industry-decided code of fair competition. Ward Pitfield, the 1934 president of the Investment Bankers Association and an influential Montreal Conservative, approved the adoption of the American NRA code for the securities industry.[15] By the end of 1934 calls for compulsory cooperation came from the major trade associations and manufacturers of rubber, newsprint, clothing, flour, canned foods, tobacco, paints and varnish, boots and shoes, furniture, plumbing and heating equipment and jewellery.

Arthur Meighen, government leader in the Senate and a prominent business figure, was a leading advocate of state-encouraged industrial cooperation. Meighen believed that left alone businessmen would engage in "unrestrained and mutually destructive competition." To prevent this, Meighen maintained that there must be "governmental supervision of the distribution of leisure and government sanction of a code suited to the character of the present industrial struggle."[16]

Attempts by Combines Act Registrar F.A. McGregor to force government action against combines were greeted coldly by government officials who accepted the argument that more, not less, industrial collusion was needed. Ontario Securities Commissioner

George Drew accused McGregor of "harassing" businessmen and particularly the rubber footwear industry. Unlike McGregor, Drew regarded the industry's price-fixing practices as a measure taken in the public interest.[17] McGregor's report of price-fixing by the Canadian National Millers Association met with a similar response from Harry Stevens. Stevens was pleased to hear association honorary president C.H.G. Short comment before his Price Spreads Commission that "a big stick of some sort" was needed to create even more cooperation in the milling industry and that government was the instrument to provide it.[18]

Stevens' basic accord with the powerful millers seems surprising in a man who became estranged from the Bennett government after taking on the department stores and the meat-packing industry. Indeed Stevens did wish to stop department stores from dictating prices to suppliers and to increase the bargaining power of meat producers. But he was not a supporter of either free competition or extensive government regulation. Unlike Bennett, he supported the interests of small business and believed that if allowed to collaborate small business could be as efficient as conglomerates. Although he opposed the bias of the Combines Act that favoured mergers and discouraged cooperation of competing firms, Stevens was not against all big business. He had high praise not only for the millers but also for the tobacco industry. The tobacco industry was dominated by its largest constituent company even more than the meat-packing industry, but unlike the meat-packing industry the tobacco industry had taken the initiative to bargain collectively with its producers.[19]

The demand for the Price Spreads Commission began with a private request from the Canadian Manufacturers Association. Many manufacturers complained to Stevens that mass buyers, particularly department and chain stores, forced them to sell their products at unreasonably low prices. Only state enforcement of wholesale prices determined by the trade organizations could reverse this trend.[20] The Retail Merchants Association, representing the non-chain retailers, joined with some manufacturers to form the National Fair Trade Federation. They called upon government to prohibit discriminatory practices by chains and to insure that all retailers paid the same price for manufactured goods.

Federation President Warren Cook, who was also chairman of the Canadian Garment Manufacturers Association, argued that the low prices received by the garment manufacturers from the chains were responsible for the low-wage pattern of the industry, which had fueled many strikes in this labour-intensive sector. Stevens' sympathy with the small manufacturers and retailers made him an enemy of the department store chains, who defended their price-dictation policies as free enterprise in action.[21]

Bennett's confrontation with Stevens was not over the fundamental issue of free enterprise, versus state regulation; neither man believed in laissez faire. The two men could not agree whether to weigh regulation in favour of big business or small business. Stevens resigned from the cabinet. In October 1934 Stevens also resigned as chairman of the Royal Commission on Price Spreads and Mass Buying. Stevens had been criticized for circulating a pamphlet accusing Sir Joseph Flavelle of a dishonest business practice. Several cabinet ministers demanded that he publicly apologize to Flavelle; Stevens chose to resign instead. Bitter after his resignation, Stevens wrote to Bennett that countless citizens suffered while "others whom you champion in such eloquent terms have been reaping rewards far beyond that which any citizen may reasonably expect to win."[22]

Bennett's New Deal

In a series of radio speeches Bennett introduced his New Deal proposals.[23] He maintained that the era of individualism must give way to an era of cooperation and government regulation. In his broadcasts Bennett stated that "reforms mean government intervention...control and regulation. It means the end of laissez faire." Government, he went on,

> ...will have a new function to perform in the economic system. It will be a permanent guide and regulator with the right and power of correction, with the duty and responsibility of maintaining hereafter in our whole industrial and capitalist system a better and more equitable distribution of benefits.[24]

A significant cross-section of Canadian business received Bennett's views enthusiastically. His later speeches to the major boards of trade, explaining the kind of plan and policies he had in mind, won him the support of powerful, top-ranking members of the business establishment: A.O. Dawson, president of the Canadian Chamber of Commerce and of Canadian Cottons; H.B. Henwood, president of the Bank of Toronto; C.H. Carlisle, president of Goodyear Tire and later president of the Dominion Bank of Canada; Colonel H. Cockshutt, president of Cockshutt Plow; Thomas Bradshaw, president of North American Life; J.D. Johnson, president of Canada Cement; Ward Pitfield, president of Ward Pitfield Investments; W.W. Butler, president of Canadian Car and Foundry; J.W. McConnell, president of St. Lawrence Sugar Refinery and the *Montreal Star*; C.J. Ballantyne, president of Sherwin-Williams Paints; James McGroady, chairman of George Weston Bread; A.C. Fraser, secretary of the National Dairy Council; and Arthur Purvis, president of CIL.[25]

There was also fairly widespread newspaper support for the announced New Deal. The *Montreal Star*, the Toronto *Evening Telegram* and the *Mail and Empire* were especially enthusiastic. Most important was the support of newspaper-chain owner F.N. Southam, president of Southam Publications. Senator C.J. Ballantyne wrote Bennett:

> I was much pleased with a visit that I had with Mr. F.N. Southam last night at his house...Mr. Southam told me that he was so taken with your first radio talk that he had the telephone put in his room and that he called by long distance his newspaper managers at Vancouver, Calgary, Winnipeg, Hamilton and Ottawa, telling them all to back your new reform policies and he showed me editorials from the *Winnipeg Tribune* and *Vancouver Province* which were most favourable.[26]

Within the Conservative Party the reaction was largely favourable. A provincial caucus of Ontario Conservative MPPs and former MPPs unanimously endorsed Bennett's program. Provincial Conservative leader and businessman George Henry announced that the remedial legislation had been endorsed in a majority of riding association meetings throughout the province.[27]

Bennett's New Deal proposals did not escape criticism. The *Montreal Gazette*, a longtime Conservative party supporter, claimed that Bennett had "shocked and startled" the people of Canada with his new plan, particularly those with strong conservative leanings. Some businessmen were never reconciled to the Bennett reforms even after the conservative intent of the New Deal speeches was made plain. Sir Joseph Flavelle, chairman of the board of the Canadian Bank of Commerce and a diehard Conservative, expressed the hope that King would win the election. Flavelle, who had been a reformist businessman before World War I, had assumed a marked anti-statist position in the postwar period. Unlike the businessmen who had decided during the Depression to reassess their attitudes towards government involvement in the economy, Flavelle's position remained largely unchanged.[28] C.H. Cahan was one of those conservative Canadians "shocked and startled" by Bennett's proposals. Cahan even criticized the legislation that he was required to present to Parliament to put the New Deal in effect.[29]

Minimum wages, maximum hours of work and a weekly vacation were some of the promises of the New Deal. Because of business criticism of NRA, the question of labour conditions was separated legislatively from industrial rationalization, through clearly Bennett supported the view of businessmen that better wages and working conditions would result from industrial cooperation. The rhetorical radicalism of the New Deal speeches (largely the work of Bennett's brother-in-law and Canadian Minister in Washington W.D. Herridge) was necessary to convince Canadians that competition was not simply giving way to government-sanctioned monopoly.

To insure cooperation and government regulation, a Dominion Trade and Industry Commission was to be established. But rather than establish a new agency, Bennett chose to turn the responsibilities of the commission over to the Dominion Tariff Board. The commission had the power to stop business practices that constituted unfair competition or unethical behaviour towards consumers. It could approve and supervise agreements that regulated prices and production in an industry where it felt competition had proved "wasteful and demoralizing." Approved agreements would be immune from prosecution under the Combines Act, whose administration, as the Canadian Manufacturers Association had requested, was removed from the Department of Labour and placed in the hands of the Tariff Board-Industry Commission. As Mackenzie King observed, the Tariff Board was too closely involved with the business community in its tariff work to be an impartial judge of alleged illegal combination.

The regulatory provisions of the act fell short of the recommendations of the Price Spreads Commission. A Commission majority wanted the new trade commission to be an agency with broad powers of regulation to protect workers and consumers. Instead it became an organization to regulate the aspects of business behaviour that the more established interests wanted regulated: price and production agreements, commodity standards labelling and the issuing of new securities. A business practice was regarded as unfair only if "intent of destroying competition or eliminating competition" could be proved.

Stevens, now an independent, was outraged since intent would be difficult to prove; the Bennett government, a defender of big business, was only interested in window dressing. The Liberals derided Bennett for the tepid legislation that followed the thunder of the radio speeches. W.W. Kennedy, Stevens' replacement as chairman of the Price Spreads Commission and a loyal Tory, wrote Bennett of his agreement with Stevens' conclusions. Kennedy said proposed Criminal Code amendments covering false advertising, discrimination in trade and evasion of minimum wage laws were "practically useless":

> All members of the Commission and I believe all members of the House are agreed that certain 'unfair' practices uncovered by the evidence are against the public interest and should be prohibited. Such practices are not static but vary from time to time.
>
> To attempt to deal with them under a rigid enactment, such as that proposed in the amendment to the Criminal Code, would be largely ineffectual and in any event, making 'the intent of destroying a competitor' the only basis

> of prohibition would only touch the fringe of the matter.
> To be effective the power to determine what is an 'unfair' trade practice must be elastic.[30]

Bennett answered Kennedy by pointing out the constitutional difficulties that blocked this kind of action. But his Commons speeches made it clear that he believed business must set its own house in order and the government's role was to make information and assistance available. Bennett ignored many Commission recommendations. A defender of the blacklists,[31] Bennett opposed Criminal Code amendments to prevent anti-union practices. A defender of big companies, he opposed a call to stop firms from engaging in activities not directly related to those for which they had been incorporated. A livestock board and fisheries board giving government substantial direct control over these industries was another recommendation that Bennett ignored.

The attitude of the Bennett government towards such monopolistic devices as the patent and the international cartel further indicates that his government opposed Stevens' idea of using government to halt the trend of industrial concentration. Stevens later recalled that Bennett, Cahan, Matthews, Ryckman and others with business connections opposed not only government controls over companies that had entered into international cartel arrangements but even investigations of these cartels.[32] Stevens and others publicly attacked Bennett for allowing some industries (like the electrical equipment industry) to hide behind patents to keep new companies from entering their fields.[33]

Bennett did not hesitate to defend big business. As he explained in a campaign speech in the 1935 election: "We have passed from an era where scarcity was the problem to an era where abundance has made distribution the most vital and pressing of all our economic problems."[34] The big companies could insure supply, and if the state developed better mechanisms for its distribution, equilibrium could be restored. Bennett was effectively carrying out a minimal regulation of corporations—rather than the more extensive control envisioned by Stevens—to prevent public antagonism from forcing a breakup of the big companies. Similarly, A.O. Dawson, president of the Canadian Chamber of Commerce, expressed the belief that industry would be in less public disfavour if governments passed legislation to prevent individual companies from following unacceptable practices.[35]

The Dominion Trade and Industry Commission, hamstrung by the restrictions Bennett placed upon it, undertook few investigations to corroborate or disprove charges by small firms that big competitors, suppliers and retailers were guilty of unethical activities. The commission's standard line was that the complaining companies should be more specific in alleging illegal activities by other firms. But if such information were available to the small firm lodging the complaint, presumably it would have gone directly to the courts. The commission reported at the end of 1942 that it had never required the courts to stop companies from engaging in illegal activity.

The Dominion Trade and Industry Commission's power to approve price-fixing agreements was removed by the ruling of the Judicial Committee of the Privy Council in 1937. A semblance of a combines act was restored by the Liberals in 1938 despite Canadian Chamber of Commerce and Conservative opposition. Stronger competitions legislation, introduced a year earlier, was defeated in the Senate and opposed by King, who showed little interest in the subject.[36]

At least twice in the 1930s the Combines Registrar reported combines in industries in which leading politicians had been involved. In 1933 he accused the Rubber Footwear Manufacturers Association of price-fixing. The report was not published; the Conservative Minister of National Revenue was E.B. Ryckman, immediate past president of Dunlop Rubber. In 1937 an unpublished report alleged price-fixing in the flour milling industry; Liberal Finance Minister Charles Dunning was immediate past president of Maple Leaf Milling.

Small business, in the form of fruit basket manufacturers in Ontario and electrical contractors in Toronto, accounted for two of four Combines Act convictions in the Depression. The prosecution of a British anthracite coal monopoly achieved indifferent results, and the conviction of four paperboard shipping container manufacturers in 1939 ended price-fixing in a small area of the vast pulp and paper manufacturing industry. Meanwhile, the courts ruled that neither Famous Players Corporation, controlling 90 percent of the film distribution industry, nor the price-fixing Imperial Tobacco Company constituted combines. They dictated terms to their clients, but they conspired with no one and therefore acted completely within the law.[37]

The competitive industries such as clothing and furniture, largely competed by exploiting labour. Larger, non-competitive companies earned greater surpluses but paid better wages. It is not surprising that organized labour gave little support to small business in its anti-monopoly campaign. State ownership of the large corporations—to insure that technological progress and economies of scale could be utilized without a further growth in private power—was the alternative presented by the CCF and even more clearly by the Communist party. It was not widely accepted.

Big business was victorious in its fight to create an economy dominated by monopolistic corporations for two related reasons: the state was dominated by the personnel and ideology of monopoly capital; and no unifying ideology opposed monopoly capital. The small businessmen who were anti-monopoly favoured a thrust in the direction of more private ownership (more firms per industry). Anti-monopoly forces within the labour movement supported public ownership. The two viewpoints had little in common except a common enemy and no serious anti-monopoly coalition was possible. Neither group had much influence with government or sufficient economic power to press its demands. Organized labour was particularly weak and divided; state intervention had played no small role in creating both characteristics. The left wing was similarly ineffectual; it was either ignored or repressed by the state. Small business, feeling betrayed by the Bennett legislation, supported the ephemeral third-party movement of H.H. Stevens in the federal election of 1935. But Stevens' Reconstruction party, while winning votes from the disaffected petit-bourgeoisie, was unable to prevent other alternate-party movements from also soaking up the votes of disenchanted electors from other social sectors. By shedding its pretence of competition and stressing the virtue of state-supervised cooperation, monopoly capital assured both its continued domination of the state and its begrudging support by a populace that felt that the most serious injustices of capitalism would now be regulated by the state.

IV

NATURAL PRODUCTS MARKETING BOARDS

The agricultural marketing board is one of the most obvious areas where the state has directly intervened in the country's economy. By the 1930s there was a considerable concentration of economic power in agriculture-related industries, and the price instability brought on by the Depression forced processors and distributors to pressure the Canadian government to institute measures to protect their monopolistic interests. The business community's call for state-controlled marketing boards to regulate all facets of the agricultural industry—from production to final sale—was in effect an attempt to restrict competition in the industry.

Farm Marketing in 1930

State intervention in the peacetime marketing of natural products was limited in Canada before the Depression. In the late 1920s British Columbia passed legislation giving the dairy and produce industries the right to form cartels. If 75 percent of the growers or dairy farmers in an area voted to establish a marketing practice (for example, a fixed price or a production quota) the decision was legally binding on all producers. In the early 1930s this legislation was ruled unconstitutional. It invaded the federal jurisdiction over interprovincial and international trade; and deducting the cost of operating the marketing board from the sale price of the commodity constituted an indirect tax, which meant that federal authority was required.[1]

Although marketing boards were rare before 1930, the state had been involved in the grading and inspection of agricultural products for well over a decade. Meats and canned foods for both export and interprovincial trade had been inspected by federally-appointed personnel since 1907. Livestock and livestock products had been compulsorily graded since 1917 and dairy products and pickled fish since 1920.

The Depression brought chaos to the marketing of agricultural products and revealed the producers' powerlessness in dealing with monopolistic middlemen and processors. Canadian Canners, the leader in the fruits and vegetables canning industry, controlled about 70 percent of industry assets and sales and set all prices for the industry. Fruit and vegetable wholesaling was in the grip of various regional monopolies, and the courts had unsuccessfully ordered the breakup of the western combine in the business. Canada Packers, controlling 59 percent of the meat-packing business, and Burns and Swift, controlling most of the rest, could among themselves determine prices paid to livestock producers.[2] Tobacco processing was almost entirely in the hands of two companies. The largest, Imperial Tobacco, bought over 70 percent of the annual tobacco crop. The dairy industry in the thirties was controlled by national and international corporations that acted as regional or local monopolies in the production of butter and commercial milk.[3] Following World War II it would be even more narrowly controlled. After the collapse of the grain pools in 1930, the storing and selling of grain was in the hands of a few large firms, and the milling industry, which constituted a combine in the opinion of the Combines Registrar, owned most of the bakeries in Canada. The farm machinery and fertilizer industries were also highly concentrated.

As sales of agricultural products dropped precipitously in the face of economic depression at home and record high tariffs abroad, the processing and distributing companies tried to cover their losses by sharply reducing prices paid to producers. Meat-packers, canneries, dairies and tobacco companies continued to earn profits throughout the Depression. Farmers, on the other hand, were often faced with bankruptcy because of their drastically decreased earnings.[4]

Pressures for a Marketing Act

Not surprisingly, many producers' organizations began to petition the government to establish agencies that would force distributors and processors to pay higher prices to the growers. But the agribusiness corporations had themselves become advocates of state intervention. The corporations were partly motivated simply by the recognition that state intervention was inevitable. For them the issue was what form the intervention would take. As John Burns, general manager of Burns and Company, saw it, the day was past "when we will be left alone to run our own business." In a letter to a Canada Packers executive Burns argued that, since producers and the public in general wanted state regulation,

> . . . is it not the part of wisdom for us to recognize this fact and work with the different governments in bringing about the new regulations and thus have something to say as to these regulations made entirely by others, imposing hardships on business which are sometimes harmful and costly and which do not accomplish what they are designed to accomplish?[5]

It was disingenuous of Burns to make it appear that business was merely bowing before community demands and sitting down with government to write rules for its own regulation. In fact processors and distributors, often led by Burns, demanded government intervention. In 1934, faced with the prospect of a butter surplus that might depress prices for some time and unable to get industry executives to agree on an export price, Burns wrote to Agriculture Minister Robert Weir:

> . . . If the industry will not deal with its surplus voluntarily, we would strongly petition you to immediately commandeer and remove from the market twenty per cent of the butter stocks held in Canada at this time.

Burns' position on this question seconded a previous resolution for federal action by Quebec and Ontario distributors meeting with Weir one month earlier.[6]

The processors and distributors wanted government to achieve two things: to pacify producers and consumers, and to provide the rationalization or stabilization within industry that industrialists as a whole wanted. The regulation of an industry whose primary producers were independent farmers rather than hired employees created special problems. No regulation was possible without the farmers' consent and participation. The crucial issue for agribusiness was finding a way to establish state-regulated agencies without giving farmers control over the prices and profits of distributors and processors. The culmination of business efforts was the Natural Products Marketing Act of 1934, a federal act that was passed concurrently by all nine provinces. Though the act was declared unconstitutional in 1937, it set the pattern for future marketing legislation at both provincial and federal levels. An industry-by-industry analysis will indicate the goals of various forms of agribusiness and the pressures put upon government to help achieve these goals.

Faced with the problem of overproduction caused by Depression conditions, wholesalers and canners of fruits and vegetables were convinced of the need for government regulation. Overproduction threatened the economic power of the leading companies in this industry because it drove growers to try to circumvent regular channels in order to sell as much of their crop as possible. Growers had seen the value of their produce shrink to a fraction of its former value. Though most growers believed total production must be cut, in the short run each grower was tempted to cut his losses by overproducing and selling surpluses at cut-rate prices to small wholesalers or directly to retailers.[7] The wholesalers, banded together in the Canadian Fruit and Vegetable Jobbers Association, encouraged growers to set up voluntary cooperatives. The cooperatives would be guaranteed a stable price for produce in return for production restrictions and an agreement to deal with the association's members only. When the voluntary system failed the association favoured government compulsion to force all growers and jobbers to operate within cooperatives. Using the forum of the Canadian Chamber of Commerce annual convention in October 1933, jobbers' association president J.S. Roger urged the government to enact legislation similar to the British Marketing Act.[8]

When the Natural Products Marketing Act and the Fruit Grading Act were passed in 1934, the outgoing jobbers' association president wrote that it was "the duty of every fruit distributor in Canada to give both these acts at least 100 per cent support."[9]

The canners had also attempted to encourage voluntary collective agreements with growers both to restrict production and to insure that produce was properly graded. Little was achieved and the canning industry, which had looked favourably on the National Recovery Administration in the United States, were optimistic about the new marketing act.[10]

The tobacco industry, like the fruit and vegetable industry, had attempted to achieve stability through grower-buyer cooperation before the marketing act was declared. And, because the number of tobacco growers was small, some success had been achieved without state involvement. But the industry leaders felt that only government involvement could insure stability. Imperial Tobacco president Gray Miller told the Price Spreads Committee:

> Now we have advised them against over-production; quite irrespective of what you gentlemen may think, our opinion is that is the crying trouble, particularly when there has been *no governmental agency* [emphasis mine] to help us try to do that. This year the Ontario government...has stepped into the situation and without that we would not have got a twenty-five per cent reduction on this year's crop.

Miller proceeded to outline a cartel-like plan for controlling tobacco production in Canada under the natural products marketing legislation. The federal Department of Agriculture would determine the annual crop, license each grower and fix his portion of the crop. It would also license all wholesalers, dealers, packers, leaf-handlers and processors. The aim of Imperial Tobacco and the four medium-sized firms, who together accounted for 92 to 95 percent of all distribution and processing, was to lock out all other competition. As Archibald Leitch, the country's largest tobacco grower, testified before the Royal Commission on Price Spreads, the growers had applied for supervision under the new marketing act of the previously voluntary agreements at the request of the manufacturers. Walter Stewart, president of Macdonald Tobacco, the number two firm in the industry, had told Leitch that the big five companies wanted regulation to ensure that smaller companies could not take advantage of the pricing agreements to buy surpluses and thereby undersell the established companies. Without regulation Macdonald Tobacco was not willing to participate in a collective agreement.[11]

The dairy industry had for some time before the 1930s been an exponent of more extensive government regulations, claiming that they would benefit the producers and the public as well as the dairy industry. A state-regulated agency would maintain public health standards and eliminate the fear of purchasing contaminated milk. The dairies and their trade associations, as well as newspaper journalists, argued throughout the 1920s and 1930s that pasteurization, already practised by the large dairies, should be made compulsory. The desire to eliminate as competitors the smaller dairies that did not pasteurize milk was also an industry aim. Fearful of having the outlets for their products further restricted, dairy farmers successfully delayed the passage of pro-pasteurization legislation in most provinces until the late 1930s. The position of the industry was summed up in the *Canadian Dairy and Ice Cream Journal*: a compulsory pasteurization bylaw

> would result in cleaning out the unresponsible producer-peddlers and the fly-by-night, pricecutting distributors, while at the same time protecting all legitimate producers, distributors and dealers.[12]

The dairy industry in the Depression faced the same problem as most industries—overproduction. With the purchasing power of Canadians drastically reduced and foreign markets largely closed, overproduction by the farmers was inevitable. The farmers, scrambling to undersell one another and to relieve themselves of huge surpluses, threatened to undermine the stability, if not the dominance, of the big companies. The companies in turn looked to government to restore stability. Borden's, an American-owned food empire and the leading corporate distributor of fluid milk in Canada, devised a plan for complete government regulation of the industry from the point of production to the point of final sale.

Like the tobacco scheme, all facets of the industry would be licensed. Each producer would be restricted to selling to one distributor, and contracts signed by the companies and the producers would insure that milk would be bought only from the contracted producers. Prices would be established for both fluid and industrial milk (milk sold for the manufacture of butter and ice cream). Similar views were expressed by the president of Silverwood's.[13]

In 1934 the Ontario provincial government of Premier George Henry (the founder and past president of Acme Farmers' Dairy of Toronto) passed legislation that accorded with the Borden's plan. Under the Ontario Control Act a provincial board was to be established with equal representation of producers and the industry and a government-appointed chairman; its task would be to regulate the sale of milk by licenses, quotas and price-fixing. The legislation was well received by both the dairy industry and industry as a whole. The Ontario division of the Canadian Manufacturers Association commented that the act was "plainly state control, but in consultation with members interested, the view was expressed that the present disturbed situation required control of this character."[14]

Quebec approved similar legislation in 1934. By 1939 almost every province had enacted legislation to control prices received by producers and to check retail price-cutting. In all these provinces the licensing and bonding of distributors restricted entry into the business. These laws all had the scope of the Borden's plan and in every case resulted from both industry and producer pressure.

To be more fully effective the Borden's scheme required federal coordination of the provincial plans. A huge butter surplus in 1934 convinced industry leaders that federal involvement was needed. A high federal tariff in 1930 had saved the Canadian market for Canadian butter, and the industry was well-disposed to look at the R.B. Bennett government as friendly to its cause. A government agency that would buy up surpluses as well as regulate imports appeared to be the best course of action. This was the view of J.A. Caulder, president of the Dairy Corporation of Canada; his view was shared by the creameries and butter distributors of Ontario and Quebec as a whole and by western creamery executives like John Burns.[15]

The meat-packers, who were later to oppose the specific marketing plans proposed by producers in their industry, had joined producers, stockyard officials and livestock commissioners to pressure the provincial and federal governments for a marketing board. A resolution passed unanimously at an Alberta conference attended by all the packers called for a "national marketing board or boards, vested with wide powers, chief among its functions to be the stabilizing of prices of livestock and livestock products on a basis that will provide adequate return to the producer." Conferences in Manitoba and Saskatchewan passed similar resolutions.[16]

Calls for government marketing programs from the industries most directly associated with the farmers were supported by boards of trade. The Regina Board of Trade had as early as 1931 decided federal action was necessary. According to the Board, thousands of eggs and laying hens had been destroyed early that year because of surpluses. Surpluses in butter and hogs further threatened farm receipts. The Board called for the immediate convening of a federal conference "of producers and the trade to evolve some national policy for marketing exportable surpluses in such manner as to prevent the demoralization of our domestic market."[17] The Associated Boards of Trade of the Fraser Valley, influenced by the Fraser Valley dairy and fruits industry, in 1933 called for a "Farm Products Marketing Act." "Experience in farm products," said the organization, had indicated that orderly marketing was only possible with "complete producer control of the product" and that this could not be achieved through voluntary means. The Vancouver Board of Trade passed a similar resolution. The Winnipeg Board of Trade's agricultural bureau had recommended taking the same position, but the Board was not able to reach a consensus on the issue.[18]

Outside of the agricultural industry, the major pressure for the Natural Products Marketing Act came from the lumbermen of British Columbia. The Canadian lumber industry, like the Canadian newsprint industry, depended largely on the American market and was therefore materially affected by the National Recovery Administration code for the U.S. lumber industry. The Canadian industry welcomed the code, believing that its provisions for production controls and minimum prices would stabilize the industry continentally. It called upon the directors of the Canadian Lumbermen's Association to take all actions necessary to implement the American Lumber Code in Canada, including requesting the Canadian government to take action.

The Marketing Act

The Natural Products Marketing Act of 1934 was in part the result of significant business pressures. When Minister of Agriculture Robert Weir presented the bill to the House of Commons he observed that boards of trade and other business organizations had joined producers' organizations in expressing appreciation for the bill. By the time Weir was finished amending the bill, industry groups reacted even more positively towards the program.

The legislation allowed a majority of producers of a primary product to establish rules for orderly marketing under government supervision. These rules would be put into effect through marketing boards established for the various primary products, and in turn a Dominion Marketing Board was to be set up to approve and regulate the work of the various marketing boards. Marketing would continue through existing channels and no board would participate directly in marketing. Through their boards producers would be able to determine minimum prices, quotas, quality grades and other regulations deemed necessary.

According to Weir the aim of the legislation was less to control the profits of the trade than to guarantee the "organized trade...that they would receive a certain quality of goods in a uniform volume." The resulting stability would allow the trade to have a "uniform quantity" at its disposal and to guarantee set returns to producers.[19]

Mackenzie King, whose government would slow down the process of creating marketing boards before World War II, correctly identified "the principles underlying the provision of this measure " as those of

> ...restricting trade and restricting production and of creating monopolies with regard to commodities that are to be produced and bought and sold and stored and exported from different parts of the country; and of creating monopolies of producers in particular occupa-

> tions, special groups controlling production and sale of different classes of products and commodities.[20]

This was what many businessmen and producers wanted. Sanford Evans, president of the Canadian Chamber of Commerce and a Winnipeg statistician, was one member of the business establishment who opposed this form of state intervention. When the Natural Products Marketing Act was first read in the Commons, Evans sent a questionnaire, blatantly biased against the legislation, to member boards of the Chamber of Commerce. Though many boards simply ignored Evans' questionnaire, the Montreal Board of Trade's legislative committee replied. Asked by Evans if it favoured empowering marketing boards "to regulate the time and place of marketing any registered product and to determine the manner of distribution of such product...", the committee replied, "yes, provided the majority in the industry concerned concur." Would the Board favour conferring on marketing boards the power "to regulate inter-provincial, import and export trade?" The answer again was "yes, provided the majority of the industry concerned agrees." Did the Board favour allowing a majority of producers in any group the right to compel the minority to surrender their produce for distribution and sale by a central board and provincial board under a compulsory marketing scheme?" The committee's one-word answer was "yes". The Toronto Board of Trade maintained a similar stance.[21]

The business community was not unanimous in its support of the new marketing legislation. Simpson's president C.L. Burton, representing the attitude of his industry, opposed experimenting with state-encouraged cartels. It was not that Burton was a free-enterprising opponent of state involvement; he had in fact encouraged governments not to slow national development by cutting expenditures on infrastructures during the Depression. In 1935 he was the most open exponent of a huge expansion of the Bennett work-relief camps. But Burton and the large retailers, importers and exporters in general opposed moves towards national economic self-sufficiency and higher, stabilized prices,[22] claiming that what lay behind their opposition was a concern for the effect these actions would have on the consumer. However, the Price Spreads Commission's revelations about the low wage and high profit pattern of department store operations casts some doubt on Burton's altruistic motives.

Burton's apprehensions about the new legislation had little effect in the business community. *Canadian Business*, the organ of the Canadian Chamber of Commerce, argued that commodity prices would be raised by the act and purchasing power and business activity could be stimulated. Export trade would not be hindered by higher prices. The one fear that the Chamber's journal did express was that producers might wish to use marketing boards to try to "avenge themselves" of alleged injustices by the trade.[23]

The degree to which vengeance might be possible was somewhat reduced by amendments to the original bill, which generally followed the changes suggested by the boards of trade of Montreal and Toronto and the Canadian Chamber of Commerce. The amended act specified clearly that neither the Dominion Marketing Board nor the boards it approved for regulating natural products could engage directly in the marketing of a product. Boards were also to be made legally responsible for compensating individuals hurt by its rulings. As the Toronto Board of Trade appraised the amendments, it was "gratifying" that "features of the NPMA approved by this Board remain while those features to which objection was taken have been modified."[24]

After an initial period of supervision by Deputy Minister of Agriculture J.H. Barton, the Dominion Marketing Board was placed under the direction of Archibald Leitch. As the second largest tobacco plantation owner on the entire continent,[25] Leitch was an atypical producer.

The schemes approved by the board were not exclusively farm marketing boards. One of the early schemes approved was the British Columbia red cedar shingles marketing scheme, in which 80 per cent of the Canadian shingle mills were integrated into the American National Recovery Administration to the point of enforcing an American-set quota for the Canadian exporters. The dry salt herring and dry salt salmon scheme was supported by "a representative number of persons engaged in the production of dry salt herring and dry salt salmon" in British Columbia. Representatives from the four fish-packing plants that had successfully petitioned the government for a marketing board would fill all but one of the board's positions. A chairman from outside the industry would be appointed by the Department of Fisheries. The national jam scheme was regulated by a board dominated by manufacturers. Nine manufacturers sat with three growers, a consumer representative appointed by the government and a businessman-chairman from outside the industry.[26]

While the original request for a board came from industry in only four of the twenty-three schemes established, the Dominion Marketing Board and the government approved agricultural products marketing schemes only when they had the support of the industries involved, as well as the growers. The dry beans marketing board was established only after "a representative number of persons engaged in the production and marketing of dry beans produced in the counties of Kent, Elgin, Huron, Middlesex, Lambton, Norfolk and Essex in the province of Ontario [had] petitioned under the NPMA." In many cases the processor had formal representation on the producers' boards, sometimes on the marketing board itself, as in the Ontario tobacco scheme, or in a parallel advisory board, as in the British Columbia tree fruit scheme. Within a year of the passage of the act, provincial marketing boards had been established for British Columbia tree fruits, herring, salmon, halibut, dairy products and red cedar shingles; Ontario tobacco, cheese, beans and potatoes; Quebec lumber; Maritime potatoes and salt fish. National marketing schemes for the dairy and jam industries were also established.

The most ambitious program for rationalization of an industry was presented by the National Dairy Council, an organization of dairy industrialists and producers whose board was dominated by industry representatives. The council's program, very similar to Borden's scheme, covered all dairy products. Though the plan won the support of the Canadian Dairy Farmers Federation, it met with a great deal of producer opposition. The producers were not at all well-disposed to a plan that fixed prices and quotas on fluid and industrial milk. A dairy products equalization scheme, to which the government contributed one million dollars, was the best the industry could achieve nationally in the face of producer opposition. To relieve the butter surplus money from the fund would be used as incentives to producers selling milk to cheese factories rather than to creameries. Even after the Natural Products Marketing Act was passed, the dairy industry achieved a high level of concentration through the actions of provincial governments.

Industries that resisted producers' marketing board plans were able to convince the government and the Dominion Marketing Board to reject the producers' plans. In 1933 the meat-packing industry, one of the industries most heavily attacked by the Price Spreads Commission, supported a call for state intervention in marketing. The livestock pools in the three prairie provinces were more radical than producers' groups in most other industries. Originally they set forth a scheme that would have removed the packers from marketing altogether, making the marketing board a selling agency for both livestock and processed meat rather than simply a regulatory agency. Leitch informed them that this was impossible within the scope of the act. But the revised scheme still included many provisions that threatened the packers. Direct sales from farmer to packer would be prohibited. Although it could have no say in the sale of meat, the central selling agency of the original plan would be retained for the sale of livestock.The central selling agency was clearly meant as a device to reduce the packers' control over price. Appearing before Leitch, the packers recited arguments about the evils of interference in the marketplace and denied the existence of price collusion in the industry. This opposition to state intervention was inconsistent with their previous stands on the issue. John Burns had earlier advocated "commandeering" butter surpluses and instituting a government-regulated marketing scheme for the dairy industry. While favouring a state-supported stabilization plan, the meat-packers were not willing to abide by a scheme that limited the powers of the trade. The Dominion Marketing Board and the Department of Agriculture's Deputy Minister were inclined to agree that the livestock pools had not presented a plan that would allow for proper cooperation between producers and packers. As Harry Stevens saw it, the leading civil servants in the Department of Agriculture were too sympathetic to the views of the packers. And the Dominion Marketing Board, unlike the Price Spreads Commission chaired by Stevens, was quite deferential to the packers.[27]

Various producer pools did not particularly want to cooperate with private industry. R.H. Milliken, counsel for the Saskatchewan Co-op Wheat Producers Limited and Saskatchewan Pool Elevators, wrote Bennett of the disappointment "of the producers' marketing associations of the Dominion" that the marketing act was "purely a regulating act and does not attempt to make possible the creation of boards which may do the actual buying and selling."[28] It was no doubt an exaggeration to say that the producers of Canada were on the whole disposed to the elimination of middlemen and the humbling of the processors. The marketing legislation would not have allowed such a turn of events. The livestock industry remained without a marketing board.

Impact of Marketing Boards

Although the Natural Products Marketing Act was not an unqualified success, there was considerable disappointment when the Privy Council ruled the act invalid in 1937. The National Dairy Council had resolved in advance of the court decision to ask the King government to establish special marketing legislation for the dairy industry. After seeing the impact of the act, Mackenzie King, who had originally opposed it on principle, hoped it would not be disallowed because he feared that chaos would result.[29] Despite the concern of the federal government, the provinces took the initiative and began picking up the pieces of the marketing legislation. Federal grading regulations disallowed under the act were quickly put back in place through provincial laws. The dairy industry control plans were provincially instituted. The Privy Council had certainly set back the cause of marketing boards, but the support for the legislation demonstrated by both industry and producers could not fail to keep the issue of marketing boards alive.

Although since the 1930s industrialists have called state interference with the free-enterprise marketing system a sin against higher economic laws, it was the businessmen themselves who pressured government to set up these boards, and it was their perseverence and their influence over government that determined much of the character of the marketing boards. To insure that they had sufficient control over the marketing boards, businessmen had very early on made it clear to government what they considered the proper function of these regulatory agencies. The boards were meant to stabilize prices to the farmer, not to redistribute the share of profits between farmers on the one hand and distributors, processors and retailers on the other. Because their conception of marketing boards insured a fixed price for farmers, businessmen were able to secure the support of the producers. The farmers would not have any say in the marketing of the final product, but they could assure themselves of a better return for their produce if they supported the processors' and distributors' demands for higher, fixed prices.

In *The Control of Competition in Canada*, Lloyd Reynolds confirms the reason behind the producers' compliance with the demands of industrialists. He also confirms the early fears of Mackenzie King for the overall impact of marketing boards:

> ...there is a tendency to fix not only the price paid to farmers but the price charged to consumers. Processors and distributors argue that they can guarantee a fixed price to the farmer only if their own returns are guaranteed and for this reason are usually able to secure farmer support for their proposals. There is thus a marked tendency towards complete cartelization of the food industries, with prices fixed at every stage from the grower to the consumer.[30]

By the time the attempt to stabilize the food industry with government aid had met with success, there had already been a significant integration within the industry. Governments had hesitated to prosecute combines and had rejected the idea that businesses in related fields should not be run by the same corporate group. Ironically, a combination of state action and inaction that corresponded closely to industry's demands helped advance a semi-monopolistic pattern within the food industry in Canada and other industries dealing with natural products. Business pressures were particularly insistent for reforms that would stabilize the marketing practices of Canada's leading export.

V

THE CANADIAN WHEAT BOARD

The Canadian Wheat Board was established in 1935 by politicians of one party ideologically opposed to a state-regulated board and was maintained by another political party opposed to it even more strongly on a theoretical level. The businessmen who joined the farmers in encouraging the politicians were also ideologically opposed to a wheat board. While most leaders of the grain trade, like the politicians, were worried that central marketing might lead to further government involvement in the trade, they were more afraid that without a central marketing agency the wheat trade would be doomed to instability. Ideology gave way to pragmatism. The board made its debut against a background of a drought that considerably reduced wheat production and a depression that greatly devalued the harvested crops.

Canada had had experience with government marketing of wheat in the emergency conditions of the Great War. In 1917 a government-controlled wheat marketing agency replaced the system of open market trading on the Winnipeg Grain Exchange. The Board of Grain Supervisors fixed the prices for wheat and was the sole marketing agency for the 1917 and 1918 crops. Until 1919 all grain futures trading was suspended. A fixed-price system had obvious benefits for the wheat grower, and at the end of the war the Canadian Council of Agriculture and the United Grain Growers opposed the reopening of the private wheat market. They called on the Canadian government to imitate the United States by establishing an agency to market wheat and to guarantee farmers a floor price. The Canadian Wheat Board was appointed to market the 1919 crop and what remained of the 1918 crop, but business pressure forced its dissolution in 1920. Though the Canadian Council of Agriculture and the United Grain Growers continued to press for the re-establishment of a board, most of the farmers' energies in the 1920s were directed towards the building of cooperative wheat pools that would act as alternatives to the private selling agencies. The pools would ensure that the farmer received most of the final sale price for his wheat; he would not be forced to sell cheaply to speculative futures traders. Between 1926 and 1930 about 52 percent of all prairie wheat was marketed by Canadian Co-operative Wheat Producers Limited, the central selling agency for the three prairie wheat pools.

The Government's Halfway Measures

With the Depression came the collapse of the voluntary pools, whose optimistic overpayments for wheat deliveries in 1929 and 1930 left the three provincial pools with a combined debt of $25 million. When the pools went into voluntary receivership, their members again pressured the government to establish a state-operated compulsory pool. The three prairie governments responded in 1931 by setting up compulsory wheat boards. Since these boards restricted international trade—an area of federal responsibility—they were ruled *ultra vires* by the Privy Council. Although farmers had already made their demands for a wheat board clear in their provincial campaigns for compulsory pooling, the federal government did not immediately move to replace the provincial boards with a federal wheat board. It was only when the trade itself offered no alternative that Prime Minister R.B. Bennett acted.

The two men most responsible for establishing the grain board in 1935 were R.B. Bennett and John I. McFarland, both leading lights in the private grain trade in Canada for many years. Bennett had acted as Lord Beaverbrook's agent in the merger that created the Alberta Pacific Grain Company, which by the mid-1920s operated over 300 grain elevators. McFarland owned 45 of the 113 elevators in the original merger and held the controlling interest in Alberta Pacific until 1926. Neither man was much impressed by the campaign for a government board. In June 1933, only two years before the board was set up, Bennett wrote Sidney Smith, president of Reliance Grain and a leading Manitoba Conservative, that "I am anxiously looking forward to the time when we will have no further responsibility in connection with the grain business."[2] In 1931 McFarland had rejected the suggestion of Agriculture Minister Robert Weir that a compulsory board be established, claiming that as a monopoly selling agency it would lack the flexibility of the private competitive system.[3] In November 1933 he was still advising Bennett that a wheat board was valueless unless it could carry out the improbable task of reaching an understanding with the international import firms that handled the wheat crop of the United States, Australia and Argentina.[4]

McFarland's entry into the government service as the dollar-a-year czar of Canadian grain marketing was the first step towards compulsory pooling. The bankruptcy of the pools was cause for alarm not only for the grain farmers but also for the commercial banks that had made large loans to the pools in the 1920s. In August 1930 the bankers had loaned $4 million to Canadian Co-operative Wheat Producers and the three provincial pools only after the prairie governments had given written guarantees for unconditional repayment if the pools defaulted. Further advances of $561,000 were made in November 1930. But the marketing agency's inability to sell its wheat for more than a fraction of the price it had paid the producers was soon abundantly clear. Fearful for their own loans, as well as the effects that forcing the provincial governments to give further guarantees might have on provincial credit, the bankers turned to the federal government. The Canadian Bankers Association and the three premiers all sent urgent telegrams to Acting Prime Minister Sir George Perley noting the necessity of federal aid to the pools. The federal government agreed to guarantee the banks for losses up to $5 million in the financing of the 1930 crop. In November McFarland was appointed general manager of Canadian Co-Operative Wheat Producers because of his acceptability to the pools, the premiers and the banks.[5] One condition McFarland stipulated was that he serve without a salary.

The government's action to save the wheat pools by preventing an even further decline in wheat prices, as Bennett justified in a letter to Canadian Bankers Association president Beaudry Leman, was necessary to protect not only the interests of the pools and other grain companies but also "the entire farming and business interests of Canada." He added that "representations have been made to the Government to this effect not only by the interests directly concerned but other important Canadian enterprises."[6]

Because of persistent producer claims that the system of marketing wheat through futures-trading worked to destabilize the earnings of farmers, Bennett set up a three-man Royal Grain Commission in April 1931 to determine whether the sale of grain futures was detrimental to the producer. Its chairman was Sir Josiah Stamp, chief executive officer of the London, Midland and Scottish Railway. The Winnipeg Grain Exchange named an industry representative, and the three prairie premiers jointly named an agriculture representative. The elevator companies argued before the commission that they could not take possession and pay for large quantities of wheat from farmers unless they had already sold wheat futures to cover their costs and allow them a profit. Millers and exporters said that since they had to sign contracts for delivery of their products well before wheat had been received, they had to hedge against the possibility that wheat price increases would make their contracts unprofitable. Only the purchase of futures made this hedging arrangement possible. Both groups were convinced that the speculators who bought and sold futures were a necessary component of the grain-selling trade. Only the farmers resented the futures speculators. Competing with each other to sell all of their wheat, farmers often sold cheaply to futures traders to avoid being stuck with unsold wheat. Only a government agency that fixed prices and quotas for wheat could prevent the farmers from competing against each other to the speculator's advantage.

Not surprisingly, the businessmen-dominated commission accepted the arguments of the trade and rejected the call of the pools to replace the speculators with a government monopoly agency for buying and selling farmers' wheat. Continuation of futures-trading was recommended, although it was suggested that a supervisor of futures trading should be appointed by the government to guard against deliberate attempts by speculators to demoralize grain markets. A supervisor was never appointed.[7]

The determination of both government and the private grain industry to leave the marketing system unchanged was complicated by a series of events that began in 1931. The fundamental problem was the near-disappearance of the speculators as grain prices tumbled. With private buyers and sellers unwilling to take hedges, the federal government—in the person of McFarland—moved in to fill the vacuum. Despite McFarland's reluctance to interfere with the private market, he revealed in his correspondence with Bennett that there seemed to be no alternative if the government remained committed to preventing the total destruction of the grain industry.[8] In 1931 and 1932 McFarland restricted Canadian Co-Operative Wheat Producers' operations to selling the carryover from the 1929 and 1930 crops and the new crops delivered to the pools' elevators. The pool selling agency operated like any other grain elevator company, selling hedges through the regular trade channels to cover deliveries at the best available price. McFarland fired the co-operative's overseas representatives and announced the end of the company's policy of trying to circumvent the grain exchanges by selling direct to millers and other large importers. He wanted to dispel the impression overseas, as well as at home, that the pool sought a producers' monopoly that would be detrimental to consumers.[9]

In July 1932 the price of wheat dropped to 38.5 cents per bushel on the Chicago Grain Exchange (a drop of 25 cents per bushel in two days and barely more than a quarter of the price that had prevailed in the late 1920s). Selling orders flooded the Winnipeg market and a nine-cent drop in the price of a bushel of wheat occurred in one day. Hoping to stave off disaster for farmers with wheat that had to be delivered, McFarland purchased almost twenty million bushels of wheat, for which no futures had been sold at prices higher than the going market price. He hoped that world prices for wheat would soon rise and surpluses held by the Canadian Co-operative Wheat Producers would be profitably sold.[10] He continued to oppose a policy of holding back large quantities of wheat in order to force up world prices.

Such a policy was supported by one of Canada's leading industrialists, Frederick Morrow. Morrow was, among many things, vice-president of a grain elevator company with elevators at Sarnia and Toronto and total capacity of five million bushels. In September 1932 he suggested to McFarland that the government should follow the example of the U.S. Farm Board. A government-regulated agency, the Farm Board was storing part of the cotton crop until prices rose. McFarland regarded this policy as self-defeating in the grain industry because Canada's competitors would supply the grain that Canada was withholding. The international agreement among grain-exporting countries to stabilize (limit) production and to establish a floor price had become a major objective of the government's wheat policy.

As the price of wheat continued to rise slowly, McFarland requested and received the support of the Winnipeg Grain Exchange in August 1933 for a floor of just over seventy cents per bushel on October futures. The speculators were largely unwilling to buy futures at this new minimum price, and McFarland was forced to buy heavily to make up the temporary desertion of the hedge-purchasers.[11] From this point it was clear that the government, if it wanted to stabilize wheat prices, would have to continue for some time to purchase large quantities of wheat. Bennett urged the Monetary and Economic Conference in London to consider the wheat problem, and a conference of leading wheat exporting and importing nations, which included eighteen European countries, Canada, the United States, Argentina and Australia, was arranged. The agreement on prices and production that was signed in London in 1933 gave the Canadian government and many industry spokesmen hope that prices might stabilize. Quotas were established as well as a minimum price of 63.02 cents per bushel.

Most leading grain merchants backed the policy of a government-supported grain market. James Richardson, president of Winnipeg-based James Richardson and Sons, congratulated Bennett on his policies, saying that he had long pressed for government involvement to insure that wheat production would not be abandoned in Canada. Reliance Grain president Sidney Smith and Alberta Pacific Grain vice-president James Murray expressed similar sentiments.[12] There were other grain merchants who were quite willing to see the number of people engaged in wheat production drastically reduced. Searle Grain, while supporting

McFarland's policies, was upset with the London agreements. As H.G.L. Strange, director of the reseach department for the company, wrote Saskatchewan Provincial Treasurer Murdo McPherson, price-fixing was the real goal of the international agreement and its effect would be to encourage farmers on marginal and submarginal land to continue producing wheat. A better idea, suggested Strange, would be to pass legislation to force enclosures of the poorer wheat lands for ranches, to

> ...declare such areas ranch land and withdraw them from all farming operations, plough up the roads, tear down the fences, destroy the buildings, offer long leases to ranching corporations, move the farmers, if they desire, to Northern areas or allow them to go on relief.

Strange added that, if the government simply did nothing and allowed market forces to operate, the result would be similar to the dictatorial program that he encouraged.[13]

Neither the grain trade nor the business community as a whole shared Strange's drastic views. Many leading businessmen believed that Canada was having difficulties combating the depression in the grain industry because there were too few rather than too many farmers. The "back-to-the-land" movement had considerable sympathy in the business community.[14]

The bankers, whose main concern continued to be the credit of the pools and the Prairie provinces, were even more supportive of the government's intervention to boost grain prices than the grain merchants. S.H. Logan, president of the Canadian Bankers Association, appearing before the Standing Committee on Banking and Commerce in March 1934, strongly defended the policies of Canadian Co-Operative Wheat Producers, which were backed by bank advances guaranteed by federal loans:

> On a good many occasions in the last two years buying power either for export or speculation has not been present in sufficient volume to take care of the legitimate hedging operations essential to the functioning of the grain market. On such occasions purchases by the Co-Operative have filled the gap. These advances by the bank

> have had the effect not of encouraging speculators but rather the contrary. In periods of weakness speculators who might have sold short have been discouraged from doing so by the knowledge that the Co-Op with the powerful support of the Dominion Government was likely, if not certain, to support the market. On the other hand, speculators for the advance would hesitate to take a strongly bullish position knowing that the large holdings of the Co-Op might come on the market in substantial volume at any time. In this way the price has been protected from severe drops in periods of poor consumptive demand and in periods of strength from rising so far above the world price as to stop the movement into export channels.[15]

McFarland could not have offered a better justification for his policies.

In 1934 the grain industry faced severe setbacks. Private speculators were not returning to purchase hedges. A 200-million bushel carryover from previous years sat in government hands with a 400-million bushel crop expected for 1935. And hopes for the international stabilization of wheat markets dissolved in November when Argentina refused to be bound by the price and quota agreements made in London. A bountiful European crop in 1934 made the prospect of additional carryovers by the exporting countries certain. That same month the government pegged the price of wheat futures at seventy-five cents per bushel.

A Temporary Wheat Board

Reluctantly, both government and grain industry leaders began to consider machinery for a greater government role in the marketing of wheat. The establishment of a wheat board, until then rejected by McFarland and Bennett, began to appear necessary. In January 1935 McFarland wrote to Bennett that James Murray was pressing the Liberal party of Mackenzie King to make the setting up of a wheat board party policy:

> It would seem as if Jim Murray would favour a wheat board always provided that it is directed by proper directors and officials. He seems to think that the elevator companies would have satisfactory margins of profit and they could not be much worse off with a board than they are now.[16]

McFarland also informed Bennett that King did not favour establishing a board and that "you need not go off the deep end for a board until you are forced later."

This negative tone about setting up a wheat board was common in the McFarland-Bennett correspondence. The board was viewed as a necessary evil. Even after an announcement of the board's impending establishment was made late in February 1935, McFarland suggested that if the drought continued the need for a board might not materialize.[17] McFarland saw a wheat board in conservative terms. Noting that the "clear heads in the grain trade" accepted the idea of a board to undertake the role the speculators had once filled, the government's leading grain advisor was convinced that:

> . . . without a public participation in a speculative way and on a large scale, the old system simply will not operate; and it is pretty well realized now that the forces which kept the old system going were not the membership of the Grain Exchange but public forces outside.[18]

Preservation of the "old system," in its essential features, was one of McFarland's motivations in supporting a government wheat-buying and -selling agency.

Although it was generally accepted that a government wheat board was a necessary evil, the powers such a board should have were contentious. Bill 98, which received first reading in June 1935, envisaged a three-man Grain Board with far greater potential power than the trade wished to devolve on the government. The Canadian Grain Board's task was to be "the orderly marketing of wheat in interprovincial and export trade." To this end it had the power to erect a government monopoly in the buying and selling of wheat. The Board could buy wheat from both producers and "other persons having possession" of wheat. All grain elevators would be subject to licensing and regulation by the Board, which would also have the power to set up elevators of its own if the cabinet approved. Oats, barley, rye and flax produced in the four western provinces could also be bought, sold and stored by the Board. Wheat contracts between the Canadian Co-Operative Wheat Producers and either its farmer-members or its customers, previously guaranteed by the federal government under various relief acts, would be acquired by the Board.

Reaction of the grain trade and the business community as a whole was unanimously negative. The major boards of trade and the Canadian Chamber of Commerce joined the industry in attacking the compulsory features of the bill that would make the Board the monopoly buyer and seller of the wheat that farmers delivered to elevators.[19] Prime Minister Bennett agreed to set up a special committee to hear the industry's point of view before drafting the final contents of Bill 98. Bennett later summed up the work of the committee:

> Evidence was given by various witnesses who said that they thought they should have another chance. A witness from Vancouver said that they had built up through all these years a magnificent organization that should not be lightly scrapped; a witness from Winnipeg made a similar observation. In the end we compromised. We provided for a board and provided that ordinary channels that had been established for the marketing of grain should still be utilized for that purpose.[20]

In its appearance before the committee the Winnipeg Grain Exchange was in a sense fighting for its existence. It rejected the McFarland-Bennett claim that the speculators had completely deserted the market. It also denied persistent rumours of deliberate demoralization of the grain market by "bear" raids ("bears" are speculators who, gambling that wheat prices would continue to drop, sold large quantities of futures at low prices on the assumption that they could maintain their profit margins by later purchasing wheat at even lower prices). The government regarded this short-selling as a means of artificially depressing the price of wheat. It was argued that despite the government's presence in the trade speculators were profiting from the farmers' misery. The Exchange, and James Richardson, denied that a significant "short" interest had invaded the Winnipeg market.[21]

Bennett and McFarland were especially unwilling to listen to Richardson. They believed that he had taken advantage of the relative lack of government regulation to promise the delivery of wheat at prices the government considered excessively low. McFarland cited Sidney Smith as his source confirming a "very substantial" short interest. As for Richardson, McFarland remembered his support as early as 1931 for putting a crutch under the market and therefore found incomprehensible his attacks against the pegging of wheat prices. Only one explanation seemed plausible to Bennett and McFarland, who wrote:

> It is rather significant that Mr. Richardson wrote you at the time he did because only a short while before he wrote you, there were persistent rumours around the Grain Exchange of evidence of Richardson selling out any long wheat he might have owned. I do not know that he had any large quantity but I do know that since these rumours were current, his people here have been talking somewhat pessimistically about the market.

In his response to McFarland's letter Bennett said, "I wholly agree with what you have written."[22]

The Winnipeg Grain Exchange claimed that if in fact too few individuals were willing to take the hedges, it was because Canadian grain was being offered at prices above those set by other grain exporting countries. This was a thinly veiled attack against McFarland's policies of not selling wheat when he considered prices too low. It was a hypocritical attack considering the support the leading grain companies had given McFarland when he reluctantly began purchasing hedges. In any event, the Exchange argued, the emergency situation of the wheat farmer was temporary, and private economic forces, if allowed to operate, would in time provide redress. In the meantime, the government should not tamper with the open market system.

But what of the fate of the wheat farmer in the interim? The

Grain Exchange suggested that the federal government subsidize the producer "by some system of price support or by other means." In response Bennett pointed out that Canada's average production of wheat exceeded 400 million bushels and that a direct subsidy would mean a large contribution from the Canadian treasury. Nevertheless, most of the large elevator companies, whose members regularly endorsed the resolutions of the boards of trade for cheaper government and balanced budgets, favoured a direct subsidy to the wheat producer. They argued that the government was correct to intervene to help the farmer, but that merely holding back wheat until the price rose would create resistance among wheat-buyers and simply leave the government with larger and larger stockpiles.

What most grain elevator companies argued for was a continuation of McFarland's policy of maintaining a government speculative presence in the market, but this presence was not to constitute one hundred percent of the speculative end of the market. The compromise—or "strategic retreat"[23] as one author saw it— was an alternative proposed by Sidney Smith, a supporter of McFarland's policies. The government would establish a fixed minimum price for wheat—as it had since November 1934—and if there were no other buyers the government would buy the wheat and sell it at international prices. In effect it would subsidize the producer. When the international price was above the minimum price set by the government, regular channels of marketing would be used. Behind all this was the belief that grain markets would soon return to normal and that the Wheat Board's minimum price would almost always be below the prices paid on the grain exchanges. The proposal would allow the speculators to realize profits when the price was high and would leave the government to absorb losses when the price was low.

The final legislation, which was passed in August 1935, removed grains other than wheat from Board jurisdiction, gave the Board the right to receive grain only from the producers and left the Board of Grain Commissioners as the final arbiter of elevator licenses. The legislation was accompanied by a warning from Bennett that a compulsory pool could not be ruled out for the future. McFarland was named chairman of the Wheat Board.

Those who feared that the Tories might use the Wheat Board to weaken the power of the private elevator and exporting companies and to rout the speculators could take heart in the Liberal victory of September 1935. More ideologically disposed to free enterprise, the King Liberals had opposed the establishment of the Wheat Board on anything but a temporary basis and had voted against Bill 98 when the government refused to consider an amendment that clearly stated its emergency nature. Both publicly and privately, King and the leading western Liberal cabinet ministers, Jimmy Gardiner and T.A. Crerar, made plain their intention to abandon the Board as soon as market conditions allowed.[24] Crerar and Trade and Commerce Minister William Euler favoured abandoning the Board at once. It was Charles Dunning, the Finance Minister and the Cabinet member closest to St. James Street, who argued that the Board could not be abandoned until wheat prices had somewhat advanced.

McFarland was forced to resign as chairman of the Wheat Board in December 1935. He was replaced by James R. Murray. Besides his position as vice-president and general manager of the Alberta Pacific Grain Company, Murray was a former secretary of the Winnipeg Grain Exchange and one of the authors of the Exchange's presentation before the Special Committee on Bill 98. When Murray assumed office, the Wheat Board held almost 300 million bushels of wheat and wheat futures. Within two months Murray disposed of 75 million bushels through futures trading. Like McFarland, Murray began his tenure of office as the government wheat salesman with the objective of convincing importers, especially the British millers, that Canadian wheat was always available on demand and at competitive prices.[25] McFarland charged that Murray and the Liberal government were succouring the speculative short sellers and abandoning the principles of the Board by selling wheat at whatever prices were offered.[26] Murray responded that the Board would have found no justification or support in the act if it had "chased the elusive bears and made them settle." The act preserved the futures market. Murray's goal was to sell wheat, not to tame speculators.[27]

Like McFarland, Murray soon came to believe that the free market alone could not be relied upon. Some cabinet ministers wanted to drop the fixed minimum price for wheat before the 1936 crop was harvested. But Murray, with the support of Dunning and by this time Crerar, convinced the government that to remove the floor price would encourage British monopoly buyers to send prices down deliberately. This would spell disaster for the future of wheat-growing in Canada. The combination of drought and bargain-basement sales would drive wheat farmers out of the West.[28]

The government now set up its third Grain Inquiry Royal Commission in Canada in twelve years. It was the job of the new Commission to offer an independent assessment of the government's view that a reasonably swift return to the grain exchange method of marketing was in order. The Commission was empowered to study the various alternative methods of marketing wheat and to inquire into all grain-handling transactions in Canada from 1930, including those of the Canadian Wheat Board. Heading the Commission was Justice Walter Turgeon, a former Saskatchewan provincial Liberal cabinet minister.

The 1936 crop was largely marketed by members of the Winnipeg Grain exchange. The minimum price set by the Board was 87.5 cents per bushel, a price below market prices for that year's crop. Agricultural Minister James Gardiner justified the Board's policy by saying that it had set a reasonable minimum price and could not stop farmers from making deliveries to outlets where a higher price could be obtained. The CCF members viewed the government's policy as an indication that the Liberal government was not concerned about providing orderly marketing and price supports for farmers, a sentiment that was openly shared not only by some Conservative MPs but also by some Liberal members. W.R. Motherwell, a former federal Liberal Minister of Agriculture in the 1920s, accused the government of committing "infanticide" on the Wheat Board. Nevertheless, the same policy of taking delivery of wheat only when the price dropped below a certain price—ninety cents— was followed again for the 1937 crop. The Turgeon report, released in 1938, stated that for 1936 and 1937, "it may be said that Canadian grain is now being marketed under the open market, competitive futures trading system.[29]

King believed the time had arrived when the government could pull out of the grain business. Gardiner was to attempt to get the pools to request government legislation to regulate the Winnipeg Grain Exchange and to peg the price of wheat each year. In return the pools and the private sector would become the selling agencies.[30]

The Turgeon Commission report supported the return-to-free-enterprise view of the government. Turgeon accepted the arguments of the grain trade that importers would resist having to buy from a government monopoly selling agency and that the availability of wheat from other countries made it impossible for a government wheat board to stabilize prices successfully. But he believed that the Board should remain intact as long as conditions were "unsettled" to meet any situation that might arise.[31]

A situation arose in 1938. Despite a drought that continued to affect much of the wheat-growing area, the price on international markets was falling; protectionist policies of many importing countries had reduced demand. The government undertook through the Wheat Board to guarantee a minimum price of eighty cents per bushel. Within the cabinet it was Dunning again who was most insistent that the minimum price be put into effect. He argued pragmatically, noted King in his diary, that "we would be saving relief in the end by giving State aid to the producers." Gardiner, the ideologue of liberalism, wrote King to urge that the minimum price be set at no more than sixty cents and that any additional money be paid in the form of a subsidy to the producer rather than as an apparent payment for wheat delivered.[32] But Sir Charles Gordon, who as president of the Bank of Montreal was still concerned for the credit of the prairie provinces, told the bank's annual meeting of shareholders that the guaranteed wheat price was a measure which, while primarily benefiting the prairie provinces, would benefit the entire Canadian business community. The *Monetary Times* argued that it made more sense to subsidize wheat sales than to have the country faced with "the loss of purchasing power and the necessity for the relief of acute distress that a smaller crop at a higher price would entail." The *Financial Times*, however, in a front-page article said that business saw "both dangers and benefits" in giving bonuses to the wheat grower. The guaranteed wheat price would have a positive effect "on debt liquidation and purchasing power", but it would be offset by the expenditure of taxpayers' money to provide the bonus and the danger that other producers' groups would want similar assistance.[33]

In 1939 the government set out to guarantee only sixty cents a bushel for wheat, a plan in accordance with the views of King, Gardiner and Crerar that the government should withdraw from the grain trade. The government's plans were opposed by a united front of western interests, in which the grain dealers and boards of trade played a large role. The Committee on Markets and Agricultural Readjustment, representing western interests, was established in December 1938 at a conference called by the Manitoba government. The committee met again in February 1939 and unanimously agreed on a policy for the 1939-40 crop year. The policy called for the continuation of the Wheat Board for 1939-40 and the setting of a guaranteed price for wheat of at least eighty cents for No. 1 Northern. Subsidiary assistance through crop insurance, "or some other method", was requested for farmers who suffered a total or partial crop failure "by reason of drought or other calamity."[34] The first delegation to present the committee's viewpoint to cabinet came to Ottawa in March 1939. The delegation's nineteen members represented farmers' organizations, the prairie governments and prairie businessmen. The businessmen were spokesmen for the considerable intersts of the North West Grain Dealers Association, Pioneer Grain and the boards of trade of Saskatoon, Regina, Edmonton and Calgary.

The Committee on Markets gave five reasons for supporting the Wheat Board's continuation: simplicity of operation; economy of administration; the Turgeon commission recommendations for maintaining the Board during unsettled conditions; protection against further demoralization of the market structure; and the fact that the state in most other wheat producing countries directly intervened in the wheat market.[35]

The last of these was soon to become the compelling reason for making the Wheat Board a permanent and compulsory pool. Both importing and exporting countries were intervening in the market, which made trading in the grain exchanges a rather small determinant of price. Wheat prices at Liverpool had declined to levels close to a record low, and Canada's Northern wheat sold at sixty cents per bushel at Fort William. But the erection of tariffs and quotas by continental European countries to protect home producers often allowed wheat prices in those countries to exceed two dollars per bushel. The Committee concluded:

> Consequently through the intervention of governments, producers in importing countries are protected from the effects of low international prices and consumers are prevented from enjoying the benefits of cheap bread. Under prevailing conditions low international prices are largely ineffective in bringing about stimulation in world consumption of wheat or in bringing about an increase in the world trade.[36]

The chief argument of the grain trade for a speculative wheat futures market—that it established the price that consuming countries would pay for wheat—was being eroded by a system of increased government restrictions, in which tariffs and quotas made low prices by exporters a negligible factor. The major exporting countries, meanwhile, were all granting bonuses to their producers. In the United States price supports were in effect for that year along with an export subsidy. Argentina was paying growers a minimum price—a price above the world market levels—and Australia was extending assistance of various kinds to its producers.

The Committee on Markets reappeared before the cabinet in April 1939 to denounce the government's announced sixty-cent guarantee on wheat and to demand that it be raised to eighty cents. It also disagreed with the kind of assistance outlined in the government's Acreage Bonus Bill. The committee felt the government was providing assistance only to farmers with poor crops and, besides a guaranteed minimum price, little to those with average or better crops.[37]

The government had begun to relent. Crerar wrote King in April that the government's wheat proposals would cost the Liberal government eight to ten federal seats in Manitoba alone. Farmers and the business community would reject the Liberal party if it abandoned the Wheat Board. The farmers had had their purchasing power greatly reduced to pay operating costs at a time when most had difficulty just paying interest on mortgage debts. The effect on manufacturing and business in general would be considerable. According to Crerar

> . . . our wheat producers are in this plight because of world forces over which Canada has no control. There is scarcely another country in the world that is not, directly or indirectly, aiding its wheat producers. Much as I dislike Government intervention in these matters and much as I dislike anything in the nature of Government subsidies or bonuses I don't think we can afford to ignore the realities of the situation facing our wheat producers.[38]

In the end the government raised the price guarantee to eighty cents and the Wheat Board marketed the crop. Ironically, the grain trade and conservative cabinet ministers had played a significant role in foiling King's plans for a government departure from the grain business.

The farmers and their organizations played an important role, perhaps the leading role, in forcing the government to keep the Wheat Board in operation. Vernon Fowke, who is critical of the overall pattern of federal wheat policies, regards the events of 1939 as a victory for the producers.[39] But his studies raise doubts that the fear of losing the farmers' votes can alone explain why the Board was first established and why it was maintained. The wheat producers did not wish to see the Board that had been established during World War I disbanded. Yet, as Fowke writes:

> For three years after the Canadian Wheat Board was disbanded in 1920 there was great uncertainty in the West concerning the form of wheat marketing organization which should be provided for the postwar years. . . The obvious possibility in view of the recent past was that the Dominion Government might be persuaded to reconstitute the Wheat Board and to continue its monopoly. In the hope that this possibility might be realized, the western Grain Growers' associations, the national Canadian Council of Agriculture and the western legislatures made repeated representations to the federal government

> and did not abandon their efforts in that direction until 1923, when it was finally made abundantly clear that the Dominion Government was not to be persuaded.[40]

Since a campaign of similar intensity to the producers' campaign in 1939 had been mounted by the farmers without success in the early 1920s, it could be argued that the Liberal government, in power for most of the period of that earlier campaign, did not have as strong a western representation as the Liberal government elected in 1935. But the fact is that Crerar and Gardiner, the leading western Canadian Liberals in the later government, were converts to the Wheat Board and not its early advocates. What was new by the late 1930s was the shift in the position of the grain trade from outright opposition to a Wheat Board in the 1920s to an acceptance of the Board, at least temporarily, as a means of coping with a changed world market structure in the industry. It was also important that eastern businessmen were less opposed to giving the farmers a minimum guaranteed price for their wheat. Dunning, referring to the eighty cents per bushel guarantee for the western wheat crop of 1938, commented in his budget speech of 1939:

> ...That guarantee may cost the dominion treasury a substantial sum of money but at the time it was given there were few, even amongst the industrial and financial leaders of eastern Canada, who did not believe it justified in view of the drastic decline in the world price of wheat and the general economic interest of the country as a whole.[41]

A Permanent Wheat Board

Wartime conditions brought an end to futures trading. Convinced by 1943 that the wheat-importing countries would continue setting import quotas, the government gave the Wheat Board the sole right to set prices for Canadian wheat, which in effect ended private futures trading. Delivery of wheat to the private elevators and marketing through private export firms continued, but fees were established by the government in consultation with these firms. D.A. McGibbon, a supporter of the futures-trading method of sale, noted that the Board had not substantially changed the marketing process. By the end of World War II, he noted:

> With the private grain trade the Board had ironed out most differences and reduced procedure in dealing with it largely to routine. But while the operations of the Wheat Board had been gradually adjusted to the use of facilities of the private elevator companies, to the functions of the exporter and to other factors in the trade, it would be difficult to prove that it had reduced the over-all cost of marketing Canadian wheat. Substantially, the Canadian Wheat Board had been superimposed on and meshed into the existing organization. Except in the elimination of a small number of futures grain brokers, no significant reduction in grain trade personnel was discernible.[42]

Farm Credit Legislation

The establishment of the Wheat Board was not the only aid given by the federal government to the wheat growers. The Canadian Farm Loan Board had been set up in 1929 to provide long-term mortgage credit for farmers, but during its first five years it "operated upon a very conservative basis." In 1934 security provisions for loans were eased but with little impact during the Depression. The government also began to make short- and intermediate-term loans to farmers with the encouragement of the chartered banks anxious to vacate the field.[43] Federal legislation to aid farmers in the repayment of their debts was also introduced. The Prairie Farm Rehabilitation Act was passed in 1934 "to assist in the planting of trees, hedges and shelter belts, to provide experimental sub-stations for guidance in the system of farming most suitable for an area." The act provided $750,000 for 1935 and a limit of one million dollars per year thereafter. In 1937 the appropriation was increased to $2 million and in 1938 to $3.5 million. But most federal funds reaching the farmers during the 1930s simply consisted of relief money.[44]

Provincial debt adjustment legislation saved many farmers from bankruptcy.[45] The business community's opposition to the legislation encouraged the federal government to pass the Farmers' Creditors Arrangement Act of 1934. Prime Minister Bennett was concerned that provincial debt adjustment boards would lack uniformity and allow "repudiation on a wholesale scale," with the result that banks and other investors would abandon those provinces that had adjustment legislation. The prairie provinces, in particular, would suffer.[46] Bennett met with representatives of the Dominion Mortgage and Investments Association in March 1934 to discuss the question of agricultural debts.[47] Later that month a special committee of the association wrote Deputy Minister of Finance W.C. Clark a four-page memorandum recommending a "farmers' creditors arrangement act."[48] The proposed legislation would allow farmers to enter into compromise arrangements with their creditors under the supervision of a government board. There would be "no general scheme of compromise"; each application from a farmer "would have to be dealt with on its merits and regard paid to the priorities of creditors."[49] The Farmers' Creditors Arrangement Act of 1934 followed the general principles underscored by the association. However, where creditors representing two-thirds of a farmer's debts had agreed to a compromise, the legislation stipulated that the government board could impose the arrangement on all the farmer's creditors. The association objected to this arrangement.[50] But while recognizing that some boards might differ from others on how to assess the capacity of a farmer to pay, C.C. Ferguson, general manager of Great-West Life (the leading insurance firm on the Prairies), called "the fundamental idea underlying the legislation...sound and logical."[51] The farmers, nevertheless, received the major benefit from the legislation. By February 1938 over 26,000 cases had been handled and over $50 million of principal and $4 million dollars of interest had been removed from a total indebtedness of close to $159 million.

The government's decision to expand farm credit in 1934 had also received support from the financial community, especially from the Canadian Bankers Association and the Dominion Mortgage and Investments Association,[52] which commented that lending institutions had lost too much money in loans to farmers to make any new loans. While the government would lose more money by increasing farm loans, the association stated that:

> . . . in the light of the national importance of rehabilitating the Western farmer, in morale as well as financially, the wider powers appear desirable and the increased risk of loss should be easily capable of justification in the national interest.[53]

Vernon Fowke has demonstrated in *The National Policy and the Wheat Economy* that the prairie provinces were involved in a colonial relationship with the dominant interest groups of Montreal and Toronto, whose purpose in the "national" plan was to extract resources for the use of central Canada and to consume goods manufactured behind tariff barriers in the Toronto and Montreal-centred regions. Within these parameters, however, the eastern businessmen, the local grain trade and the federal government had a common interest in preserving a minimum standard of living on the prairies in order both to ensure that wheat-growing continued to be a viable economic activity and to prevent the total collapse of this hinterland area. The Wheat Board and the price stabilization policies of the early 1930s that preceded it accomplished little more than this. A pattern of low farm income and subsequent decline in farm population; a lack of sufficient employment opportunities outside the capital-intensive extractive industries; a low-wage pattern in the small manufacturing sector; and decline in population relative to Canada as a whole have been the fate of Saskatchewan and Manitoba since World War II. Oil-rich Alberta has been spared this fate, at least temporarily, though it remains to be seen to what degree a province whose wealth is controlled by American multinational oil corporations can eventually escape a fate of unbalanced development.[54]

The farmers' organizations in the 1930s presented few alternative policies. The Canadian Council of Agriculture, once powerful enough to spawn the Progressive party, had temporarily folded. The wheat pools were under a government trusteeship. Farmers' ideology, despite a favourable attitude to cooperatives, had historically been pro-free enterprise. Though farmers in the 1930s wanted a wheat board, most remained suspicious that "creeping socialism" would result ultimately in the socialization of their land. While the farmers of Saskatchewan were more willing than most to support a fundamental restructuring of the entire economy, many farmers were content to continue complaining about high tariffs, high freight rates and bankers' conspiracies and to endure their economic lot fatalistically.[55]

What little was done by governments of the 1930s—the McFarland purchases and sales and later the Canadian Wheat Board—was done begrudgingly and only with the widest collaboration and compromise with the business interests. Although western farmers may have had the greatest input in the process that led to a permanent Wheat Board, they were not the sole beneficiary. As with marketing boards and unemployment insurance, it is fair to say that while the Wheat Board was an advantage to the farmers, it was equally advantageous to the business groups involved in the grain trade because it preserved more than it changed. It gave a state guarantee of profits to the traders and elevator companies and allowed them to increase their concentration.

Although the marketing boards and the combines legislation substantially reduced competition in the industries involved and insured that a few monopolistic firms would continue to dominate certain economic sectors, the stability of the entire business community depended upon the overall performance of the Canadian economy. During the Depression the business cycle touched bottom. Businessmen's efforts to improve general economic conditions failed, and the business cycle showed no signs of correcting itself. The business community began perceiving the state as an agency for smoothing out the business cycle. Throughout the thirties businessmen pressed the government to become an active participant in the economy by establishing a social insurance scheme, providing aid to the construction industry, becoming involved in the mortgage-lending field and setting up a central bank.

VI

SOCIAL INSURANCE

Until the twentieth century state-supported social welfare programs were virtually non-existent. In the largely rural Canada of the nineteenth century help for the poor, sick and aging member of the community was provided by the family and by local religious and charitable organizations. Increasing urbanization and industrialization did little to change the prevailing view among Canadians that those who needed financial assistance and health-care services were the responsiblity of relatives and friends rather than the state. Although few Canadians wanted to see the state become involved in providing these welfare services, governments gained considerable community support for their public education and public health programs. Free elementary education and municipal and provincial public health services were established in Ontario by the end of the century. The public education debate had focused on the benefits of providing industry with a literate work force and the need to keep unemployed young people from turning to crime. Public health measures were seen as essential to fight cholera and smallpox epidemics. In an urban environment families and charitable institutions were unable to provide sufficient funds and services. The state was called in to fill the gap. Since neither crime nor cholera could be contained within the ghettoes of the working class and the poor, the wealthier classes supported a minimum of state measures.

Other social legislation came slowly. Workmen's compensation legislation existed in all provinces except Prince Edward Island by 1920. An American study of the introduction of compensation indicates that it was viewed by large corporate interests as a means of fending off the more radical employer-liability type of legislation that made employers legally responsible for employees injured at work. Although there is no study of the origins of workmen's compensation in Canada, Canadian corporations were sufficiently interested in seeing compensation legislation enacted for the Canadian Manufacturers Association to draw up a set of proposals for a system of collective insurance under government control. The CMA also joined with labour to encourage governments to adopt insurance legislation.[2]

The high rate of unemployment before World War I and the high rate expected at the war's end prompted the Ontario government to name a Royal Commission on Unemployment in 1914. The Commission rejected the idea of a government-run unemployment scheme, though it urged the province to provide financial assistance for company and trade union unemployment programs.[3] The end of the war brought federal pensions for war widows and provincial legislation providing mothers' allowances.[4]

Throughout the 1920s the Trades and Labour Congress pressed unsuccessfully for universal old-age pensions, unemployment, health and disability insurance. A Royal Commission on Industrial Relations had endorsed the principle of compulsory contributory state insurance in 1919. A similar scheme was proposed by the Select Standing Committee on Industrial and International Relations in 1928 and received the support of the House of Commons in May 1929. Despite the further support of church organizations, social service agencies and the 1919 Liberal convention, no universal programs of social insurance were legislated in the 1920s.[5] The only program of social legislation passed at the federal level in the 1920s was a pension scheme, a concession forced out of Mackenzie King in 1926 by CCF leader J. S. Woodsworth.[6]

The Depression brought the question of the state's role in providing for its citizens into sharper focus. The business community and other conservative groups that had previously resisted social insurance and legislation regulating working conditions slowly began to change their views. Altruism was not the motive. A. E. Grauer, writing for the Royal Commission on Dominion-Provincial Relations in 1939, summed up the new attitude that began to make certain social reforms acceptable to conservatives:

> Since the Great War, the Great Depression has been the chief stimulus to labour legislation and social insurance. The note sounded has not been so much the ideal of social justice, as political and economic financial expediency. For instance, the shorter working week was favoured in unexpected quarters not because it would give the workers more leisure and possibilities for a fuller life but because it would spread work; and the current singling out of unemployment insurance for governmental attention in many countries is dictated by the appalling costs of direct relief and hope that unemployment insurance benefits will give some protection to public treasuries in future depressions and will, by sustaining purchasing power, tend to mitigate these depressions...
>
> It is pertinent to note that differences in form of government do not seem to have mattered in this development. Labour legislation and social insurance are as characteristic of fascist Italy as of democratic countries and remain a fundamental of the communist system of Russia.[7]

Social insurance was intended to stabilize a destabilized economy and not necessarily to redistribute wealth. That later studies should indicate that wealth has not been significantly redistributed would only validate the view of conservatives who believed social reforms, if carried out in a certain way, would reinforce rather than disturb the status quo.[8]

Since unemployment insurance had not been an issue in the 1930 election, Prime Minister Bennett was in no hurry to introduce legislation. During the early thirties he balanced his endorsement of the principle of unemployment insurance with his insistence that it needed a great deal of preliminary study. However, Bennett was very firm about what form of unemployment insurance he would not consider. He rejected out of hand the proposal of A.A. Heaps and the small Labour caucus for a non-contributory plan financed by a steeply-graded income tax. This plan was also backed by the Communists, whose importance in the nightmares of Bennett and businessmen should not be underestimated. A Communist campaign among organizations of the unemployed, trade union locals and labour councils in support of a non-contributory scheme resulted in a deluge of requests for Bennett to pass the Left's version of unemployment insurance.[9] Bennett's rejection of this plan was phrased in the type of encomium to the monied classes that he would soon be careful to avoid on public platforms. Chiding Heaps he said:

> May I say to my friends from the West, do you realize how difficult you are making it for the West by the attitude that some of you continue to take? Do you realize in your denunciations of what some of you call "St. James Street" and some of you call "the banks" and others "the moneyed interests" that it is upon them we have to rely largely for our taxes?...What good on earth can any member accomplish by pursuing the course that my honourable friend has pursued tonight and that some other honourable gentlemen are pursuing here, crying aloud, calling upon high heaven in denunciation of wealth, money and means and then in the same breath crying aloud to tax it.[10]

With this attitude it is not surprising that Bennett insisted that "insurance involves premiums and premiums should be paid by the joint action alike of the insurer and the insured themselves and with the assistance of the state."[11]

Social Legislation and the Business Community

The St. James Street interests, which Bennett defended against the western attack, were also looking favourably at the wisdom of a program of unemployment insurance. The *Financial Times* reflected an increasingly common view that a compulsory state insurance scheme was a means of forcing workers to save money in good times as a hedge against unemployment. With extreme condescension this crusty Tory journal advised in 1932 that workers, unlike corporations, did not have the good sense to build reserves "against distress in the event of future unemployment." Two years of Depression had indicated that workers' savings were crucial. The *Financial Times*, like Bennett, was interested as much in the financing of unemployment insurance as in the principle itself. Britain had not assessed high enough premium contributions to keep its insurance fund solvent when employment dropped precipitously, and most of the payments it was making at that time were from general revenue rather than from the insurance fund. The newspaper believed the government's only financial responsibility to the insurance fund should be administrative, and that all benefit payments should come from premium contributions.[12]

Though the 1935 legislation (the first legislation for social insurance in Canada) called for some state contribution, five-sixths of the fund was to be provided by employer and employee contributions. As J.S. Woodsworth observed, insurance premiums would force many workers receiving low wages to pay direct taxes for the first time, effectively decreasing their take-home pay. While supporting the bill establishing unemployment insurance, Woodsworth repeated the Left's proposal for a non-contributory "tax-the-rich" scheme. Bennett simply reiterated his former arguments that unemployment insurance was based on the same principles as any private insurance scheme—benefits would accrue to those who paid. Bennett had long believed that more people should pay income taxes. Only three to four percent of working Canadians earned a taxable income ($3,000 per year in 1930). Bennett believed these "men of means" were treated unfairly since they also paid taxes on dividends, and the money from which dividends were received was in turn subject to corporation tax. Insurance programs since the 1930s, as well as direct income taxes on a larger segment of the population, have been a major way of preventing new government programs from redistributing wealth.[13]

The need to counter the Left's version of insurance programs was not the major motivation behind increasingly wide business support for social insurance. Social insurance, as Grauer noted, was the result more of expediency than of any particular desire for social justice. There were several interrelated reasons for various industrialists and financiers to campaign during the Depression for insurance programs. It had become clear that an urban society could not rely on an approach in which relatives, charity organizations and municipal governments bore the burden of caring for unemployed, sick and aging citizens. With high unemployment concentrated in certain urban centres on the one hand and certain provinces on the other, local responsibility could only mean municipal and provincial bankruptcy. The danger that unemployment would bring national bankruptcy became an argument for an insurance program that would provide for workers trapped at the bottom of the business cycle without diminishing the financial resources and credit standing of junior levels of government. It was also argued that the availability of a fund that could be released when the economy went into a recession would maintain the purchasing power of the newly unemployed and prevent another depression. Still another argument for the stabilizing effects of unemployment insurance reasoned that it would allow employers to introduce new labour-saving technologies without having to worry about the effect on the workers displaced; they would be taken care of by insurance until they found new work. Since technology was likely to replace more and more jobs and since full employment was never likely to be achieved, old-age pensions began to make sense as a means of removing older workers from the labour force and replacing them with more energetic young people, whose anger at being unemployed presented a major threat to the existing order.

The chartered banks were major exponents of unemployment and other forms of insurance aimed at preventing municipal and provincial bankruptcies. No one was more forthright in his support for these programs than Sir Charles Gordon, who as president of the Bank of Montreal and Dominion Textiles was second only to Sir Herbert Holt in assets over which he had trusteeship as a corporate officer or director. Writing to Prime Minister Bennett at the beginning of 1934, Gordon decried the wasteful spending that direct relief by the municipalities entailed. He could see no end to these expenditures and noted that the provinces and municipalities were getting so deeply in debt that they were

> ... threatening to strangle their general credit to the point where it would be difficult if not impossible to carry through refunding operations for any maturing issues,

> letting alone the funding of money for any new capital undertaking.

The need to prevent future recourse to extensive direct relief convinced Gordon of "the urgent desirability of invoking some system of unemployment insurance." The British Parliament's recently reorganized unemployment insurance scheme was presented as a model because it covered four-fifths of all working people. Gordon concluded his letter to Bennett suggesting that "*for our general self-preservation* [emphasis mine] some such arrangement will have to be worked out in Canada and that if it can be done soon so much the better."[14] On other occasions Gordon supported old-age pensions and other social legislation. He drew on twenty-five years of British experience with social legislation to indicate that it was possible to prepare for difficult times for individuals and the economy as a whole without endangering stability. It was his view that direct relief always endangered stability.[15]

The Bank of Nova Scotia's executives cautioned against expectations that unemployment insurance would completely obviate the necessity for direct relief. But they endorsed the principle as going at least part way towards decreasing the burden of relief on national and local budgets. Like many advocates of insurance, the bank advised that a workable insurance scheme must be tied to a better-developed and nationally-coordinated system of employment bureaus along the lines of Great Britain's. Only in this way could insurance become part of a scheme for re-employing the unemployed rather than a fund for "malingerers."

The cities and provinces most burdened with relief and most in danger of ruining their credit joined the bankers in pressing the government for unemployment insurance. British Columbia had supported federal unemployment insurance since 1928; Alberta since 1930; Saskatchewan and Manitoba since 1931. Cities supporting unemployment insurance included Vancouver, Ottawa, London, East Windsor, Port Arthur, Nanaimo, Sudbury and Leaside.[16]

Most manufacturers also saw unemployment insurance ultimately as a cheaper way of taking care of the unemployed. In a series of articles published in *Canadian Machinery and Manufacturing*

News in 1934, businessmen observed that relief involved huge public expenditures released "in a haphazard and sometimes wasteful manner" and that the work ethic was undermined by relief:

> Relief penalizes the conscientious workers who save their money in good times and favors the spendthrift element. Unemployment insurance does the opposite, benefits being based on savings of the worker, enforced though it may be, and not simply on need. Relief money comes from so many sources and passes through so many hands that petty grafting is inevitable. The businesslike set-up of a proper unemployment insurance program would do away with this.[17]

The magazine's series on unemployment insurance included favourable articles by officials of Massey-Harris and Gutta Percha Rubber. O.H. Shenstone, Massey-Harris' factory superintendent, had met previously with Bennett's executive assistant, R.K. Finlayson, to express his support for unemployment insurance, which he saw as a program of advance planning for recessions.[18] The creation-of-purchasing-power argument for unemployment insurance was used by men like Chrysler of Canada president John D. Mansfield. Mansfield and his American boss Walter Chrysler were supporters of the New Deal idea that a combination of social measures and industrial cartels was needed to correlate production and consumption.[19]

Technological change and the resulting loss in jobs was cited by Arthur Purvis, president of C.I.L. and Dunlop and chairman of the King government's National Employment Commission, as a further reason for adopting insurance programs. Purvis viewed some instances of unemployment as "a national responsibility" rather than a company responsibility. This responsibility should be socialized by both an unemployment insurance scheme and the expansion of employment services and retraining programs.[20] Purvis's familiarity with technological change and unemployment was corroborated by Conservative MP maverick Tommy Church, in whose riding the Du Pont plant operated:

> I know of one industry in Canada presided over by the chairman of the commission. What did he do in the very week during which this report was signed and presented? What did this representative of the Du Pont dynasty do?—this gentleman who is supposed to have the interests of the Canadian working class at heart? I will tell you what he did in one industry. He and his fellow directors and managers introduced into the industry of which he is the head a machine that put out of employment seven or eight men who in all their lives had never been off the payroll. That is one thing he did in one of the industries of which he is a director and it indicates how he solves the unemployment problem.[21]

Other employers had experienced difficulties in introducing technological and management advances. In 1929 Canadian Cottons endured a bitter strike in its Hamilton plants where layoffs accompanied the introduction of assembly-line techniques. Perhaps it was this experience that led company president A.E. Dawson to support a fairly extensive program of social insurance. Speaking on employer-employee relations to the Canadian Chamber of Commerce in September 1934, Dawson urged the government to set up a fund for sickness, unemployment and old age. He proposed that the fund be financed by a compulsory employee contribution of five percent with equal contributions from employers and government. A reasonable pension for workers retiring at the age of sixty-five would be one of the benefits of this program.[22] Although these insurance programs promised some benefits to the workers, the primary motive of Dawson and other trustees of capital was not predominantly altruistic. Although many of these men may have wanted to see an improvement in workers' living standards, their first responsibility was to their corporations and fellow managers and directors.

There was by no means a unified industry position on unemployment insurance at the time of its introduction by the Bennett government in 1935. The Canadian Chamber of Commerce and the larger boards of trade had been largely unable to reach a consensus on the issue. The Canadian Manufacturers Association, led by smaller manufacturers unable to absorb the costs of insurance as well as the larger firms, opposed an unemployment insurance scheme. The CMA, however, did support legislation replacing the needy-poor pension with a universal contributory old-age pension scheme funded through pooling employer-employee-state contributions. The British Columbia CMA supported a federal health insurance scheme. It was not the principle of insurance that was in question; it was rather the efficacy of dealing with unemployment in this way.[23]

Influential businessmen opposing unemployment insurance included CPR president Edward Beatty and Sir Thomas White, vice-president of the Canadian Bank of Commerce. In Beatty's opinion, railway employees had job security and did not need insurance.[24] While not absolutely opposed to unemployment insurance, White, Canada's wartime Tory Finance Minister, disagreed with the view of some bankers that it would greatly benefit business. He believed that it was an unfair proposition since it would hit all industries, whether or not they were subject to great shifts in available employment, and that it would encourage "abuse" as a means of escaping employment.[25] The Winnipeg Board of Trade shared White's view. Disagreeing with the judgment of many businessmen that insurance schemes were cheaper than relief, the board predicted that under conditions of high unemployment the fund would become bankrupt as it had in Britain and the state would be called upon to pay the difference.[26]

The long list of businessmen who applauded the Bennett proposals in the New Deal radio speeches indicates a fairly widespread business support for some form of social insurance. Social insurance and government spending, along with greater government regulation in the economy, were the fundamental themes of the speeches. Financier Ward Pitfield, who had seen the legislation before it was announced, called it "the finest plan I have ever seen to combat unemployment."[27]

Leading businessmen-politicians had also publicly supported unemployment insurance. Raoul Dandurand, Liberal leader in the Senate and one of the leading French-Canadian businessmen, saw insurance as necessary in an urban society. Referring to the back-to-the-land movement that had attracted considerable support in business quarters as a partial solution to unemployment, Dandurand argued that there were too many unemployed young people, city-born and bred, to allow such a policy to absorb most of the unemployed:

> When I think of them and of the inevitably slow process of reabsorbing into industry those who are now unemployed, I feel more and more concerned that *if our capitalist system is to survive* [emphasis mine] we shall have to establish a contributory unemployment system to tide our people over periods of economic depression.[28]

Quebec's Premier L.A. Taschereau, a director of many corporations, supported a federal unemployment insurance scheme—with provincial cooperation—to ease the relief burden on provinces and municipalities.[29]

On the other hand, Arthur Meighen, a supporter of American New Deal policies for compulsory cooperation within industries and legislated minimum wages to increase purchasing power, opposed insurance schemes. Meighen wanted "a measure of disgrace" to be attached to relief and therefore felt it should remain "on a basis of charity." Relief by insurance would make people feel they had a right to collect relief while unemployed.[30]

The Unemployment Insurance Scheme

Unemployment insurance was in fact the only insurance legislation introduced in the 1935 session. As the Canadian Chamber of Commerce observed, the legislation included the features considered most important by businessmen, whether or not they supported this form of insurance. It was national in scope, contributory, involved only a small direct contribution from the state, and was tied to an expansion of employment offices. In other words, it appeared to be a coordinated federal policy for handling future unemployment. The ineligibility of those already unemployed answered the objections of those who feared an insurance program introduced under Depression conditions would quickly become a "dole."[31]

Bennett made reference to the British example when he introduced the insurance legislation. In Bennett's view, the employment services were the "very foundation" of insurance since they gave the government the ability to insure against abuse and at the same time to provide for mobility of the labour force. With no apparent distaste for uprooting people from their homes, the founder of work relief camps in Canada noted that the advantage of an unemployment service with compulsory registration for eligibility was that it allowed the labour office to

> ...transfer labour from one point to another and provided there is unemployment at one point and requirements at another, the labour may be transferred from the point where there is a surplus to the point where it may be utilized.[32]

Maximizing the efficiency of labour in the production process was not Bennett's only motivation. He had come to accept all the reasons that various businessmen had suggested for insurance. Not least of these reasons was the need to weaken the Left, whose proposals for a non-contributory insurance scheme had gained considerable support. Referring generally to his New Deal proposals, Bennett wrote to a New Brunswick publisher:

> ...Tim Buck has today a very strong position in the province of Ontario and he openly demands the abolition of the capitalist system. A good deal of pruning is sometimes necessary to save a tree and it would be well for us in Canada to remember that there is considerable pruning to be done if we are to save the fabric of the capitalist system.[33]

Bennett's fear of the socialists was compounded by his feeling that the era of scarcity had given way to a period of abundance where distribution, rather than production, was society's major problem. Promising a universal old-age pension scheme in the 1935 election, Bennett argued that this would be a means of easing the task of younger people seeking jobs. The age of retirement was to be lowered to sixty. "Labour-saving machinery, elimination of duplication and growing concentration of business make it impossible to ever supply again work for all the people," commented Bennett.

On the other hand, these advances meant increased production. If the state had some role in the distribution of the benefits of this increase in national income, more and more people could legitimately be removed from the labour force and provided for by the state.[34]

The Bennett unemployment insurance scheme covered only 56 percent of working people in the country; civil servants, bank employees, seasonal workers and employees earning over $2000 per year were ineligible. The Senate added the bank employees to the list of eligible workers. Ironically, the bankers who had pressed for an insurance program objected to coverage for their own employees, claiming bank employees had secure jobs and needed no protection against joblessness. The CMA argued unsuccessfully for a sliding scale of contributions based on an industry's job stability record. Unions called for a scheme that covered all employees, especially seasonal workers most likely to require unemployment assistance.[35] Although no unemployment insurance scheme would satisfy every sector of industry or society, the Bennett plan on the whole followed the tried and safe British path and incorporated the features that organized business considered essential.

The unemployment insurance legislation was submittted to a court test by the federal Liberals. It was ruled *ultra vires* by the Privy Council. The federal government was committed to reintroducing it through joint action with the nine provincial governments. Mackenzie King had always been shy to battle the business leaders, but he met with only slight opposition and much encouragement. As the Depression continued the growth of business support for state social insurance legislation paralleled the increase of business interests in favour of orderly state marketing. The Ontario Associated Boards of Trade and Chambers of Commerce congratulated King on his efforts to join with the provinces in securing an amendment to the British North America Act to permit unemployment insurance and labour employment agencies under federal authority.[36]

Thomas Bradshaw, president of North American Life and one of King's first choices for membership on the National Employment Commission (he was unavailable), approved of the proposed five-year national plan. As part of such a plan Bradshaw encouraged a commission to "draft a comprehensive scheme of old age pensions, unemployment insurance, etc. and after exhaustive analysis of the risks involved, to determine who should be the contributors, the basis of contributions and the benefits to be allowed."[37]

The new business ideology of conservative state planning to maintain stability in the capitalist system was crystallized in the 1938 report of the National Employment Commission. Arthur Purvis, one of Canada's most powerful industrialists, chaired the commission; his vice-chairman was veteran Trades and Labour congress president Tom Moore. Their general concurrence on the best means with which to attack unemployment reflects the conservative ideology of the American-dominated and crafts-structured unions in the Trades and Labour Congress. Professor Blair Neatby has suggested that the real input into the Commission's findings came from Queen's University professors. There is no evidence to indicate that Canadian businessmen respected the economic wisdom of academics unfamiliar with boardrooms and stock markets. Purvis listened to the Queen's economists when they corroborated what he already believed. Like many Canadian businessmen, Purvis had been swayed by the British formula for reform, and he had applauded the Bennett reforms. The views of the Commission, as expressed in his report, were not new.[38]

In Purvis's report the government's role included providing financial aid to Canadians cast aside in the play of private economic forces and employing these financial schemes along with other measures to lift the economy when it began to sag. Ten years earlier, this attitude towards government intervention would have been labelled socialistic. His report called for unemployment insurance, a national network of labour exchanges, expanded federal vocational education programs, a comprehensive housing policy (including subsidized rental housing for the poor) and state loans for home improvements. The emphasis was on strengthening the role of the central government in dealing with unemployment. Restricting the role of local government in relief programs was considered necessary both to reduce the cost of dealing with unemployment and to tie unemployment policies to overall national economic goals. The success of unemployment insurance, the

Employment Service of Canada and unemployment aid depended upon a unified administration.[39]

Mackenzie King was privately horrified by the undiplomatic disregard of provincial rights that the commission's report represented. He feared that its publication might embarrass the Royal Commission on Dominion-Provincial Relations, which was then in the midst of hearings. Most of his cabinet resisted the idea that the federal government alone should or could handle all relief programs. Since 1934 organized business, through the Canadian Chamber of Commerce, had pressed government to establish a commission on unemployment and greeted triumphantly both the appointment of the Purvis investigation and the final report. The Chamber of Commerce regarded federal control over unemployment as essential.[40] Along with other business organizations it wanted to make local governments as weak as possible in most jurisdictions and to strengthen correspondingly the central authority.

King was more right-wing than the business community on the issue of allowing constitutional barriers to delay necessary, non-radical reforms. He regretted having named Purvis chairman and paradoxically branded his report an "academic treatise" and a reflection of the views of "a big businessman and a Tory at heart, not understanding methods of politics..." King's dismay over business disdain for constitutional considerations was matched by the business community's consternation over the provinces' use of their constitutional powers to block reforms. *Canadian Business* was angry with three provinces—Quebec, Ontario and New Brunswick—that were refusing to support King's plan for federal unemployment insurance. Calling the provincial reaction a "constitutional fetish," the house organ of the Canadian Chamber of Commerce editorialized:

> The people of all provinces will have an opportunity of passing on this social security legislation through their representatives in the federal parliament and we cannot see the necessity for hesitancy on the part of the provincial governments at the present time. The unfortunate fetish

> of provincial "rights" is ever with us but it is high time we learned that progress can best be kept on the march by the centralization of government consistent with "individual" not "provincial" freedom.[41]

More and more industry groups and individuals were adding their voices to the demand for unemployment insurance. The Royal Commission on Dominion-Provincial Relations, which was not empowered to deal with the merits of social insurance, nevertheless heard calls for legislation from such groups as the Retail Merchants Association and the Ontario Association of Real Estate Boards. The arguments of these groups were familiar ones. Contributory unemployment insurance, the merchants argued, had a "tendency to increase purchasing power." And the real estate men saw social insurance as a means of dealing with "mass unemployment" in a system of mass production without resorting to relief, the cost of which was largely borne by municipal property taxation. If the housing industry was to be revived the burden of this taxation must be lessened, and unemployment insurance was the "only one long-term answer to this condition."[42]

Unemployment insurance did not become a reality until July 1940 when a change of heart in Ontario and New Brunswick and a change of government in Quebec gave King the support of the nine provinces he needed to petition the United Kingdom for an amendment to the British North America Act giving the federal government exclusive jurisdiction over unemployment insurance. The amendment constituted, according to H.M. Cassidy, "the first and only modification of the original distribution of social service responsibilities."[43]

Unemployment largely disappeared when the country mobilized for the war, and some elements within the business community began to have second thoughts about the need for insurance. Appearing before the special committee on the insurance bill, the Canadian Chamber of Commerce refused to take a position on the legislation, arguing rather weakly that money should not be diverted from the war effort and that legislation could wait until the war ended. On the other hand, the Canadian Life Insurance Officers Association declared itself "very sympathetic" to the principle of unemployment insurance and congratulated the government for "a very responsible act." The Retail Merchants Association reiterated its support and was joined by the British Columbia Lumber and Shingle Manufacturers Association. It was particularly pleased that seasonal workers would be covered by the bill and gave "one hundred per cent" support.[44] Despite the last-minute reservations of some businessmen and a few members of the cabinet, King did not face a struggle with industry in passing the unemployment insurance scheme. There is little in King's career to indicate that this extremely cautious politician would have withstood an organized attack on a reform measure. A few recalcitrant provinces, rather than the business community, had been the only threat to the scheme, and they had provided only a temporary obstacle.

In the thirties King's caution in dealing with the provinces and his fiscal conservatism made him unwilling to consider other insurance programs, despite considerable business support for a universal old-age pension scheme (provided, of course, that it was funded by contributions rather than from general revenues). The CMA continued throughout the decade to press for a compulsory contributory pension scheme and told the Royal Commission on Dominion-Provincial Relations that the existing non-contributory deserving-poor scheme put "a premium on thriftlessness and fraud." However, business support for federal social insurance programs could not break down the obstinancy of certain provincial governments, particularly in Quebec, to an extension of federal power. Universal old-age pensions were not established in Canada until 1951.[45]

Health insurance, which enjoyed some industry support, was also not legislated in the 1930s. Bennett's Minister of Health D.M. Sutherland said the government was awaiting the recommendation of an insurance plan by the Canadian Medical Association. But no such plan was put forward. In British Columbia a health insurance proposal by Liberal Premier T. Dufferin Patullo was supported by 59 percent of the voters in a province-wide referendum. Despite this demonstration of popular support, Patullo buckled under the opposition of organized business and organized medicine. The program was not introduced. The business community certainly appeared to have the upper hand. Its opposition slowed down certain reforms as effectively as its support insured the adoption of others.[46] Just how effective the business community was in determining government action is best indicated in the statements of government leaders attesting to the crucial factor of private enterprise approval. Referring to the Municipal Improvements Bill, Charles Dunning stated in his 1938 budget speech:

> We must follow policies which will enable it [private enterprise] to work in accordance with its essential principles. The most important of these principles is that decisions as to whether the individual shall spend and consume, or shall save and invest, or shall save and hoard, are left to the individual's own initiative. If therefore the answers to the questions as to whether plants are to be built or extended, new houses are to be erected and industry is going to expand or to stagnate, depend upon the decisions of tens of thousands of individuals who are free agents and not regimented sheep, it follows that governments must pursue policies which create confidence rather than fear and uncertainty, which give leadership and guidance and encouragement rather than stifle initiative and paralyze new enterprise.[47]

Although it is debatable whether there were tens of thousands of "free agents" in the 1930s economy, Dunning's point is clear. It was essential that the voice of private economic power ring loudest in the ears of those holding political power; it was essential that politicians accept the principle that investment decisions should be made by the private sector. And this is the principle that guided the introduction and adoption of social welfare legislation. The campaigns of other, less influential groups for unemployment insurance and old-age pensions, which preceded business pressure for these insurance schemes, had little direct effect on government action. The threat posed by the discontent of unemployed workers did have some part in the business community's push for state-sponsored reforms. As businessmen recognized at the time, there was a happy coincidence between reforms necessary to maintain corporate stability and reforms necessary to appease the working class.

The actual form of the social legislation was conservative in the sense that it constituted forced savings by the poor rather than redistribution from rich to poor. Legislators like Bennett and Dunning continually insisted that social reforms must be largely paid for by the beneficiaries whether through deductions from wages for insurance premiums or deductions from wages for income tax. It is not surprising, therefore, that the era of the welfare state in Canada, while host to an expanding productivity that fattened the national pie being divided, brought about little redistribution of wealth. The wealthy had become supporters of the welfare state early enough to guide its beginnings and gradual evolution.

VII

THE CONSTRUCTION INDUSTRY

While the economy as a whole shrunk drastically in the Depression, the construction industry almost ceased to exist. The value of construction in 1929 accounted for about 10.5 percent of national income; by 1933 construction had dropped to less than 20 percent of the 1929 figure and made up less than 3 percent of national income.[1] About two-thirds of the workers directly employed by the industry in 1929 found themselves jobless by 1933. Skilled tradesmen were the first to be hit; the building materials manufacturing industry, directly dependent on the level of construction, suffered correspondingly; and the lumber industry, its ability to export blocked by high tariffs, found that its domestic market had shrivelled into insignificance.

With private industry in the doldrums, the contracts available for new buildings and improvements were negligible. Insecure and largely impoverished Canadians were investing in homes at a rate that amounted to about 17 percent of the 1929 peak investment. Public works expenditures by all levels of government had dropped from an average of about $75 million in the 1926-1931 period to $18 million in 1933. The construction industry needed the kind of support that only the state could provide. Among the areas where both business and government proposed action were home-building, mortgage-lending and public works.

The Construction Industry's Demands

Almost from the beginning of the depression, the business community looked to government for a solution to the inevitable drastic decline in construction that accompanied and magnified economic recessions. The usual remedy prescribed was the preplanning of public works. As early as August 1930 the outgoing president of the Retail Merchants Association advocated setting up a government research bureau to predict the onset of trade depressions and to time public works to coincide with the economic downturn. In this way government works could "absorb the shock of the unemployment in certain commercial enterprises, thus sustaining employment and consumer demand."[2] Sir John Aird, president of the Canadian Bank of Commerce, commented in his 1930 report that public works planning must take into account that prosperity had never lasted longer than six years in the past.[3]

In the same speech Aird called for governments to balance their budgets during economic depressions. The contradictory desire to have both public works and balanced budgets with stable taxation levels was held by many businessmen and politicians. Keynesian ideas of deficit spending to spur recovery were the views of a minority among both groups. But support for the idea of a government reserve fund set up in good times to be released in difficult times tended to follow Keynesian theories.

In its submissions to government the construction industry looked largely to state planning and subsidies for both immediate recovery and long-range stability. The Canadian Construction Association, the national association of contractors, proposed in 1931 that a national board be established to release funds for construction when the index of unemployment reached a certain level. Government contributions and compulsory levies on employers and employees would provide the necessary funds for the Association's plan. State intervention to provide stability in the construction industry was justified on the grounds that it would provide a reserve that could be used to nip unemployment in the bud, thereby preventing depressions.[4]

The umbrella organization of the entire construction industry—including lumbermen, manufacturers and construction contractors—was the National Construction Council of Canada.[5] Its message to government during the Depression was that the market economy could not be allowed to dictate either the timing or all the financing of development. One of its briefs said:

> There must be some external force come along and say to the people who are building: "Stop"—not to the industry itself but to the customers of the industry. They should be told when a certain point is reached: "These things should not be done; things are going too fast; put the brakes on the industry" and not have our Customs House built in 1929 at the very peak of everything, but in 1933 when we need the business.[6]

A construction finance corporation under federal auspices was suggested as a means of deciding the merits or the necessity of proposed construction projects. The corporation would assist approved projects with banking services or provide, where necessary, direct financing.[7] Private financial institutions, claimed the building industry representatives, were discouraging the industry's recovery by reducing the volume of available credit and charging high interest rates. Basing its evidence on trade journal reports, the National Construction Council said a cheap-money, easy-credit policy would result in an additional $83 million of private construction. "Permanent financial machinery" was needed to prevent private overspending in boom times and bank parsimony in recessions from ruining the construction industry. The organization declined to elaborate on whether such machinery would include a central bank; but there is little doubt that the proponents of controlled inflation could draw encouragement from the Council's proposals.

The National Construction Council drew on John Maynard Keynes to justify "the judgment of this industry that the resources of the state should be utilized to stimulate industry by the provision of easier credit and cheaper money."[8] The figure of 200,000 unemployed construction workers was said to be only a third of the story. Using Keynes' assertion that for every one person employed directly in construction work two more are employed indirectly, the industry's collapse could be cited as the reason for the unemployment of 600,000 Canadians. Since the industry stimulated further employment, it was inexcusable for government funds to go to direct relief that had little effect on economic revival.

Government money and government controls of building activity were essential but meaningless without intensive economic research, argued W.D. Black, vice-president and general manager of Otis-Fensom Elevator. In his pamphlet, *Stabilization of Canadian Construction*, Black repeated the Council's proposals for government regulation of development. First, careful research must be done of population trends, regional growth, the growth of new industries, the anticipated obsolescence of buildings and the purchasing power of money. In the Black proposal the board that would receive these statistics and make decisions on proposed building projects would have representation from government, finance, building and labour interests. Black's proposals were discussed at a conference in Toronto and received the support of Major L.L. Anthes, president of the Canadian Manufacturers Association and owner of a Toronto foundry. Planned economy must replace laissez faire, said Anthes.[9] Conference participants called for slum clearance which the construction industry generally regarded as a legitimate area of government activity. The Canadian Construction Association pointed to Britain's alleged achievement in the elimination of slums.

Dominion Housing Act and Public Works

The Public Works Construction acts of 1934 and 1935, as well as the Dominion Housing Act of 1935, were seen by the industry as "due chiefly to representations made to the late [Bennett] government by the construction industry." Bennett had encouraged the organization to draw up a detailed plan of public works and had provided federal funds for most of these projects.[10] But the government did not go as far as the industry wanted in instituting state responsibility for the amount of building that occurred.

The public works acts attempted to divert some funds from direct relief to construction. Federal cost-sharing on municipal public works (according to a 25 percent federal–75 per cent provincial-and-municipal formula declared by the federal government in 1930) had only a modest effect in encouraging municipalities—penniless after they had met their relief payments obligation—to carry out projects. The federal government's spending on its own public works from 1931 to 1933 was only $29 million. The public works acts committed $40 million to federal public works in 1934 and $78 million in 1935. But the overall federal attitude towards state involvement in construction, while mildly inflationist, fell short of the view of the National Construction Council that a construction regulation and finance corporation was needed. Although the 1935 public works appropriation was slightly higher than the figure for 1929, it could hardly compensate for the three-year near-hiatus in public works spending from 1931 to 1933.

There was a precedent, however modest, for federal government spending to activate house-building. About $23.5 million had been loaned to the provinces by the federal government from 1919 to 1924 to build homes in congested districts. In the 1930s both business and government were won over to the need for a state presence in the house-building business. Building industry pressure was fortified by pressure from the financial community. The president of the Investment Bankers Association of Canada urged Bennett in 1933 towards "national action" to unfreeze the mortgage situation. The Dominion Housing Act of 1935 embodied the major proposals of the Dominion Mortgage and Investments Association and the Ontario Mortgage Companies Association, organizations which included the largest loan, trust and life insurance companies in the country.[11] In a telegram to Finance Minister E.N. Rhodes, T. D'Arcy Leonard, solicitor for the Dominion association and secretary of the Ontario organization, outlined the companies' idea of the "soundest housing scheme." The ideal scheme would allow the existing mortgage-lending firms to lend up to 80 percent on approved new houses—60 percent from company coffers and 20 percent from government coffers. The government, rather than making a direct loan to a home-buyer, would make its loan to the mortgage company and assume the losses if the borrower defaulted.

In the *Journal of the Canadian Bankers Association*, Leonard justified government assistance to the housing industry on several grounds. Because of the number of workers directly employed in the industry and indirectly in manufacturing building materials and in supplying lumber, Leonard concluded that "no other industry is so interwoven into the fabric of our economic life." The house-building industry which in normal times provided about a quarter of all construction in Canada, was at a standstill because second-mortgage lenders had abandoned the market. First-mortgage lenders were as ready as ever to make loans. By loaning the 20 percent second mortgage to those considered eligible for a first mortgage by the lending companies, the government was taking the place of the temporarily non-existent second mortgage lenders. The Minister of Finance was empowered to make loans up to $10 million at an interest rate of 3 percent to approved lending institutions for re-loan to borrowers, including construction companies, at a rate not exceeding 5 percent. The unusually low interest rate for the 20 percent of a mortgage beyond the first 60 percent was considered a further incentive to Canadians considering building or buying a new home.

The loan companies greeted the Housing Act with enthusiasm. Thomas Bradshaw, president of North American Life Assurance Company, telegrammed Rhodes that his company, unable to find borrowers for residential construction, believed the legislation would stimulate home construction. North American Life, he said, was prepared to loan "considerable mortgage money on suitable properties."[12] Similar sentiments were expressed by W.H. Somerville, president of Mutual Life of Canada.[13]

The lumber business was also pressing the government to get into the mortgage-lending field. *Canadian Lumberman* carried frequent editorials supporting the concept of the federal government entering at least the second-mortgage business and perhaps the first-mortgage area as well. The Ontario Retail Lumber Dealers Association wrote both the federal and Ontario governments that some money should be diverted from relief to the setting up of a fund for loans to respectable citizens planning to build homes but unable to receive loans from the private loan agencies.[14] Canadian industry as a whole supported the Housing Act. In *Canadian Business* Henry Morgan, executive member and future chairman of the Canadian Chamber of Commerce, endorsed the principle of the legislation and said it should be a prelude to further government activities to activate building.[15]

Stimulation of construction was one of the aims expressed by the government in introducing the housing act. The others were slum clearance and the provision of adequate, cheap housing for the working poor. But government interest, like industry interest in this aspect of the housing problem, was more on the level of rhetoric than action. An economic council, reminiscent of the Black plan supported by the Canadian Manufacturers Association and the National Construction Council, was included in the 1935 legislation. Acting Prime Minister Sir George Perley stated that the council would investigate the possibility of slum clearance and possible economies and efficiencies that might be introduced in housing construction.[16] But no council was named. The King government in the prewar period did little more than the Bennett government to tackle the problem of housing for low-income people.

Business attitudes towards a government role in insuring a minimum standard of housing were ambiguous. Few in the 1930s were still willing to say that private market mechanisms would eventually handle the problem. Citing the British example, leading businessmen saw slum clearance as a priority for relief work. Many other businessmen insisted that times of prosperity rather than depression were compatible with a government attack on slums. The need-for-a-balanced-budget argument was made by those who saw urban renewal as a distant aim. Second-mortgage lending by government would involve only a small number of dollars compared to the stimulus the economy as a whole would receive. Slum clearance would involve large direct injection of government money into the economy. T. D'Arcy Leonard argued that when prosperity returned it would be proper for the government to vacate the mortgage-lending field and to concentrate its finances on slum elimination and prevention. What was desirable had to give way to what would stimulate the private sector.

The companies themselves were not willing to take losses to build homes. At a meeting with Department of Finance officials, the construction and finance company associations said loans were not being made outside the large cities because there were no funds for making appraisals and supervising construction in the smaller centres. The government was then convinced "to bear the cost of appraisal and supervision charges in centres other than the cities in which the lending institutions have their head offices." Certain expenses would be socialized, but the interest charges would still be paid to the private lenders.

The Home Improvement Plan

The Dominion Housing Act received Liberal support. The Liberal government elected in September 1935, encouraged by the construction and finance organizations, sought further ways to stimulate building activity. Liberal anti-unemployment measures, such as they were, tended to originate with the National Employment Commission headed by Arthur Purvis. Purvis had recommended in an interim Commission report in September 1936 that the government establish a Home Improvement Plan (HIP). Nineteen days later the Canadian Bankers Association, acting on behalf of all the chartered banks, wrote Finance Minister Dunning that the organization supported the Commission proposal and would immediately begin making loans in accordance with the plan if the government promised to introduce the legislation in the next session and make it retroactive. The government gave its guarantee.[17]

HIP was modelled after an American home-improvement plan. To encourage loans for residential repair the government would guarantee approved lending institutions against losses incurred on loans. A limit of $7.5 million was set on government loans and no institution could collect losses exceeding 15 percent of its total loans. According to *Canadian Banker*, the loss rate in the American plan (under which $500,000,000 had been loaned) was about .5 percent.[18] Why the Canadian—or the American—financial community needed government guarantees for loans that had only a .5 percent risk of default was not explained by the bankers' association journal. The fact that they did require such guarantees is one piece of evidence that reform often meant little more than an assumption by the state of financial obligations that a conservative financial community refused to bear alone. With the blessings of the banks and loan companies, the three and four letter government agencies, using public money but allowing the private finance companies to be their agents and make profits accordingly, began to appear.

As with the Housing Act, the financial community stressed that the stimulus to the entire economy went far beyond the public dollars spent. *Canadian Banker* editorialized that the American experience with an improvement plan, coupled with community movements for house improvement and modernization, showed that for every person making a loan for improvements three more were making repairs without a loan. People would follow their neighbours in making repairs to their homes.

In HIP's first year, $12.8 million was loaned to over 32,000 borrowers. With loans of $17.3 million made to 4000 families in two and a half years under the Housing Act, residential construction from 1 May 1937 to 30 April 1938 had reached $52 million, more than double the 1933 amount but less than a third of the 1929 figure.

This success, however modest, encouraged Dunning to sponsor further programs to cajole money-lenders into unfreezing funds for building houses. The National Housing Act of 1938, said Dunning, was designed for that purpose:

> Vitally important is the cooperation of the life insurance companies and I do say that this legislation is designed to cast out fear on the part of those investment institutions also, and to encourage them, as partners with the Parliament of Canada, to make advances for the purpose of building homes not merely in our larger centres...but also in the smaller centres throughout the country.

The new Housing Act continued the 60–20 private lender-government split on mortgages for homes valued under $4000. It also introduced a 25 percent government second mortgage for homes valued under $2500 if a private lender would assume a 65 percent first mortgage. In response to a request of the Ontario Associated Boards of Trade to encourage building in small and remote communities payments were to be made to lending institutions to defray costs involved in arranging the loans. A twenty-dollars-per-loan maximum plus mileage allowance would be granted the lender. The total available guarantee for home improvements was also increased.[19]

Most welcome from the business community's standpoint was a section in the act that provided for federal payment for three years of a portion of municipal taxes for houses built between 1 June 1938 and 31 December 1940. The government would pay 100 percent of municipal taxes the first year in which the house was taxed,

50 percent the second year and 25 percent the third year. Dunning expected the program would cost the federal government under $5 million. This measure was first suggested by the Dominion Mortgages and Investments Association as a means of stimulating construction.[20]

According to the *Financial Times*, the 1938 budget was well received by the business community. The "outstanding constructive feature," it said, was the assistance provided the building industry, through both the housing legislation and the generous provision for public works. In its monthly review the Bank of Nova Scotia reflected business pessimism that the economic depression might persist for some time. Under such circumstances, it argued, the government was doing the job that must be done.

Industry could be well assured that the government shared its reticence in seeing these social measures as more than just pump-priming to stir the private sector. Mackenzie King commented in his diary that the budget was "following the example of priming the pump to a greater extent than I would like," but added:

> However Britain's announcement this morning that she was arranging to make large expenditures once armaments were being reduced, made it almost imperative that we should meet our unemployment problem by some addition to the purchasing power and aid to construction in our country.[21]

Mortgages

More ambitious than the 1938 program was the stillborn Central Mortgage Bank of 1939, forerunner of the Central Mortgage and Housing Corporation. Since government second-mortgage activities had been an insufficient incentive to mortgage-loan companies, the government would also provide money for first mortgages. The Mortgage Bank would be empowered to issue government guaranteed debentures to a value of $200 million. Any incorporated mortgage-lending institution could join the bank if it agreed to an adjustment of currently-held mortgages. The Mortgage Bank would assume half of the losses incurred in the adjustment.

The Dominion Mortgages and Investments Association, collective spokesman for the lenders, had already presented Dunning with a plan for a central mortgage bank and supported the bill in principle. But they opposed an adjustment for urban homes and demanded that the terms of adjustment for urban homes be less liberal than those for farms. They readily accepted that existing farm mortgages should be adjusted to put a maximum of five percent annual interest on farm debts. Few farmers were able to pay even that rate and the federal government was bailing out the companies for half of the losses incurred in adjustment. Urban dwellers who had borrowed at steep rates were often able—though with considerable hardship—to pay these rates. In fact surveys conducted by the organization indicated a reasonable repayment level by urban borrowers.[22]

Some members of the government committee felt that the privilege of access to the Central Mortgage Bank should be accompanied by some concessions on the part of the Bank's beneficiaries. Dunning, however, had no intention of coercing lending institutions either to join the Bank and make new loans or to adjust old loans. Changes must be made to cajole companies into joining the plan:

> ...There are about three companies with large investments in the smaller type of urban homes covered by the act, that it is very desirable should become member companies because of the benefits which would accrue particularly in constituencies like your own [to Ralph Maybank, Winnipeg South] and I am trying to find the way not to set up an idealistic piece of legislation which won't work but keeping it within the bounds of reason so it will operate.[23]

Dunning moved amendments that raised the adjustment rate on non-farm mortgages to 5.5 percent and excluded from adjustment all loans made after 1 January, 1936. T. D'Arcy Leonard consulted members of his organization and brought the committee the news that most, if not all, companies would now join the Mortgage Bank.

The companies continued to chafe at the adjustment rate on non-farm mortgages. J.L. Ralston, Dunning's successor, would not agree to an industry suggestion that only farm mortgages be adjusted. And since Ralston, like Dunning, would not force the companies to join the Central Mortage Bank, the legislation was suspended in February 1940.[24]

In the 1938 session Dunning also introduced legislation for low-rental public housing. The interim and final reports of the Purvis Commission had called for "assistance for low rental housing for those unable to afford to pay an economic rent" as part of "a comprehensive housing policy." The Purvis report was adopted by business because Purvis had stressed that there was one criterion for the usefulness of a public expenditure: its ability to stimulate private spending. Purvis saw assistance to low-rental housing "as a means of stimulating employment in the construction industry in which there was the greatest lag."[25] Purvis and Dunning had received representations not only from the construction industry but also from some boards of trade and leading individual businessmen in favour of taking some action on the problem of the slums.

The Dunning program would allow the municipalities to decide whether public housing should be placed under municipal auspices or under the control of a limited-dividend private corporation. Thirty million dollars would be available in loans to municipal programs that had received government approval. Interest on the loans would be set at 2 percent per annum to municipal housing commissions and 1.75 percent per half-annum to private housing corporations. Accommodation in low-rental housing would be limited to those making less than five times the fixed minimum rent, and rent would be set at a maximum of 20 percent of family income. Other families would be considered only if there were not enough families at this income level to fill vacancies.

Dunning told the House that the legislation had been inspired partly by a project that Montreal businessmen had been evolving for two years. The project involved 400 units at a cost of $2700 per dwelling. In support of the plan, which had been worked out in detail, Dunning commented: "I hope if this bill passes parliament they will be able to consummate the project on which they have been working for the past two years."[26] A loans program, however, could do little to stimulate bankrupt and near-bankrupt municipalities to build public housing.

Business determination to maintain a government role in the house-building field was demonstrated by business leaders in 1942 when, at C.D. Howe's instigation, the government dropped the Home Improvement Plan and considered dropping the National Housing Act. Howe argued that non-war housing could wait until the war ended. The Canadian Construction Association, the Canadian Builders Supply Association, the Canadian Lumbermen's Association, life insurance executives and several boards of trade, as well as labour organizations and the Canadian Conference of Mayors, successfully pressured the government to retain the Housing Act. The general secretary of the Canadian Builders Supply Association pointed out that the American government was giving the banks a 100 percent guarantee on credit involved in private housebuilding. *Timber of Canada* reported that the prewar tendency towards centralization of population in the urban centres had been accelerated by the exigencies of war, and government aid to house-building was necessary to prevent an absolute fiasco when the soldiers returned. *Building in Canada* argued that even before the war, "at least 200,000 additional homes were needed to provide reasonable accommodation for the people." The "bold enterprise" of the Americans in housing was contrasted with the "half-hearted efforts" of the Canadian government.[27] By 1941 22,123 units had been built under NHA and DHA and almost $74 million had been loaned. HIP loans approached 100,000 with a value of almost $40 million.

Public Works Planning

While generally supportive of advance planning of public works, the Canadian business community had mixed feelings about the value of make-work projects hastily designed to reduce the numbers of people on relief rolls. Despite these mixed feelings the $40 million public works appropriation in 1934 was commended by the Chamber of Commerce, which hoped that this type of public spending would be "contagious" and encourage private spending. Its enthusiasm was no doubt prompted by the fact that many of its leading members were direct beneficiaries of the expanded works program. In its 22 June commentary on the legislation the *Financial Times* remarked:

> While the majority of industries, as well as chain stores and departmental stores, may be expected to benefit in some degree from the program of the federal government, the most direct and substantial benefits will accrue to the construction, cement, structural steel, builders' supplies, dredging, steel and iron and paint companies.

Particular beneficiaries would include Canada Cement, Dominion Bridge, Canadian Dredge, Gypsum Lime and Alabaster, Steel Company of Canada, Dominion Steel and Coal Company, Sherwin-Williams and C.I.L.

Since 1934 the Chamber of Commerce had repeatedly submitted to the federal government a proposal for a national employment commission that would decide the best ways of committing public funds to achieve recovery. The Purvis Commission, the result of the agitation of the Chamber of Commerce and others, opposed public works designed principally to provide employment. Public works were costly and the taxation burden they created discouraged private investment. Only those public works that stimulated the private sector (roads to mining or tourist areas, improvement of dock facilities, etc.) should be approved. The Chamber of Commerce supported the Purvis approach. So did the government. Labour Minister Norman Rogers told the Commons that the government was carrying out the Commission recommendation to end the practice of joint federal-provincial-municipal public works and would in future concentrate its spending on federal works aimed at developing the tourist industry.

Advance planning of public works—so that public works would be held back until the economy was sluggish—had become an accepted dogma by most businessmen during the Depression. The construction industry, retail merchants and the president of the Bank of Nova Scotia had mentioned early in the Depression that public policy in the 1920s had erred in not paying attention to the timing of public works. Others who had added their voices in favour of such a policy by the late 1930s included the Canadian

Manufacturers Association, the Montreal Board of Trade and Arthur Purvis.[28] Since no public works had been held back in the previous period of prosperity, advance planning could only be instituted for the next recession.

Few businessmen were opponents of the expensive federal-provincial highways-building program, which would provide a national highway system. Though highways-building had added to the federal debt in the 1920s and placed severe strain on the provincial governments' budgets (especially the Maritimes'), industrialists believed government had a duty to build the infrastructure needed to make cheaper the carrying on of national business.[29]

Regulated Wages

The construction industry saw a usefulness for the state as a stabilizer in its role not only as a spender but also as a potential regulator of conditions that previously had been partly determined by the market. Heavily unionized, the construction industry in some areas faced a labour market in which wages for particular jobs had been partially stabilized by the unions. Unionized firms faced competition from non-unionized companies, a situation that undermined the union's ability to guarantee companies that increased labour costs would be uniform throughout the market and would therefore not be a factor of competition. Only state enforcement could insure stability of the wage factor. Ontario's Industrial Standards Act of 1934 (and similar acts in other provinces) allowed the state to enforce agreements over wages and hours voluntarily entered into by employer and labour groups representing a substantial majority of workers in the industry. State enforcement of voluntary collective bargaining agreements required the support of both employer and employee groups; either group could call for a meeting with a representative of the Minister of Labour to determine whether this support existed.

The Toronto District Construction Council, which included 95 percent of Toronto contractors, was one of the first employer groups to ask the provincial Labour Minister to approve an industry agreement establishing standard rates of wages and hours for the industry in Toronto. Bricklayers, carpenters and labourers were covered under the ensuing agreement. Within a year the Home Builders' Association was complaining that the labour component of building costs was prohibitive and that the Industrial Standards Act was being unevenly enforced. While the members of this association wanted a return to a competitive labour market in construction, the Toronto Building and Construction Association, "composed of the larger contractors and sub-contractors in the building industry in this district," did not. The organization's secretary wrote Labour Minister D.A. Croll that it wanted to continue to enter into contracts with the international building craft unions and have the government guarantee the uniformity of wage rates and hours. It advised Croll to counter the propaganda campaign led by the Home Builders' Association by making some amendments and by increasing the finances available for enforcement of the act. In construction as in other industries the established companies wanted stability and were willing to use the state apparatus to enforce rules which, whatever their overall merits, made it difficult for smaller, less established firms to compete. Croll followed the advice of the large firms and the agreements were renewed.[30]

By 1938 one or more building trades were covered by Industrial Standards Act agreements in twelve Ontario cities. In Quebec standardized labour conditions in the building industry were met with early and near-unanimous support. By 1938 all but a few townships in the province were covered by voluntary state-enforced collective agreements. Some building trades in Edmonton, Calgary, Halifax, Dartmouth, Regina and Saskatoon were also covered by agreements.[31]

By 1938 the construction industry had come to see state involvement as integral to its stability. Only planned government spending would insure that the vulnerable construction industry would have a cushion when the private sector was not building. Only government guarantees to the lenders would insure that sufficient credit was available. Only government spending would expand the house-building industry to include some of the slum-dwellers. And only government enforcement would guarantee uniform wages and hours throughout the industry.

The belief that capitalism, as a result of technological and administrative innovations, faced long-term structural problems of employing the available work force had led to support of various programs of social insurance. Cyclical unemployment, which might also be reduced through judicious insurance programs, was regarded as a special threat to a future in which even at the top of the business cycle unemployment would be already high for structural reasons. Keeping construction at stable levels through government regulation and spending became the better part of conservative logic under such circumstances.

If regulating the construction industry would contribute to economic stability, there were even greater benefits in regulating the money supply. The debate on the establishment of the Bank of Canada—like the debate on the construction industry—was whether or not government regulation might smooth out the economic cycle.

VIII

THE BANK OF CANADA

Several recent studies have pointed out that the conservatism of Canadian bankers was particularly evident in their choice to invest their funds in "safe" places—government bonds, the extractive industries, commerce and established manufacturing industries. Their credit policies were especially cautious. As new high-technology industries began to develop in the twentieth century, in the early stages the banks refused to extend credit. Only later when many of these industries were either absorbed by large American concerns or established as subsidiaries, did the bankers change their credit policies.[1] These conservative bankers were often the leading business supporters of social insurance, marketing boards and other forms of government intervention. This kind of state involvement had the conservative consequence of reinforcing the status quo and it was this aspect of certain government interventions that appealed to the bankers.

One reform that did not carry great favour among most bankers was the setting up of the Bank of Canada in 1934. Despite the fears of the bankers, the Bank of Canada changed very little. While its establishment was supported by many members of the business community, as well as by non-business interests, once in operation its record could not help but produce relief among the bankers. Their economic power had not been compromised and the decisions carried out by the Bank were in accord with bankers' views.

The Central Bank Debate

One of the early calls for a central bank had come in 1917 from E.L. Pease, president of the Canadian Bankers Association. Vice-president and managing director of the Royal Bank of Canada, Pease had expressed a need for a central bank to Minister of Finance Thomas White. Through the Finance Act of 1914 the federal government had already assumed some of the duties of a central bank. As the likelihood of war had increased, the banks had experienced a run on their gold reserves as speculative depositors hurried to convert their Dominion and bank notes into gold. In consultation with the bankers the cabinet suspended the convertibility of both Dominion and bank notes. The Finance Act extended the prohibition on convertibility and provided for government advances to the banks in return for the banks depositing specified securities with the government. Rediscounting (banks borrowing government notes), however, was not widely used. Pease believed a central bank, which would be a permanent rediscounting bank, would allow the commercial banks to "liquefy dormant assets, thereby increasing our resources for the general benefit." Banks would be more likely to increase their loans if a permanent reserve fund was available from which the banks could borrow. The Canadian Bankers Association asked the government to renew the Finance Act. At the time the association informed the government of its intention to formulate a central bank plan. Finding a formula acceptable to all the banks turned out to be a difficult task. On the whole banks feared that the central bank would become a competitor. Banks were also unwilling to risk losing the right of note issue they had always enjoyed in Canada (there were restrictions requiring, on request, the conversion of bank notes to Dominion notes or gold). The Bank of Montreal, the country's leading bank, held a monopoly of the government's accounts and did not wish to turn them over to a central bank. The issue was shelved.[2]

The Depression inevitably reopened the debate. The central bank issue became part of the larger debate on the question of what role, if any, the government should have in spurring investment, particularly when private investment was insufficient to keep the economy buoyant. To the MPs representing the United Farmers of Alberta, like G.G. Coote, it seemed clear that a shortage of purchasing power existed and that it could only be restored by inflating currency and increasing government control over private lending practices. In the United Farmers of Alberta scheme, and even more clearly in the ideology of the Social Credit party, the banks were choking small investors and consumers by refusing to make more loans. The banks could only be humbled by the establishment of a government bank, which would have control over the amount of currency issued. The Social Credit theory was simplistic in the extreme, divorcing banking operations from the operation of the existing industrial system as a whole and generally relying on conspiracy theories in which bankers and communists were allies in an unholy crusade against virtuous small businessmen and farmers.[3]

The monetary cranks of the Social Credit variety who regarded inflation as a panacea were not the only participants in the debate on the central bank. Support for controlled inflation, by no means unanimous in the business community, was strong in many sectors of the economy. Various components of the construction industry drew on John Maynard Keynes to justify demands for state intervention to provide "easier credit and cheaper money." The National Construction Council of Canada denounced the banks for not cooperating with the construction industry in providing the credit needed to lift the industry from its doldrums.[4] Lumbermen in Parliament tended in particular to be in favour of central banking. Wilfrid Hanbury, a lumberman and Vancouver Liberal MP, in April 1931 called for a "federal reserve system," as the American central bank was called. A federal reserve would increase the money available for loans and the result would be more money invested in industrial expansion. "More and cheaper money would increase the purchasing power of the Canadian people."[5] Chubby Power, scion of a family in the lumbering business, pointed out the necessity of inflation to keep Canada from pricing itself out of world markets.[6]

The need for a government agency that could quickly adjust Canada's money supply as other countries inflated their currencies was stressed by the major importing and exporting industries. The grain merchants, like the lumbermen, urged on the government the importance of international cooperation to achieve a standard of value "to which domestic payments can be immediately and accurately reflected."[7] Reacting to the fact that fluctuations of various foreign currencies relative to the Canadian dollar had caused some instability in the industry, the North Western Grain Dealers Association gave this guarded sanction to a central bank:

> The question whether the establishment in Canada of a central bank similar to the Bank of England in its functions would assist in stabilizing the rates of exchange by which grain exporters are affected is a large one involving many expert considerations. But the membership of the association is certainly of the opinion that anything which can be done to reduce the fluctuations in exchange rates ought to be done in the interest of all concerned, and especially of the producers.[8]

In general the west favoured a central bank and a cheap-money policy that would make Canada's wheat competitive in world markets and give farmers and merchants easier access to bank loans. A Winnipeg Board of Trade questionnaire showed 71 percent of the respondents in favour of a central bank.[9] A Canadian Chamber of Commerce poll showed a majority of Manitoba, Alberta and Saskatchewan—as well as Prince Edward Island—businessmen in favour of a central bank. Majority opinion in the other provinces was opposed. The Chamber of Commerce brief summed up the arguments of businessmen for and against a central bank. The opponents were not convinced that countries with a central bank had weathered the Depression better than Canada or that such an agency could be set up without political patronage, which would hurt financial confidence and undermine the central bank's attempt to end instability. Supporters stressed the central bank's potential role in stabilizing foreign exchange and domestic price levels, influencing the expansion and contraction of credit and securing greater elasticity in interest rates.[10] Among leading eastern Canadian businessmen who supported central banking were E.W. Beatty and C.L. Burton,[11] two men who did not support many other reforms of the decade.

With the exception of some small manufacturers who urged Bennett to establish a central bank, manufacturers as a group took no position on central banking. If the intricacies of banking had prevented the manufacturers from taking much interest in the central banking issue, they were not alone. Labour made only two representations to the Royal Commission on Banking and Currency, set up in 1933 to investigate the central bank issue. The Trades and Labour Congress official journal did not address the issue until 1934, after the government's decision to set up the bank had been made known.

While the commercial bankers were opposed to a central bank, the investment dealers were not of the same mind. A.E. Ames, head of the second largest investment company in the country, had helped in the drafting of the Liberal party proposal for a central bank constitution. The proposal, prepared before the Royal Commission on Banking and Currency had reported in 1933, closely paralleled the views expressed in the commission's report. Investment Dealers Association president Ward Pitfield wrote Bennett and told a Chamber of Commerce annual convention that the commercial bankers were too parsimonious and that investment was suffering accordingly. "National action" was required to create a "substantial extension of internal credit at reduced rates," though Pitfield was not specific about the form this "national action" should take.[12]

The Montreal Stock Exchange, also critical of the commercial banks, would not directly endorse a central bank. It argued before the Royal Commission on Banking and Currency that Canada lacked a true money market and that the banks had done little to help create one. Even before the Depression, the Canadian banks had charged substantially higher interest rates on loans than the American banks, with the result that Canadian brokers would borrow in New York or Boston to finance the issuing of securities in Canada. Interest was paid by the brokers to American banks rather than to firms within the country. In the opinion of Stock Exchange president I.G. Beaubien, it was necessary for the banks—if not of their own volition then aided by the state—to pool a certain amount of their reserves in order to have a fund available that would allow the banks to be less cautious about loans. Though Canada's economy did not yet have a turnover comparable to Britain or the United States, Beaubien believed a reserve system would make it possible to create a money market to compete with London and New York.[13]

The commercial bankers, on the other hand, did not see the need for Canada to develop its own money market. Their presentation to the Royal Commission consisted mainly of home truths about the structure of the Canadian economy. It was a dependent economy relying on external markets as much as on internal markets and on external investors as much as on internal investors. In particular, said the Canadian Bankers Association, "the very intimate and continuous business relationship existing between Canada and the United States is a factor which can never be left out of account in any study of the Canadian financial situation."[14] The large number of American branch firms in Canada was a considerable source of deposits for Canadian commercial banks. Canada's securities market was limited and the success of most large bond issues depended upon large subscriptions by Americans. About 40 percent of the capital investment in non-farm business and government securities in Canada was held externally. If the central bank was purchasing securities on the open market in an attempt to expand its reserves and create conditions allowing low interest loans, many of the securities it would receive would be securities formerly in American hands. Such imports of securities would "cause a pressure on the foreign exchange market...and a consequent diminution of the market base in Canada." Unlike the Montreal Stock Exchange, the bankers did not believe a central bank would do much to change this dependent economic structure, and in fact they seemed to see no reason for changing it.

The bankers also repeated their objections to surrendering their right of note issue. They made clear their intention to recoup financial losses in this area by closing unprofitable and marginally profitable bank branches in small communities. Finally, the bankers suggested that since a central bank could not be free of political interference they preferred simply to remain under the Finance Act. The act allowed them to make loans from the government, but it did not give the government considerable powers to regulate the volume of currency in the country.[15]

Ironically, it was the Canadian economy's dependence on the external factors that made both R.B. Bennett and Mackenzie King decide that Canada must have a central bank. Britain had abandoned the gold standard in September 1931, and the resulting rapid fluctuation of exchange rates was wreaking havoc in the Canadian economy. In October 1931 the Canadian dollar was at a discount of 11 percent, and the calling of loans obtained in New York before the discount ruined three leading brokerage houses in Montreal, which explains the interest of the brokers in a central bank or similar agency for regulating the currency.

The commercial banks were in the vanguard of businesses calling for restoration of the gold standard. The Bank of Nova Scotia argued that stabilization of price levels required a world-wide effort to return to the kind of system of stable exchanges that the gold standard had provided.[16] But the report of the monetary and finance commission, approved by the World Economic Conference in July 1933, had this to say about the steps necessary to restore the gold standard:

> The Conference considers it to be essential, in order to provide an international gold standard with the necessary mechanism for satisfactory working, that independent central banks, with the requisite powers and freedoms to carry out an appropriate currency and credit policy, should be created in such developed countries as have not at present an adequate central banking institution.[17]

The views of the conference placed the country's bankers in an awkward position. A return to the gold standard, eagerly sought by the bankers, meant that Canada should set up a central bank, a measure the bankers resisted.

Within days of the conference Bennett established the Royal Commission on Banking and Currency, whose mandate was to determine whether a central bank was advisable and what role it should take with existing banking institutions. At its head was Sir Thomas Macmillan, a director of the Bank of England. The majority report of the Macmillan Commission carried the signature of only three of the five members. The two banking representatives, Sir Thomas White of the Canadian Bank of Commerce and Beaudry Leman of the Banque Canadienne Nationale, filed dissenting reports on the central banking question in which they almost totally rejected the findings of the majority. Macmillan's report accepted the views of both the domestic advocates of a central bank and the World Economic Conference:

> In the first place from a national point of view, the central bank, within the limits imposed by law and by its capacities, should endeavour to regulate credit and currency in the best interests of the nation and should, as far as possible, control and defend the external value of the national monetary unit. In the second place, from the international point of view, the central bank, by wise and timely cooperation with similar institutions in other countries, should seek, so far as may be within the scope of monetary action, to mitigate by its influence fluctuations in the general level of economic activity.[18]

While Sir Thomas White simply reiterated the bankers' views about the unlikelihood of a central bank substantially improving the domestic situation by regulating the currency, he did concede that in the broader context of "the promotion of intra-Imperial and international trade," the government might have reason to establish a central bank. But he did not believe that such considerations had been made known to the Commission. White was not against moderate inflation, and considering the bankers' support of the government's construction and insurance programs, it seems unlikely that most bankers found the federal government's programs too inflationary. (Bank of Montreal president Sir Charles Gordon praised Bennett for his program of moderate inflation.) White wrote Bennett after the banking commission had finished its work to recommend monetary inflation. He called on Bennett to amend the Dominion Notes Act to change the 40 percent reserve of gold for bank notes to 25 percent and to make a new issue of treasury bills to the banks at a low rate of interest. Such moderate inflation was justified on the same grounds all inflationists used:

> . . . This would materially assist in your financing of relief and public works expenditure and would thus tend to reduce unemployment and by stimulating trade, to cause a rise in the domestic price level.

Bennett responded to White saying that he was in full agreement with White's recommendations and that the government planned to follow his course of action.[19]

The spectre of inflation was not the worry of White and his fellow bankers. Long-term considerations ofst how far a central bank might go to curb the bankers' power were joined to short-term consideration of the loss of profit that would result from the bankers' losing the right of note issue. The threat to close rural banks in order to recoup this loss continued.[20] Bennett was angered by the bankers' opposition to the central bank and dismissed their objections as narrow and self-interested.[21] But Bennett's views on banking, as expressed both before and after his decision to establish a central bank, indicate that he did not contemplate using it to produce more than the kind of moderate inflation that even the bankers deemed advisable when faced with a drastic shrinkage in national credit and the consequent necessity of federal relief spending. Bennett entertained ideas of the role of banks that were common in the rhetoric of bankers. Calling the banking system "the sheet anchor of Canada in this period of depression" while ignoring the multiplier-effect created by extra dollars in circulation, Bennett summed up the business of banking as "the maintenance of an equilibrium between demand deposits and demand loans and between time deposits and time loans" so that anyone could be sure that a cheque drawn against his deposits in a bank would always receive cash. Like most bankers, Bennett appeared ignorant of the power over demand that the moneylenders held. He made it seem that availability of money for loans was always related to business demand for money, when in fact this demand was always tempered by the bankers' willingness to supply credit.[22]

More than a year and a half later and with the decision to establish a central bank already made, Bennett commented in a radio speech that Canada did not intend to follow the inflationary policies of the American government. When applied in the past in other countries, these policies "destroyed large capital assets... and in some cases resulted in a complete transformation of their institutions."[23] The Canadian government believed that the government's contribution to recovery must be:

> ...to restore to owners and employers of capital that

> confidence which comes from a realization that the period of low prices is past. This confidence is now apparent and must not again be subjected to undue risks and dangers.[24]

Central Bank Legislation

It was this philosophy that guided the drafting of the central bank legislation. Recognizing the split over the issue in the business community, Bennett and Finance Minister E.N. Rhodes carefully delimited the powers of the bank. The two banker-members of the royal commission who had opposed the establishment of the central bank nevertheless pronounced themselves pleased with the central bank that had been set up. Beaudry Leman believed the legislation did not go far enough in making the bank the controller of the volume of credit in the nation. But he added that:

> ...On the other hand, it may have been the part of wisdom to shackle and fetter the new species introduced in the Canadian fauna in order that no one be scared. As it becomes evident that the animal is tame, it will no doubt be found desirable to loosen and even remove some of the chains.[25]

When Finance Minister Rhodes introduced the central bank legislation, he stressed the same points put forward by the Macmillan commission majority: the need for a bank to cooperate with other central banks and to provide at home a state regulatory role over the volume of credit. Like Bennett, Rhodes pointed to the need for some control over the general price level in order to maintain investors' confidence. The central bank's role would be an indirect one: by its purchase or sale of securities it would affect the rate of rediscount and thus the availability of credit in the country. The "shackles and fetters" to which Leman referred were the strict limits on the securities that the bank could trade. The bank was prohibited from having direct interest in any industrial or commercial undertaking and from making loans or advances on real or immovable property. Thus the fear of the commercial bankers that the central bank could contribute adversely to Canada's balance of payments problem was partially undercut by severe restrictions on which securities the bank would be trading on the open market. The bank was restricted to trading only government securities, though many of these were held outside the country.

The bank was to be privately-owned but with profits limited to 6 percent. Private ownership was meant to meet criticisms from business that a central bank could not be immune from political pressure. And as the first governor of the bank Bennett appointed Graham Towers, assistant general manager of the Royal Bank of Canada and a direct descendant of John R. Richardson, one of the founders of the Bank of Montreal. He did so despite advice from Deputy Finance Minister W.C. Clark that it would be wiser to make an appointment from outside the banking community since none of the bankers was sufficiently trained as an economist (Towers did, in fact, have training in economics).[26]

Towers' appointment was not fortuitous. Despite the bankers' solid public opposition to a central bank while the Macmillan commission held its hearings, the Royal Bank had maintained a fairly consistent stance in favour of a central bank since World War I. The Royal Bank's vice president, managing director and assistant general manager shared the view that the other chartered banks had not fully grasped the issue of a central bank and that it was the role of the government to adopt monetary policies that would stabilize credit. Although the bank's general manager did not join his colleagues in breaking the bankers' solidarity in 1933, he supported the establishment of a central bank once economic conditions had improved. Towers himself had publicly supported central banking for Canada as early as 1930. Since it was this bank which listed Prime Minister Bennett as one of its leading shareholders, its pro-central banking attitude perhaps weighed as much in Bennett's decision as the combined opposition of the other nine chartered banks.

The Bank of Canada under Towers did not make the radical changes in banking policy the bankers feared when they appeared before the Macmillan commission. When it began its operations in March 1935, it did so with an elected board whose members to a man had been chosen from a slate of officers prepared by the Canadian Chamber of Commerce.[27] Following the advice of the

Macmillan report and striving to placate bankers' criticism of the dangers of political interference in the government agency, Bennett set the Bank of Canada up as a private institution. Shares with a total value of $5 million were sold to the public and the 12,000 shareholders chose as their directors the well-established industrialists whom the Chamber of Commerce designated as its choice.

In 1936 the Liberals under Mackenzie King issued another $5.1 million of Bank of Canada shares for government purchase in order to make the government the majority shareholder. Two years later under pressure from the opposition parties, King decided to have the government buy out the private shares and become the sole shareholder in the Bank of Canada. He did this with great reluctance and without any intention of using the government's ownership of the bank as a means of countering private banking decisions. As he wrote in his diary, he continued to believe that directors elected by the private sector acted as a necessary brake against hasty decisions by the bank. But such a brake could be provided "by a type of men who will be appointed as directors." If radicals were in power, the "safety device" of elected directors could be removed. As it stood, King intended that the changes resulting from public ownership would be "very little or nothing."[28]

The "type of men" leading the bank had at heart the interests of the private bankers and business in general. Arguing before the House Standing Committee on Banking and Commerce in 1939 that the central bank was following a policy of moderate inflation, Towers repeated the bankers' original warning that proponents of the central bank were ignoring the Canadian economy's dependence on outside interests. For Towers it was an argument for restraining the activities of the bank. Towers laid special stress on one aspect of the lack of self-sufficiency in the Canadian economy—Canada's role as an exporter. In Canada, he argued, about one-third of national income consisted of receipts from goods and services sold abroad, whereas the same figure for the United States was about one-twentieth. The result was that, while the Americans could increase demand for goods available by expanding the money supply and deficit spending, with so much of the demand for their goods outside the country Canadians could not achieve as much with similar policies.

> Deficit spending in Canada can have little direct influence upon the course of foreign demand for our products. It can do little to increase domestic consumption of things which we normally export. . . .
>
> An export economy is in the position of having very little influence over the level at which many of its most important prices are set. It should, therefore, do all it reasonably can to keep its cost flexible and to avoid introducing elements of rigidity through borrowing on fixed terms. Otherwise its competitive position in foreign markets may be adversely affected. . . .[29]

Not only could inflation not affect demand for the exportable portion of Canada's production, but much of the new spending power it did create would not encourage new production in Canada, since many of the extra dollars would be used to purchase imported goods. Overall, the dependent nature of Canada's economy limited the effectiveness of monetary tinkering. But Towers was not advocating the use of monetary policy or any other government policy to reduce this dependence. Instead, he emphasized that government policies covering both the money supply and taxation must include "precautions. . . to prevent discouragement of private initiative and expenditure."[30]

The policy of modest inflation carried out by the Bank of Canada increased the currency in circulation in Canada from $163 million on 31 March 1935 to $238 million on 31 December 1938. Deposits in the chartered banks jumped from just over $2 billion to close to $2.5 billion. But the $75 million increase in circulating currency did not satisfy the extreme inflationists of the Social Credit party or Socred-leaning Liberals like Walter Tucker. Tucker proposed in 1938 that the government issue an additional $560 million in Bank of Canada notes to finance construction of highways, irrigation projects and other public works.[31] The response of Finance Minister Charles Dunning indicated the government's support for the cautious policies of Towers. Such vast inflation, he said, would "destroy the confidence of the business world with the soundness of conditions." The "retarding of private business enterprise" would more than offset any increase in purchasing power created by an ambitious program of public works.[32] Dunning supported credit expansion by government intervention as a means of combating deflation while emphasizing that credit expansion must be regarded as "a very dangerous weapon requiring the use of expert technique as well as great wisdom and caution." And it was as important to be ready to tighten credit when the time came as it was to have made it easier to obtain in the first place.[33]

In his National Employment Commission report, Arthur Purvis probably expressed majority business opinion of the central bank several years after it had begun operation:

> It is to be hoped that the establishment of the Bank of Canada will make available for the future ability, experience and technical devices for a prudent control of credit such as did not in the past exist. That control can accomplish much toward the lessening of fluctuations in business and employment to the degree that the Bank can give wise and independent leadership to business and governments and to the degree that such leadership is understood and accepted.[34]

The policies followed by the Bank of Canada under Towers gave the commercial bankers little cause for complaint and the fears expressed by the bankers before 1934 ended once it had been established. Royal Bank economist Donald Marvin commented that the bank's policies had produced the "salutary" effects that the Royal Bank leadership had expected.[35]

Although the central banking concept had its detractors in the business community, it had significant support among leaders of important sectors of the economy: grain, lumber, construction, railway, retailing, investment banking. The clamour for inflation from the Left and from Social Credit gave the business supporters of the central bank an edge over the bank's opponents (although international pressures played as large a role as internal popular pressure). The bank that was established, however, did not have the chastening effect on the commercial bankers that the populists had expected. Instead, its governor, himself a banker, and the ministers of finance used the bank to carry out a limited control of credit—"a prudent control of credit," in Purvis's words—which businessmen on the whole approved as necessary for the social welfare programs they had encouraged. The Bank of Canada's domination by a "type of men" sympathetic to the commercial banks and to private investors' fears insured that it would in the short run have little effect upon the power and privilege of the financial elite.

The imposition of a central bank on the commercial banks was the only change in the banking system that occurred in the 1930s, despite the vociferous attack by popular organizations against these institutions. The attacks had been strong enough that in 1934, when the charters of the banks came up for their dicennial review, Bennett agreed with Chubby Power's call for a sweeping investigation of the Canadian banks and bankers by a select committee of the Commons. Review of bank charters every five years, restriction of bank dividends to 6 percent per year, and an end to interlocking directorships between banks and the financial institutions were proposed by some members of Parliament. These proposals were rejected by the government and by business.[36]

Bankers and Entrepreneurship

The conservatism of the bankers went deeper than their desire to hold the status quo by opposing a central bank. Large Canadian firms with close ties to the banks were often unable to obtain bank loans without paying high interest rates and without government loan guarantees. Despite its close ties to banks and particularly to the Bank of Montreal, the CPR was able to get a $60 million five-year loan in 1934 only after a government guarantee had been secured. Even then the loan was at a rate of 5 percent interest at a time when the banks were paying only 2.5 percent interest on savings. Prime Minister Bennett, though providing the requested guarantee, believed the interest rate too high.[37]

The government had guaranteed private company borrowings

before the 1930s. At various times before this decade the major railways had had multimillion dollar loans guaranteed by the government. In the case of the Canadian Northern Railway (later expropriated by the government and merged with several other railway systems into the Canadian National Railway) over $200 million of private bonds had been guaranteed. When the railroad had been unable to pay its bondholders, the government had been forced to make payments on its behalf. So expensive a lesson in the dangers of the government taking risks on behalf of timid moneylenders should have argued against continuing the practice. But the evidence of the 1930s indicates that the bankers and leading industries still wanted government guarantees provided for certain major loans and that the government in turn was willing to provide the guarantees.

E.P. Neufeld has commented that the "entrepreneurial spirit among bankers seems to have dimmed in the period after the First World War." He argues that the banks did not expand their operations into such new areas as personal instalment credit and did not "persevere with corporate security type of lending after their initial unfortunate experiences." After 1910 "their conservative attitude" caused them to edge "persistently toward more liquid assets."[38]

The Canadian financial community's conservatism was also behind the government's entry into the fields of lending that businessmen considered necessary but too risky for private lenders. The government's new role in the home mortgage field was greeted enthusiastically by the mortgage companies. A similar enthusiasm prevailed when the government entered the field of short and intermediate term loans for farmers. The Canadian Bankers Association told the Macmillan commission that bankers did not wish to assume the risk involved in these loans and that the responsibility for the loans should be socialized.

> Assuming that the need for credit in this form is clearly a matter of sufficient national importance to warrant some action being taken by the authorities, consideration should be given to the creation of an institution financed on the public credit and to the placing upon it of the responsibility for meeting all legitimate demands.[39]

The Life Insurance Companies

The life insurance companies, like the banks, came under attack during the Depression. A Montreal financial journal, the *Journal of Commerce*, charged the officers of Sun Life and Metropolitan Life with incompetence and fraud. Repeating the journal's charges in the Commons, Michael Luchkovich, United Farmers member for Vegreville, maintained that Sun Life had used the funds of its policyholders to inflate the securities of pulp and paper and power companies and had invested in other speculative ventures at the risk of heavy losses to the policyholders. It was further charged that Sun Life president T.B. Macaulay had issued a large dividend to stockholders to convince them that the company was in strong shape; he had then sold most of his stocks at a high price before the near-insolvency of Sun Life became clear. North American Life's directors, under guise of making the company a mutual, allegedly siphoned off close to $1.3 million.[40] Without disputing the charges, Bennett rejected Luchkovich's call for an inquiry. He wondered aloud whether members of the House of Commons might not also on some occasion have been guilty of "slight errors of judgment in their investment" and asked them to consider the "human equation"—a touching but confusing request considering that swindling was the charge. Claiming that the reputation of the companies and the credit of the country as a whole was at stake, Bennett asked that the House "dispose of this resolution quietly and expeditiously and decline to refer it to any committee at this time."[41] The Liberals supported him, although Mitchell Hepburn, MP for West Elgin, insisted Sun Life was indeed insolvent. Privately King believed Luchkovich correct and later wrote in his diary that he had been reliably informed that both Sun Life and Bennett had been involved in catastrophic investments in Samuel Insull's fraudulent holding companies for hydroelectric firms in the United States and in the Swedish match trust (both of these corporate groups had collapsed). It was only his fear that a crisis might be precipitated if the matter was exposed in Parliament that caused him to encourage Hepburn and others not to raise the issue.[42] The federal Insurance Act was redrafted between 1932 and 1934. Arthur Meighen, Conservative leader in the Senate and Vice-president of Canada Life, was given the responsibility for the new Act, and he apparently passed the job of redrafting it on to Newton Rowell, counsel for the Canadian Life Insurance Operators Association.[43]

Life insurance companies were restricted by the legislation to investing 15 percent of their assets in common stock holdings. Sun Life, according to one author, was the only major company that exceeded this limit at the time. Therefore, the effect of the legislation was simply to compel Sun Life to fall in line with the other companies. The government had been willing to allow insurance companies to invest 25 percent of their total assets in common stocks; it was at the request of the insurance companies that it reduced this figure to 15 percent.[44] At the same time the government was effectively disciplining Sun Life with its legislation, the insurance industry as a whole was chastising the company with its request for the 15 percent limit. The insurance industry expressed satisfaction with the final legislation.[45]

An attempt in 1935 to place a maximum on the interest insurance companies could charge policyholders, who made loans from the companies using their policies as collateral, was quashed by Bennett. Dissident Conservatives had joined opposition forces to propose amending the Insurance Act by setting a limit of 5 percent interest on these loans. Bennett left his sick bed to scuttle the bill. His argument was a familar one: the confidence in Canada of investors at home and abroad would be destroyed by the legislation.[46]

Most of the leaders of the life insurance companies joined the bankers as supporters of moderate inflation, insurance programs, marketing boards and other stabilization measures. The presidents of Sun Life and North American Life, vilified by opposition MPs, were supporters of reform. T.B. Macaulay praised the Bennett government for its public works program and encouraged easy-money policies to restore purchasing power.[47] Thomas Bradshaw, president of North American Life, so favoured planned capitalism over the laissez faire variety that he told his company's annual meeting in January 1936:

> Whatever we may think of Soviet Russia's five-year plan, or that set forth in the recently issued book, *The Next Five*

> *Years*, and to which general support was given by a group of 152 of Britain's outstanding men and women, representative of all shades of thought, there is much to be said for the intelligent planning of the future over a definite term of years and adhering as closely as possible to program.[48]

The life insurance companies' willingness to rely on the state for certain ends was evidenced by their encouragement of federal legislation to deal with the problem of debt-ridden farmers. Provincial debt adjustment acts in the West made collection of debts from farmers difficult, and the companies that had loaned to the farmers (particularly Great-West Life, the leading insurance firm on the Prairies) pressed for federal action. C.C. Ferguson, general manager of the company, urged the federal government to enact legislation to allow a system of orderly repayment of farmers' debts that took into account their ability to pay.[49] The Farmers Creditors Arrangement Act, which provided government supervision for arrangements to repay debts, met with Ferguson's enthusiastic approval. Government-appointed boards would determine whether a farmer was able to repay all or only part of his debts and what his repayment period should be. Though recognizing that some boards might differ from others on how to assess the capacity of a farmer to pay, Ferguson called "the fundamental idea underlying the legislation. . . sound and logical." It was "the first attempt to attack the basic problem of adjusting farm debts according to the capacity to pay."[50]

The insurance companies, like the banks, had sympathetic ears in the Depression governments. There was no attempt to limit the power of the financial community in the 1930s. The establishment of a central bank, which could be viewed as a government limitation of private sector power, did not shake the financial community. Considering the agitation against the banks and insurance companies in the 1930s, it is remarkable that so little change occurred. The close connections of the government leaders with the financial and industrial community and their belief that no policy should be followed if it discouraged private investors clearly defined what actions they were prepared to take.

IX

DOMINION-PROVINCIAL RELATIONS

The conservative premises that led Canadian businessmen to press for various reforms in the 1930s also guided their decision to come out in support of a strong central government. Although provincial governments had treated them generously,[1] businessmen felt that the security of their enterprises depended upon centralization. They wanted one government that was willing to provide funds for and to coordinate programs designed to guarantee a stable level of purchasing power in the country—public works, social insurance and mortgage loans—while curtailing expenditures that industry considered unnecessary and wasteful.

The provincial governments had often opposed extending federal power. Until 1949 the Judicial Committee of Britain's Privy Council was the final arbiter on constitutional matters, and with its support provincial politicians were able to curtail centralization. In fact the Judicial Committee prevented federal expansion into some areas that the provinces were willing to surrender (the marketing of natural products, for example). The business community's inability to achieve the kind of centralization that it felt was essential to keep Canadian industry healthy was the result as much of obstruction from Britain as of opposition from Canadian politicians.[2]

Nowhere was the business community's desire for centralization more evident than in the hearings of the Royal Commission on Dominion-Provincial Relations, which were held throughout Canada in 1938. The Canadian Chamber of Commerce appeared before the commission with a high-powered delegation that included officials of the Hudson's Bay Company, Bell Telephone, Royal Trust and Greenshields-Hudson-Racine. The Chamber of

Commerce had been campaigning since 1933 for a commission to reappraise the division of powers among the various levels of government and regarded the appointment of the commission, headed first by Newton Rowell and then by Joseph Sirois, as a triumph for the organization.[3]

In making its presentation to the commission the Chamber of Commerce interpreted a series of quotations from the Fathers of Confederation, which seemed to indicate that they had wanted a strong central government, from a business perspective:

> We thus see that the Fathers of Confederation very definitely had in mind the consolidating of the country into a strong federal union, under one strong central government and the reducing of the local or provincial governments to a point *where their operations were inexpensive* [emphasis mine] and dealing with purely local matters. With these intentions of the Fathers of Confederation, we agree.[4]

There were many factors that made this accord with the Fathers of Confederation appealing to the Chamber of Commerce. In the first place it felt that the uncoordinated handling of the relief situation had led to too much expenditure and to spending on public works that had no multiplier effect on the economy rather than on works that would stimulate private investment.[5] The Chamber of Commerce concurred with the National Employment Commission recommendations that the federal government should take all responsibility for unemployment programs.[6] Hastily-conceived provincial and municipal programs, the commission had said, "are likely to be determined by immediate political consequences."[7] The fear that too many levels of government meant too many handouts to nonbusiness groups was recurrent in business briefs. The Chamber of Commerce wanted not only limitations placed on the powers of junior levels of government but also a reduction in the number of legislators at every level. Direct costs incurred in paying these legislators were not great, but the indirect costs of having so many legislators anxious to appease electors' demands for their own political ends were "enormous."[8] The feeling that Canada had too much politics because it had so many levels of government and so many legislators at each level was commonplace in business rhetoric in this period.

The Chamber of Commerce wished to place under federal jurisdiction responsibility for not only unemployment but also insurance, security frauds prevention, labour regulations and old age pensions, areas in which the provinces continued to play an important role. The constitution was largely on their side. In the Chamber of Commerce scheme personal and corporate income taxes would be collected only by the federal government, with provincial subsidies to be determined by a dominion grants commission. The provincial acts by which companies incorporated would be made uniform. The poorer provinces would be asked to surrender control over their own borrowing to Dominion supervision; in turn all provincial governments would be given stricter control over the borrowing of their municipalities. All provincial or "sectional" barriers to interprovincial business were to be removed.[9] In general the Chamber of Commerce, the senior body of Canadian business, was prepared to have the federal government go a long way towards centralizing power in the Chamber of Commerce's hands.

The Montreal Board of Trade placed its support of a wide extension of federal power within the context of the broader political ideology of the state's salutary and conservative role in the economy. The board noted that from the onset of the Depression all levels of government had been engaged in "haphazard" emergency expenditures. In their view, governments failed to appreciate the "permanent nature" of the unemployment problem and therefore had made little effort to go beyond "temporary and expedient methods" of financing relief. Much could be achieved by government expenditure if it was carefully coordinated and if the need to "give a compensatory stimulus to the production which may be checked by the taxation necessary to meet the expenditures"[10] was kept in mind. The board elaborated with Keynesian cogency:

> ...Taxation for the purpose of social services transfers purchasing power from the richer to the poorer classes, raises the standard of living of the poor, increases their demand for commodities and thereby tends towards

> industrial stability and prosperity. Furthermore, in a period of economic depression, heavier government expenditures, whether paid for by taxes or by loans, are justified and necessary in order to fill the gap resulting from the fear and inactivity which paralyze private enterprise.[11]

The Montreal Board of Trade repeated the Chamber of Commerce's list of jurisdictions that should be placed under federal control to allow for the sophisticated national planning required to achieve economic stability. Rejecting provincialist views of Confederation common in the province of Quebec, the predominantly English-speaking Montreal board claimed that "one of the purposes of Confederation was to make Canada a national unity in which business would be conducted under a common set of regulatory conditions throughout the Dominion."[12]

The desire for uniform conditions for business operations, as well as for coordinated and therefore less expensive government, led most boards of trade and other industry groups appearing before the Commission on Dominion-Provincial Relations to encourage federal control in the areas suggested by the Chamber of Commerce. Since many industries had experienced what they believed to be provincial "discrimination" against national companies, they urged that federal power be strengthened to avoid the uncertainties in business that dealing with many governments entailed. The Canadian Life Insurance Officers Association, for example, complained of "an apparent tendency to treat citizens of one part of Canada as foreigners for the purpose of taxation in another part of Canada, thus promoting sectionalism and impairing national unity." The association noted that Nova Scotia taxed non-resident life insurance agents fifty dollars while resident agents paid only five dollars.[13] The association represented 45 Canadian and foreign companies that handled 99.8 percent of life insurance policies in force in Canada. Since most of these firms did business in more than one province, the association proposed that the provinces control only legislation governing life insurance contracts and the licensing of insurance agents, and that all other matters— licensing of companies, solvency, company investments, inspection and reports—be left solely in federal hands.[14] The life insurance companies had been pressing these demands throughout the decade and had won the support of the federal government. But the Ontario and Quebec governments had resisted turning over to Ottawa all the powers that the companies wanted surrendered. A compromise reached in 1934 left the provinces in control of British and foreign companies—unless a province decided to have Ottawa carry on the regulation—but gave Ottawa the right to grant for all companies a certificate of solvency. In the view of an historian of Queen's Park-Ottawa relations, the large joint-stock companies in Ontario depended on Ottawa to protect them from the province and from the mutual and reciprocal insurers who were effectively client companies of the province. The compromise of 1934 was largely a victory for the national companies.[15]

Retail chain stores felt they were also victims of discriminatory and unjust taxation by provinces and municipalities. Taxes had been imposed on chain stores and not on their independent retailer competitors. Nova Scotia and Prince Edward Island had province-wide taxes on chain stores; New Brunswick's tax on non-resident-owned businesses hit the chains and not their competitors. Most Quebec municipalities had some form of special tax on chain stores. Montreal, for example, introduced in 1933 a levy of $150 per store on chains of twenty or more stores, with a smaller tax on chains of less than twenty stores. The tax was increased to $300 for chains of ten or more in 1935. Trois Rivières' annual tax on each chain store was $2000. According to the Canadian Chain Store Association, these taxes constituted an indirect regulation of trade and commerce, and they urged the Commission to recommend an end to this interference with trade.[16]

The life insurance companies, while conceding that the provinces had the constitutional right to pass legislation regarding contracts, wanted to restrict this right through an amendment to the British North America Act that would guarantee the civil rights and liberties of citizens and prevent deprivation of property rights by one group for the benefit of another. Civil rights was an area of provincial jurisdiction and such a proposal would involve a major shift of power away from the provinces. The life insurance companies were still smarting from the sting of debt adjustment and postponement legislation passed by prairie governments in the early Depression years to save farmers from bankruptcy. The insurance companies had looked to the federal government for Farmers Creditors Arrangement legislation that would take the place of the more radical provincial legislation. Fear of "irresponsible" and "parochial" behaviour by provincial governments, which might be concerned more with the immediate interests of their citizens than with the interests of national and international business organizations, caused life insurance and other companies to press for a stronger central government. Governments at local levels were under the same pressures as legislators at higher levels representing small constituencies: they took a local rather than a national view of things. The insurance companies therefore wanted more than limitations against interference by a province or municipality in relations between a policyholder and his insurance company. Since the life insurance companies were the leading source of long-term funds for public borrowers, they wanted a national council to be established to pass judgment on all public borrowing. Such a council, it was argued, would be free of local and partisan influences.[17]

The fire, automobile and casualty insurance companies shared the perspective of the life insurance companies. Appearing before the commission, the All-Canada Insurance Federation, representing 200 companies in these lines of insurance, asked for a division of responsibilities that paralleled the life insurance executives' demands. The federation also wanted to limit the total taxation on individuals and corporations and felt this could best be done by having all taxes paid to one central authority, which could allocate money to other jurisdictions by prior arrangement. The other jurisdictions, however, would have no power to tax on their own behalf.[18]

Provincial and Municipal Borrowing

The belief that the provincial and local governments had mismanaged their finances and should not be allowed to carry on their own borrowing unaided by the federal government was expressed in many commission briefs. The Chamber of Commerce wanted the borrowing of poorer provinces supervised by a federal loans council. The Associated Boards of Trade of British Columbia wanted borrowings by all provinces and municipalities controlled by the federal government.[19] The Investment Bankers Association wanted grants to provinces tied to federal review of provincial spending:

> Where the attainment of budgetary equilibrium is impossible because of permanent or temporary disabilities, it seems evident that rigidities can be removed only by a national sharing of the disabilities in the way of grants approved by all the parties concerned and continued only as sound fiscal policies are pursued.[20]

The loans council idea, which was so popular among the businessmen, had the support of both finance ministers of the 1930s. In the final months of the Bennett government, E.N. Rhodes had begun consultation with the provinces.[21] The consultations continued when the Liberals took power. At a dominion-provincial conference in December 1935, Charles Dunning proposed setting up a national loan council that would supervise provincial borrowing. The provinces, however, were not willing to allow the establishment of a body that would interfere with their activities unless they received some new source of income as a compensation for a voluntary cutting back of their existing authority.[22] Dunning offered the provinces the right to apply sales taxes on manufacturers and wholesalers, and in the 1936 session he introduced an amendment to the BNA Act that would give the provinces the powers of indirect taxation previously denied them. While wanting to see a loans council set up, the Canadian Chamber of Commerce and other business organizations thought the price was too high if it included this amendment. It was thought that indirect taxation placed in the hands of the provinces would be used for "discriminatory and retaliatory" purposes. A province might decide to place a tax on goods manufactured in other provinces and exempt the same goods if manufactured within the province. This use of taxation would clearly violate federal control of interprovincial trade, but the Chamber of Commerce was nevertheless convinced that the amendment would give the provinces leverage to limit the established federal jurisdiction in this area. The amendment was dropped and the loans council was not established.[23]

Business concern with how the provinces handled their finances was particularly acute in 1935 when the Ontario Liberal government of Mitchell Hepburn repudiated hydro contracts signed by previous Conservative governments. The Liberals claimed the contracts resulted from shady dealings between the Conservatives and the power companies. Hepburn's later relations with the power companies were so good that Mackenzie King thought the Ontario premier was an ally of these enterprises. At the time Hepburn was regarded as a threat by most of the financial community. Ottawa was asked to intervene. While Rhodes' sympathies were with the business community, an election was in the offing and he dared not act against what had been a popular course of action with the general public if not with business.[24]

Business demands for a federal response were greeted positively in 1936 when the Alberta government unilaterally reduced the rate of interest it would pay on the province's outstanding debt. Dunning informed the province that its request for a federal loan would go unheeded as long as the province refused to abide by its contracts.[25] Other Alberta ventures between 1937 and 1939 were formally disallowed by the federal government after an extensive campaign by businessmen across the country. The Social Credit government of William Aberhart, whose ideology was a peculiar amalgam of implacable hostility to financiers on the one hand and support of free enterprise on the other, was using its early years in office to attempt to humble the financial leaders. Reduction of the provincial debt by the provincial government without consultation with its creditors was followed by government legislation that reduced a tax on banking reserves. The Canadian Chamber of Commerce led the business attack on the legislation, claiming that it was antinational and antibusiness and would hurt the credit of the country as a whole. King was convinced of the validity of the business argument and was especially concerned that some of the legislation would result in the bankruptcy of certain companies. In June 1938 he disallowed the Act for the Security of Home Owners and the Act to Impose a Tax on Certain Securities in the Year 1938. In all eight pieces of Alberta legislation were disallowed by the federal government between 1937 and 1939.[26] The Alberta events had been a great lesson for the business community on the dangers of provincial power unchecked by a strong central government.

The banks, like the insurance companies, had reason to feel that they were being "discriminated" against by junior governments. The unsuccessful Alberta legislation was merely the worst example of the long list of legislative actions directed against banks and other financial corporations by provinces and municipalities. The rates of local taxation, it was charged, were higher for banks than for other corporations, particularly in Quebec. The Canadian Bankers Association was anxious about this Depression-born legislation, which they considered to be directed against their members' operations and expressed before the Royal Commission on Dominion-Provincial Relations the banks' desire to have bank taxation "centralized in the hands of the Dominion Government, from which they derive the right to do business." If this was not possible, a uniform method of municipal taxation on banks, decided at a national level, would be acceptable. Having to cope with local prejudices and twists of popular opinion was not acceptable to the bankers.[27]

The Manufacturers' Concerns

The Canadian Manufacturers Association largely shared the views of the financiers and retailers. They also believed that there was a tendency among some provinces to "discriminate against companies having their head offices outside the taxing province or against domestic companies. . . importing goods from outside jurisdictions for sale within the taxing provinces." While some smaller manufacturers no doubt benefited from barriers limiting the entry of out-of-province competitors, manufacturers as a whole regarded such provincialist policies as retrograde and harmful. The New Brunswick Corporations Tax Act was cited as an example. A 1936 amendment to this legislation taxed at the retail level sales of goods manufactured outside the province. The Canadian Manufacturers Association felt this legislation violated Section 121 of the BNA Act, which provides that articles of growth, produce or manufacture of any province should be submitted free into all other provinces.[28]

The manufacturers, though less sanguine than the Montreal Board of Trade about the merits of inflation as a means of fighting depression, did believe that the timing of public works to periods of recession was a wise public policy. It was also necessary that public works be of a type that would stimulate recovery in the private sector rather than simply provide relief for the unemployed without influencing overall recovery. Proper planning of needed public works to be carried out at times most useful to the nation's economic well-being was possible, in the association's view, only if the responsibility for such a program was not diffused among many levels of government. It was essential that the federal government assume the major role in accumulating data on the economy and in releasing or withholding funds for public works according to what its projections for the economy dictated.[29]

The Canadian Manufacturers Association joined the Canadian Chamber of Commerce and other organizations in asserting that only the national government should have the power to initiate programs of social insurance. Provincial schemes would mean "overlapping and needless expense and inefficiency." Even worse, if some provinces had a social insurance scheme that other provinces did not have, the manufacturers in the provinces where the scheme existed would be placed at a disadvantage. For example, the proposed British Columbia health insurance plan, which included a levy on all employers in the province, would increase costs for manufacturers in British Columbia without increasing the costs of their competitors.[30]

Reiterating the Chamber of Commerce stand against provincial taxing of corporations, the manufacturers argued that there should be only one income tax on all business concerns and that it should be collected by the federal government. The association suggested that the federal government divide the tax among the provinces on the basis of sales made in each provincial jurisdiction as a percentage of total sales nationally. According to the association, the existing situation created "a lack of certainty, uniformity, equality and finality in the system of taxation governing Canadian industry."[31]

The tariff was one aspect of national policy that had benefited manufacturers for many years. But areas of the country in which the manufacturing sector was small, particularly the Prairies, continued to groan under the burden of higher prices created by the policy of protection legislated for the advantage of the manufacturing regions, chiefly southern Ontario and the Montreal region of Quebec. The manufacturers wanted to protect the tariff from the vagaries of politics and therefore responded favourably to the arguments of the boards of trade of Edmonton, Winnipeg and Regina for a system of national adjustment grants to compensate poorer provinces for disadvantages resulting from protection. What was particularly encouraging to the Canadian Manufacturers Association was the acceptance of protection by the Prairie boards of trade. If national adjustment grants were the price of making the tariff a permanent feature of Canadian economic life, this seemed a fair price to the association, despite its rhetoric about balanced budgets. Ironically, the manufacturers were calling for these grants at the same time they were calling for an end to provincial corporate income taxes. In the association's view the provinces were to surrender to the national government the right to raise revenue as they chose; the federal authorities in turn would have the responsibility when apportioning revenues to consider that some provinces required more money than others because of the effects that certain national policies had on these provinces.[32]

The Real Estate Industry

That bankers and manufacturers with national interests should favour centralized control is not surprising. But even in the real estate business, where provincial or local companies and individuals were more influential than national operations, there was strong support for weakening the local governments in favour of central power. The Ontario Association of Real Estate Boards, for example, told the Rowell-Sirois commissioners that too many responsibilities had been placed with municipalities, responsibilities that were reflected in ever-increasing municipal real estate taxes. Taxation increases instituted to pay for relief expenditures in the Depression had exacerbated an already serious problem of excessive taxation. The real estate business joined the bankers in favouring unemployment insurance as an alternative to supporting unemployed workers who previously had been looked after by the municipal relief rolls. Unemployment insurance would make unemployment a national rather than a municipal or even provincial responsibility and would significantly reduce the burden placed on real estate. The Ontario association also wanted education and hospital costs to be borne by central governments (chiefly the provinces) and not by municipalities. More rigid controls on municipal borrowing were also advocated.[33] In arguments similar to those of the Ontario association, the Vancouver Real Estate Exchange observed that all of the population benefited from the municipal improvements that were paid for solely by property-holders. Federal government expenditures should replace major municipal expenditures so that all of the population would be taxed to pay for relief and improvements.[34]

The Dominion Mortgage and Loans Association, representing the major lenders of money to purchasers of real estate, shared the views of the real estate industry. Appearing before the Rowell-Sirois Commission, the association argued that too much of the tax burden had been placed on real estate during the Depression and that in the future relief must become a federal responsibility.[35]

The natural resources companies had generally done well at the hands of the provincial governments. Not surprisingly, therefore, the mining industry was notably absent from the proceedings of the Royal Commission on Dominion-Provincial Relations. The hydroelectric companies used the support of the provincial governments as a lever to change the federal government's mind on the question of power exports. Having originally opposed power exports, King decided in February 1938 to propose the Export of Power Act, which gave each province the right to decide whether it wished to allow power export. After a province declared that it was satisfied that a contracted export was surplus to the needs of the province, the federal government would automatically allow the sale to go ahead.[36]

There were resource companies that shared the concerns of the rest of the business community in supporting a transfer of provincial jurisdictions to the federal government. The Primary Products Publishing Company, H.R. MacMillan Export Company (a lumber exporter), British Columbia Packers (a fish-packing firm) and a number of ranching organizations wanted the federal government to have the exclusive right to establish marketing boards for natural products. When the federal marketing board legislation had been found *ultra vires* by the Judicial Committee of the Privy Council, the British Columbia government simply re-established many of the federal boards under provincial jurisdiction.[37] Primary Products Publishing Company was opposed to compulsory marketing[38], but the majority of British Columbia lumber companies and fish-packing firms favoured the legislation. Therefore Primary Products' desire to transfer power to the federal government might be seen as simply an attempt to throttle the marketing legislation by placing it at the discretion of a Mackenzie King cabinet, which was less disposed to marketing boards than its Conservative predecessor. The British Columbia lumbermen had only turned to the province for marketing legislation after the announcement of the court decision on the federal legislation. The Associated Boards of Trade of British Columbia, in which the lumbermen and fish packers played an important role, advocated the Canadian Chamber of Commerce program for a shift towards a strong central government.[39]

The one business organization that argued before the Rowell-Sirois Commission against shifting more power from the provinces to Ottawa was the Montreal district of the Quebec Chamber of Commerce. Representing mostly French-Canadian small businessmen, the organization's views did not have the same economic power as the Montreal Board of Trade, whose members were largely English-speaking and whose leadership consisted of important men in Canadian business. But the views of this French-Canadian petit-bourgeoisie were indicative of what would be the fate of attempts to whittle away provincial jurisdictions in Quebec. The Montreal district urged that governments work together to produce uniform legislation and to end duplication in the collection of taxes. Ending duplication in the provision of public services should be encouraged if it could be accomplished "without unduly limiting provincial powers and affecting Quebec autonomy."[40] Similarly, while uniform legislation on apprenticeship, wages and hours of labour was desirable, it should be achieved through interprovincial agreement. When one of the commissioners asked whether such a goal could not be more easily achieved by having federal jurisdiction in these matters, organization representative Rene Morin answered:

> We are very sensitive on matters of autonomy in the province of Quebec. You must realize there are special reasons why this should be so in the province of Quebec on account of its difference in religion and race.[41]

Among the business organizations appearing before the commission only the Montreal district of Quebec's Chamber of Commerce called on the federal government "to leave with the provinces the entire responsibility of unemployment relief." Decentralization, it claimed, would result in more efficiency and less expense. Going even further against the grain of business opinion as a whole, the organization urged the federal authorities "to give up to the provinces certain sources of taxation which should provide the necessary resources to meet such costs."[42]

Everett Hughes notes that an analysis of all Montreal firms rated in the *Dun and Bradstreet Directory* showed that those of greatest "estimated pecuniary strength" were nearly all controlled by English-speaking businessmen. French-speaking businessmen were only prominent among owners of firms with assets of less than $20,000.[43] The French-speaking businessman was generally a provincial businessman. Since he did not operate in nine provinces, he was not worried about uniform industrial and labour legislation as much as the managers of national and multinational firms who composed the Montreal Board of Trade. Gerald Fortin suggests that the French-Canadian small businessman, threatened by the English-Canadian capitalist, traditionally pushed the provincial government to protect himself against "*les étrangers*." He could not, however, expect special dispensation from the national government.[44]

French-Canadians who had achieved positions of responsibility in the English-speaking business world tended to share the views of their fellow big businessmen. Senators Charles Beaubien and David L'Esperance, two French-Canadians well integrated into the operations of St. James Street, supported R.B. Bennett's call at the 1938

Liberal-Conservative convention for a greater concentration of authority in a central government.[45]

The Report of the Royal Commission on Dominion-Provincial Relations, published in 1940, shared much of the philosophy of the leading business groups and its "recommendations concerning the reallocation of the burdens of government between the Dominion and the provinces"[46] were largely along the lines suggested by business. Indeed it had the sensitivities of the investors in mind in making its report:

> It is this need for a larger national income which has governed us in the recommendations which we have made for simplifying our financial system, for carrying as economically as possible the great burden of public debt, for cooperation in the direction of future governmental investment through borrowing and for eliminating those features of our fiscal system which involve a high cost of tax compliance or which have a marked tendency to check investment and so to reduce employment.[47]

While cognizant of the sensitivity of certain provincial governments towards any circumscribing of their constitutionally-protected jurisdictions, the commissioners argued that their aim was one of "adapting the Canadian federal system to meet the stresses and strains that have developed during the seventy years which have elapsed since it was devised and so enabling national unity to be maintained." In order to ensure equality of conditions throughout the country, certain powers must reside solely with the federal government. Social insurance programs in particular should come under federal jurisdiction. Relief of unemployed workers and of farmers beset by major natural or market disasters must also become federal responsibility. Corporate and personal income should be collected by the federal government and redistributed to the provinces according to a formula that would give poorer provinces more tax revenue than they could have collected. It was claimed that such an adjustment of the allocation of tax revenues would compensate have-not provinces which had failed to prosper from national policies protecting industry.[48]

The commission report's emphasis that its recommendations

were governed by the need to encourage investment in order to create a larger national income indicates that the business community's overwhelming support of centralization played a major role in the commission's deliberations. The major question raised by business support of a stronger federal government is whether, as industry believed, a strengthened central government would ignore local interests in favour of national interests. Clearly, the CCF and the Canadian Chamber of Commerce had opposing views on what constituted national interests. It was industry rather than the Left that understood that a remote federal Parliament was likely to be both more easily pressured by vested interested groups than local governments and less sensitive to local needs. The CCF were correct in believing centralization would mean greater funds for redistribution of wealth among regions and income groups. But naively assuming that the vote was sufficient ammunition against arbitrary government actions, they did not address themselves to the question of how grass-roots democracy could be preserved once local government powers had been drastically reduced.[49]

Some CCF intellectuals were quite aware that "what kind of nationalism?" was the crucial question. As Frank Underhill observed in an irreverent summary of Canadian history, the nation had already undergone two periods of intense nationalism. The first followed Confederation and was marked by the "economic nationalism" of the National Policy.

> The nationalism of these years was a businessmen's nationalism; its policy was that of material expansion and consolidation under the leadership and control of (and primarily for the profit of) groups of business leaders in Montreal and Toronto. Confederation itself was not a democratic movement; it represented the ambitions of business leaders to build up a great economic empire in the northern half of North America....

The second period, "again under the leadership of ambitious business expansionists," came in the first decade of the twentieth century; its main achievement was the building of transcontinental railways.[50] The real question was: If there was to be a third period of nationalism, would it be another businessmen's nationalism or a more popular nationalism that would challenge the control of the economy by a small segment of the population?

Using the exigencies of war as a rationale Mackenzie King, aided by a friendly Liberal government in Quebec and a temporarily cooperative Hepburn Liberal government in Ontario, was able in January 1941 to persuade the provinces to surrender corporate and income tax to the federal government in return for a federal allocation of 5 percent of these taxes to the provinces. Permission had been won earlier for a constitutional amendment that allowed the federal government to establish a national unemployment insurance scheme.[51] Although further national insurance schemes—contributory pensions, hospital and medical insurance—would be instituted later, the overall thrust of postwar politics was to restore the provinces to their previous positions of authority. Largely under the leadership of Quebec's provincial nationalist, Premier Maurice Duplessis, and his successors, Ottawa continually increased the percentage of tax revenues disbursed to the provinces. Quebec nevertheless reintroduced its own income and corporate taxes, and the other provinces soon followed. Quebec also began to opt out of many national insurance schemes and to operate its own programs. Although the constitution appeared to allow this kind of provincial action, Quebec's militancy in asserting its provincial rights made Ottawa hesitant to engage in a constitutional battle that might provoke separatist sentiment in the province.[52]

H.V. Nelles and Christopher Armstrong have observed in "Private Property in Peril: Ontario Businessmen and the Federal System, 1898-1911" that the financial and national business community wanted to remove regulatory functions from the control of the "unpredictable" local legislatures. The financial community wanted the central government to use its regulatory power to stablize the economy in accordance with business objectives, and controlling the behaviour of the provinces was one aspect of this stabilization. Businessmen were frustrated in this endeavour because "the decentralized Canadian federal system prevented escape from the volatile provincial level to Ottawa."[53] In the 1930s the national business and financial community not only had the same attitude towards dominion-provincial relations, it also had even more reason to fear the "unpredictable" provinces. The various forms of "discriminatory" taxation, the debt adjustment legislation and the wasteful relief programs all seemed to indicate that the provinces and municipalities required an overlord. The business community's perspective on the issue was fundamentally undemocratic. Fearing local restrictions on their economic power, businessmen preferred to proclaim their nationalism in order to concentrate power with the level of government that they felt was most removed from "parochial" interests and most attuned to "national" interests—the interests of the business community.

The constitutional barriers that had stood in the way in the previous generation continued to prevent the absolute concentration of power called for by the businessmen. Had they had their way, a federal agency would have supervised provincial borrowing, and most of the power and income sources at the disposal of the provinces would have fallen to the federal government. Although it is debatable whether the provinces really caused as much inconvenience for the national businessmen as businessmen themselves believed, it cannot be assumed that whatever increase in centralization occurred since the 1930s occurred against the interests of big business in Canada.[54] Indeed the reverse is true: the business community was left with less centralization than it had advocated.

The pressure for centralized government was another facet of industry's push for state-sponsored stability in the economy. Businessmen desired government intervention in specific economic sectors to reduce competition and to increase coordination of the money supply, insurance programs and construction. Too many levels in government was a source of instability and inefficiency, preventing the overall planning of the economy in the interests of big business.

Not everyone agreed that this was the only way to plan the economy. The business version of reform was opposed by other groups in Canadian society that had different interests, different ideologies and their own programs for reform.

X

THE RADICAL ALTERNATIVES

The business community's success in reshaping the role of the state according to its changed needs ought not to obscure the fact that there were organized groups with very different views about the changes required in the relations of power in the political and economic spheres. The business view that capitalism could be regulated for the good of industry and thereby for the good of all was rejected by many class-based organizations representing workers and farmers. A section of the intelligentsia also rejected the notion that capitalism was reformable. From the opposite ideological viewpoint the urban petit-bourgeoisie, aware that the tendency of reform was in favour of their larger opponents, organized unsuccessfully to turn the clock back to a mythical Canadian past in which the independent commodity producer had the upper hand and in which big business was unknown. In rural Alberta similar complaints led to the formation of the Social Credit Party, which in its campaign against the banks divorced the banks' operations from the workings of the economy as a whole. While few of these groups were revolutionary, their programs and demands indicate that a significant minority of Canadians did not believe that the new ideology of corporate liberalism emanating from important boardrooms and echoed in government programs would produce a Depression-free Canada.

The CCF

The Co-operative Commonwealth Federation, a left-wing social democratic electoral party, was the major organized opposition group expressing anti-capitalist views, though always with the questionable assumption that a majority of ballots in favour of socialism would by itself put an end to the capitalist system. Although the Cold War would cause a recasting of CCF thinking along the lines of the British Labour party's alternative to destroying the capitalist system,[1] the CCF's program and rhetoric from 1932 to 1939 suggested that the commanding heights of the Canadian economy would be progressively socialized under a CCF regime. Disgust with the human misery that the capitalist system had produced in the Depression caused CCF leader J.S. Woodsworth to write during the 1935 election:

> We believe that the Canadian people must aim at nothing less than the establishment of a planned and socialized economic order which will make possible the most efficient development of all our resources and the most equitable distribution of the national income. The great obstacle which stands in the way of this today is the monopolistic concentration of economic power in the hands of a small group of financiers and industrialists who exploit the masses of the people for their own private profit and who refuse to allow the machinery of production to work at full capacity unless they can levy toll from it.
>
> The essential task before us is to oust this arbitrary, irresponsible plutocracy from power and to bring our economic institutions, as our ancestors brought our political institutions, under public control and administration.[2]

The Regina Manifesto, the CCF statement of principles adopted at its first national convention in 1933, rejected the "present capitalist system" as a system of "domination and exploitation of one class by another" and proposed that it be replaced with socialism. Much of the manifesto consisted of a plethora of costly emergency measures designed to use state funds to refuel a paralyzed economy. These measures, however, would leave "untouched the cancer which is eating at the heart of our society." Concluding on a tough note, the manifesto stated:

> No CCF government will rest content until it has eradicated capitalism and put into operation the full pro-

> gram of socialized planning which will lead to the establishment in Canada of the Co-operative Commonwealth.[3]

The CCF's radicalism was a product of several disparate phenomena: class-conscious labour movements, especially in western Canada; the radical farm tradition of the Prairies; and the new-found radicalism of middle-class professionals in Montreal and Toronto. This latter group through the League for Social Reconstruction served as the CCF's brains trust and produced *Social Planning for Canada*, a well-researched dissection of the Canadian economic system. League members had also played a key role in drafting the Regina Manifesto.

Members of the League for Social Reconstruction were largely WASPs, professionals and residents of either Toronto or Montreal. Frank Underhill notes that the men who produced *Social Planning for Canada* were, with one exception, either Canadian-born and Oxford-educated or British-born and educated at Cambridge or the London School of Economics.[4] Not surprisingly, given their backgrounds, the men of the League were evolutionaries rather than revolutionaries. They were élitists moved by a middle-class version of noblesse oblige. Although their concerns for the underdog were genuine, they were mixed in with a curious middle-class consciousness in which a fetish was made of planning and technique, and the assumption was that technicians and professionals were the capitalists' natural successors as society's leaders. The key words to an understanding of League doctrines are "efficiency," "order," "planning," and "education."

Underhill summed up much of the thinking of League intellectuals in a *Queen's Quarterly* article published in November 1932, entitled "Bentham and Benthamism." Praising Bentham for his devotion to efficiency and political democracy, Underhill argued that what was needed in the 1930s was a new Benthamism that recognized the need for economic democracy as well as political democracy. This new Benthamism was to be found in the Fabian brand of socialism:

> The ideal which Bentham advocated of a mathematically complete political democracy at the bottom with a bu-

> reaucracy of administrative experts at the top is exactly the ideal of such socialists as Mr. and Mrs. Sidney Webb in our own day.[5]

According to League for Social Reconstruction leaders, political power must be transferred from the owners of capital to the people, who in turn must vest power in the genteel hands and bleeding hearts of socially-minded experts. This process would occur through "democratic and orderly means," as stated in the preface to *Social Planning for Canada*. Socialism would come not as a result of a cataclysm that would pit producers against owners but as the result of an accumulation of reforms legislated by a socially-minded government employing socially-minded technicians.

The preamble to the Regina Manifesto, which was drafted by prominent members of the League for Social Reconstruction, stated that the CCF's aim was "a proper collective organization of our economic resources such as will make possible a much greater degree of leisure and a much richer individual life for every citizen." Not surprisingly, the first plank in the CCF platform was "planning." Planning, it said, was needed for efficient development of national resources and equitable distribution of national income. It was proposed that a national planning commission, consisting of "a small body of economists, engineers and statisticians assisted by an appropriate technical staff," would work with the managing boards of socialized industries to insure that production, distribution and exchange were properly coordinated. Import and export boards, socialized finance, socialized utilities, socialized medicine and a host of milder reforms were included in the program.[6]

The middle-class influence of the League led the CCF to support the type of bureaucratic statism that was easily caricatured by its opponents and that was generally unappealing to working people and farmers who feared a system of state regimentation. The CCF and the League brushed away criticisms of the bureaucracies they were recommending by noting that powerful private bureaucracies were performing an antisocial planning function and that public bureaucracies controlled by the people's representatives could plan in the public interest. Many CCF members believed that capitalism was exploitative because it robbed the individual workers of the right to be part of the process of determining what was to be produced, and when and how it was to be distributed. Party leaders were mainly concerned with the question of distribution. Canada's transformation to the "welfare state" along with the Cold War caused a mellowing in the CCF's radical critique by the late 1940s.[7]

The Trade Unions

The CCF's criticism of the Canadian economic system was shared by a number of farm and labour groups. Among trade union groups the All-Canadian Congress of Labour in particular put forward an analysis similar to the Regina Manifesto. With about 50,000 members this Canadian labour organization was less than half the size of the larger, more conservative and American crafts-dominated Trades and Labour Congress. Because of its more radical political views, the All-Canadian Congress of Labour was largely ignored when the government appointed trade unionists to government commissions and committees.[8] Though its president, A.R. Mosher of the Canadian Brotherhood of Railway Employees, was a founding member of the CCF, the congress did not have a formal link with the party and declined to support it even nominally at election time. Although the critique of the ACCL was similar to the CCF's, it believed the workers themselves rather than a disinterested group of social servants drawn from the middle classes should run nationalized industries. Indeed, its Trades and Labour Congress opponents accused the All-Canadian Congress of Labour, as well as the remnants of the One Big Union, of wanting "to build up an industrial form of organization by which they could exercise a dictatorship over all other classes of the community."[9]

The ACCL leaders saw the Depression as a problem that was made insoluble by the capitalist system. It could only be halted by either a drastic change in the economic system or war. The national government therefore was urged to "take over the industries which provide the essentials, food, clothing, and housing, and to operate them for the common welfare, distributing the product to all citizens who are willing to do their share of the necessary work."[10] A convention recommendation supported the idea of having a government organization set up to enroll "a voluntary labour force from the unemployed" and with the means to acquire and operate farms, food factories, fisheries, textile mills, clothing factories, timber camps, sawmills, quarries and mines. The entire output of these industries would be used to provide food, clothing and shelter for the workers in the organization. This was regarded as a first step towards the establishment of a worker-run socialist economy.[11]

But just how was such major change to come about? The ACCL was clearly opposed to violent means of overthrowing the state and yet shied away from supporting the CCF. In fact, it appeared to believe naively that the Conservative and Liberal governments would consider putting the major private corporations out of business. Although the congress supported such reforms as the unemployment insurance bill and the forty-eight-hour work week, it was convinced at times that these reforms were instituted for the benefit of the capitalist class. In February 1936 the *Canadian Unionist* argued:

> Government, as the organ of the ruling class, is constrained to adopt social policies which over-ride the immediate economic interests of the ruling class....Without state intervention in the form of relief works and doles, the free competition for jobs would result in wages so low that, if prices did not also fall, the workers would perish of slow starvation and, with the loss of consumptive capacity, production would decline till capitalist property lost all its value; and, if prices declined, profits would be too small to support the capital structure of modern industry and the credit or debt structures of government....
>
> The very self-preservation of the capitalist state itself is conditional upon its making itself the instrument of social policies interfering with the free operation of the mechanism of the economic system.[12]

Other editorials in the *Canadian Unionist* made it clear that while the congress believed further "palliative measures" would be introduced by the government, it was convinced that none of these measures, short of mobilization for war, would even temporarily solve the problems of capitalism.[13] The essential point about the All-Canadian Congress of Labour is that despite its radical political views it played a marginal role in the political arena. No doubt its need to compete with the Trades and Labour Congress and to keep its locals functioning despite Canada's anti-labour laws and the unemployment of many union members was uppermost in the Congress' priorities.

The All-Canadian Congress of Labour united with the Congress of Industrial Organization in 1940 to form the Canadian Congress of Labour. Although this new organization endorsed the CCF as the political arm of labour in 1942, the CCF received only nominal support. Funds were to be committed to the CCF by the decision of member unions and only a minority of the unions undertook to affiliate with the CCF and later with the NDP. The labour movement in Canada, having suffered state repression before and after World War I and a reduction in membership during the recession of 1920-23, had retreated to a defensive position in which bread-and-butter unionism was the major goal, even when the rhetoric of certain union leaders implied otherwise.[14]

As for the Trades and Labour Congress, the Depression brought little change in its generally conservative views. These views had in the aftermath of World War I caused the more radical western members to leave the congress. If the Trades and Labour Congress did not move particularly close to the radicalism of the CCF and the All-Canadian Congress of Labour, its official stance on a number of issues in the 1930s indicated an apparent leftward shift. It had always supported public ownership of utilities (including the private railways) and in 1932 it added the banks to the list of utilities that should be nationalized:

> Believing that the banking and credit system, controlling as it does the economic destiny of practically the entire community, is in its nature and manner of functioning actually a public utility and that the private banking system as now constituted, though custodian of the people's money and savings, is not directly responsible to them for its actions but works primarily for profits and dividends for shareholders, often with very little consideration for

> the general welfare. Therefore the Trades and Labour Congress of Canada supports the principle of nationalization of the banking system.[15]

While the congress welcomed the establishment of the Bank of Canada as a step in the right direction, it continued throughout the rest of the decade to press for public ownership of all banking and credit institutions.[16] At its 1936 convention the Trades and Labour Congress came out in favour of the progressive nationalization of the resource industries and urged the federal government to set up a public ownership commission to study and report on fields in which public ownership might be extended for the public benefit. Private control of natural resources, stated the resolution, had been "to the detriment of the majority of the people."[17]

The Trades and Labour Congress directed its demands for the nationalization of the key sectors of credit and natural resources to governments that shared the ideology and many of the personnel of big business. Apparently its leaders regarded the state as a neutral arbiter in the struggle between social classes in the country. The congress clearly saw itself as working within the system and concentrated upon winning legislation that would make the organization of workers easier. It also attempted to get more labour representatives on government boards, while rejecting the right of other labour federations to have representatives appointed to the boards. With its obsequious attitude towards the old-party governments, it is not surprising that the Trades and Labour Congress rejected any affiliation with the CCF, despite recurring resolutions from western delegates at the national conventions.[18] Considering the generally pro-public ownership principles of the organization, it would be incorrect to say that it was part of a new consensus that regarded state regulation as an alternative to both socialism and laissez-faire capitalism. While some of its leaders did hold this view, the conventions indicated support for a considerable expansion of social ownership. But the search for respectability in the eyes of the state and industry kept the congress away from political action to back up its social goals.

The most radical labour federation of the 1930s was the Communist-led Workers Unity League, which organized about

40,000 workers. It was active in the mines and logging camps of northern Ontario, in the garments trades and furniture factories in major cities and in the relief camps of British Columbia. The Workers Unity League with the Communist Party had spearheaded the petition for non-contributory unemployment insurance in Canada, which called for using a tax on profits, rather than employee deductions, to finance unemployment insurance. Although 94,000 signatures were collected[19], the Trades and Labour Congress and the All-Canadian Congress of Labour did not support the Workers Unity League. Its only support came from labour representatives in the House of Commons.

The Workers Unity League and more generally the Communist Party were the victims of extensive state repression in this period.[19] Although pluralists assume that workers exercise free choice in their union affiliations,[20] the state in Canada played a major role over a long period in repressing such unions as the Industrial Workers of the World, the One Big Union and the Workers Unity League. Following the Winnipeg General Strike in 1919 Bennett's Labour Minister, Gideon Robertson, stated that from the point of view of the state a trade union had to be defined as an organization that accepted existing property relations and agreed to enforce contracts arrived at between labour and capital.[21] The capitalist state was an adversary of all trade unions; in the case of revolutionary unions, it was a relentless foe which refused to recognize these unions and the rights of their members.

Conservative craft unions in the Trades and Labour Congress had cooperated with the state in the past in its offensive against radical competitors. In the 1930s the TLC was largely silent about the repression of the Workers Unity League. *Labour Leader*, the conservative Toronto labour newspaper which spoke for the right-wing of the Trades and Labour Congress, commented:

> ...We fear that this red organization will cost Canadian industry many millions in lost time and wages unless sufficient cooperation is extended by all friends of legitimate labour organizations so that *together* we may successfully combat this new menace to peaceful progress *as we have done with other revolutionary groups that have gone before* [emphasis mine].[22]

The large number of unionists arrested or deported, as reported in *Canadian Labour Defender*, the newspaper of the largely Communist Canadian Labour Defence League, indicates the extent of state repression in the 1930s, particularly during the Bennett years. No doubt the paper was correct in its assertion that many of the people arrested for attempting to organize trade unions were in no sense communists. Over 200 political militants were reported to have been deported in the years 1932 and 1933 alone. In December 1932, the *Canadian Labour Defender* could report that several hundred persons were in jail at that moment across the country for having taken part in unemployed demonstrations and in demonstrations against conditions in hostels for the unemployed.[23]

The Farmers Movement

Labour radicalism in the 1930s was paralleled by left-wing radicalism among certain sectors of the Canadian farming population. Two radical farm organizations affiliated with the CCF—the United Farmers of Alberta and the Saskatchewan section of the United Farmers of Canada. Both groups rejected the notion that capitalism could be reformed.

The Alberta group's position was a curious amalgam of socialism and social credit. In 1935 the social credit doctrine would become the basis for the formation of a right-wing alternative to the United Farmers of Alberta, which buried the farmers organization as a political force in Alberta. As the provincial government during the Depression years, United Farmers of Alberta failed to protect the farmers from their creditors and had hidden behind the constitution to cover up its insensitivity. Although its anti-bank campaign was founded on false premises, Social Credit appeared to be a progressive alternative to the United Farmers of Alberta do-nothing government.[24] Unable to influence the entrenched MLAs of a party that had governed Alberta since 1931, it was discredited as an organization as well as a government.

Before the Depression, the United Farmers of Alberta had been little more than a radical populist movement concerned with bargaining for a better deal for farmers within the existing system.[25] From 1930 its conventions began to sound a more radical note.

While the 1930 convention placed the organization's traditional emphasis on voluntary cooperatives as the means of side-stepping industrial monopolies, it urged that the government's policy regarding natural resources be first, "development in accordance with the principles of public ownership and second, proper conservation to make these natural resources of value to succeeding generations in this province."[26] Had the government listened to this advice, the pattern of Alberta resource development might have been a very different story. By 1932 the United Farmers of Alberta was willing to admit that while cooperatives still had a role to play, direct state involvement was necessary to run many of the privately-owned industries. Its goal was defined as:

> A community freed from the domination of irresponsible financial and economic power, in which all social means of production and distribution, including land, are socially owned and controlled either by voluntarily organized groups of producers and consumers or—in the case of the major public services and utilities and such productive and distributive enterprises as can be conducted most efficiently when owned in common—by public corporations responsible to the people's elected representatives.[27]

Both the United Farmers of Alberta and the Saskatchewan membership of United Farmers of Canada shared the problem of explaining to farmers their stand on the nationalization of land. Neither organization supported collective farming, but both had difficulty convincing the farmers that despite what the daily newspapers were saying the farmers' organizations did not want to impose Soviet-style *kolkhozes* on the Canadian farmer. Their policy was simply to nationalize land that was not being farmed by farmer-owners and to lease it without right of purchase. This would eliminate the possibility of foreclosures of farms by banks, since non-farmers would not be allowed to own land. No consideration was actually given to state ownership of farm operations, despite the accusations of opponents.[28]

The difficulties that a group like the United Farmers of Alberta had in winning farmers to its program reflect the overall problems that radicals faced in the Depression. The economy was dominated by monopolies; the possibilities of an individual purchasing his own farm or business and being successful were fast declining; and the ability of the capitalist economy to provide jobs was clearly in doubt. But workers and farmers held on to the illusion that prosperity would return and with it the opportunity of becoming an independent commodity producer. While the Liberals best capitalized politically on the desire of people to turn back to better times, the success of Social Credit in Alberta shows on a regional basis the illusions that kept people tied to the dominant ideology and left them suspicious of revolutionaries.

The Social Credit

Social Credit insisted that capitalism was not the problem; the problem was the banking system. From the point of view of the independent commodity producer and the aspiring independent commodity producer, usurious credit and lack of credit was a congenital problem. The farmer's operating costs were high and the prices he received for his product were low. Without credit his earnings would always lag behind his expenses. Small businessmen faced the same dilemma. The Alberta and Saskatchewan farmers groups attacked the view that the marketplace was the best determinant of either the value of the farmers' product or the workers' labour. Those who wished to view themselves as independent commodity producers would not agree that there was exploitation in the process of production (as opposed to the process of exchange). While the one-crop economy seemed to have convinced many Saskatchewan farmers that they were little more than exploited employees of the Winnipeg Grain Exchange, other farmers believed they could win in the marketplace if they could have a constant line of credit. The banker, divorced from the operations of the economic system as a whole, became the villain.

Few Social Creditors would have read Major Douglas' mad tract, *Social Credit*, which uses the Czarist forgery—"Protocols of the Elders of Zion"—as a document to prove that a group of Zionist moneylenders had a master plan to capture the world's money supply and to enslave the people.[29] Many would have read, however, such Social Credit picture-book tracts as Louis Even's *Salvation Island*. In this pamphlet five shipwrecked men use their talents to establish an economy based on independent commodity production. Their lives are temporarily ruined by the arrival of a long-nosed banker, Oliver Glucksterlingmann, who pulls them into an endless debt cycle. Soon enslaved by the Jewish banker, the men are only rescued when a copy of Major Douglas' book washes ashore. It exposes the uselessness of Glucksterlingmann and points the way to freedom—the ousting of the "foreigner."[30] (It is strange that one can speak of natives and foreigners when one is talking about a deserted island.) *Salvation Island* revealed a great deal about the people who supported Social Credit. There are no corporations and no workers on this island; there are only independent commodity producers who deal with each other through barter. That such an economy could be seen as having parallels with the monopoly capitalism of the 1930s indicates the extent to which illusions can be sold to the people as commonsense.

While many Canadians, particularly workers and farmers and a small but influential group of middle-class professionals, rejected the existing economic system, this radical thrust could not carrv the majority of the people. State repression played an important role, keeping the working class unorganized and toeing the line. Generally, though, many of the powerless and the unorganized looked to the powerful and the organized for reforms. Many others were fatalistic and looked to no one for either reform or revolution. Few more than half the people even bothered to vote in the mid-Depression federal election of 1935. Despite the overall ideological hegemony of the ruling class, the reforms passed had so far failed to produce an ideological consensus on the question of the causes and solutions of Canada's economic problems.

XI

BUSINESS AND THE REFORM PROCESS

Addressing a Conservative party summer school in 1933, economist Harry M. Cassidy advocated a set of economic and social measures that would significantly increase state involvement in the Canadian economy. To place this program within a context acceptable to conservatism, Cassidy said its ideological aim was:

> ...maintenance of the economic and social status quo, involving protection of private property rights of the economic system known as capitalism and of social stratification based upon it; coupled with a willingness to extend the power and influence of the state, as in the direction of social reform, insofar as this may be necessary to protect and defend the essentials of the status quo.[1]

This conservative ideology was shared by a businessman-Conservative, J.M. Macdonnell, who told the summer school gathering that the Conservative party should adopt the concept of state planning. Macdonnell cautioned Conservatives against the dangers of leaving private economic forces to correct the Depression. Referring to the opinions of Sir Arthur Salter, a British statesman whom Canadian businessmen and politicians often quoted in the 1930s, Macdonnell advocated state action to achieve higher price levels. Increasing the money supply was the particular measure Macdonnell endorsed on this occasion.[2]

In an earlier address to the Canadian Institute on Economics and Politics, Macdonnell again rejected the program and argued that it was necessary to:

> ...remove the grit from the individualist machine and make it run smoothly—meanwhile allowing the process of the last century to continue viz. the gradual socialisation of those things which the sense of the community agrees should be socialized.[3]

Though paying tribute to President Roosevelt, Macdonnell quoted Salter to indicate the direction in which Canadian businessmen wanted to see Canada go:

> If we are to have a planned and directed economic system, it is from inside that system that we must find those who will, for the most part, plan and control, and they must do this through their own institutions. The Government can and must play a part only and, even for that part of encouragement and general guidance, they will, in my view, need to utilize the assistance of those who are actively engaged in the economic activities of the country to a much greater extent than at present.[4]

The problem for businessmen and governments in the 1930s lay in defining the boundaries between the activities best left in private hands and those that should be socialized (even if responsibility for the socialized activities was, as Salter advocated, largely to be given to the leaders of the private sector). With the type of semantic confusion common to businessmen in the 1930s, Macdonnell called for "individualism unified by the state."[5]

The Reform Process

The reform process of the 1930s indicated a significant willingness among businessmen and governments to experiment with programs of mild inflation, social insurance, government loans, government marketing boards and countercyclical spending. There was no unanimity in the business community on these programs, but each program had important advocates within the business community. In every case the reform agencies established by governments were closer to the mould advocated by the business supporters; the proposals of supporters within other groups consistently took second place. Marketing boards did not replace private distributors; they generally gave distributors stronger holds over their industries. Insurance programs were financed largely by contributions from those who were to receive benefits rather than by general tax revenues. Government programs to stimulate construction involved government funds, but the actual lending of funds was done by private companies. And construction was carried out by private construction companies. The Bank of Canada, while receiving the sole right to issue currency, did not take away from the commercial banks any of their power over investment decisions.

To what degree had business used the state to preserve the status quo? The Depression was not ended by the reform process of the 1930s; the beginning of the war and the government mobilization of the economy for wartime purposes brought an end to the high unemployment that had plagued Canada for nine years. But the die had been cast. Canada would never again return to the comparatively low level of government involvement that had characterized its economy before the Depression. The war saw a widespread movement for unionization of the mass-production industries and an increase in the electoral strengths of both the CCF and the Communist Party. The working class' threat to bourgeois hegemony, terrifying enough in the 1930s, would be strengthened by greater organization. The programs begun in the 1930s were extended by the King Liberals during wartime. Not only did the Conservatives support most of the Liberal reforms, they attempted to outdo the government party by advocating a state-regulated private-enterprise economy. A Conservative conference in Port Hope in 1942 unveiled a program, largely the brain-child of Macdonnell, that committed Canadian Conservatives to support state planning for full employment; "a comprehensive security plan" including unemployment coverage, accident and sickness benefits, health insurance, maternity benefits, children's allowance and retirement pensions; export marketing boards; slum clearance and planned public works. The preamble to this program indicated the continuing rhetorical confusion over what all this was intended to bring about. "Individual initiative," it said, must be "strengthened" and economic activities must be freed from "bureaucratic controls."[6] Clearly, however, the policies advocated—whatever benefits they might provide individuals—involved state initiative, and regardless of who was to run these programs, their bureaucratic nature could not be disguised.

Rhetorical consistency was the aim of neither businessmen nor politicians sympathetic to business. The sympathetic politicians were interested in using the state machinery to make up for shortcomings in the private sector and to encourage the private sector to resume investment in order to re-employ the unemployed. The businessmen themselves were unabashedly interested almost solely in earning a profit and still maintained that profit-making was the well-spring of the economic progress that had preceded the Depression.

There were important businessmen who continued to believe that the private-enterprise system could find its own remedies unaided by the state. But with the economic wreckage about them so evident, business-oriented governments could be excused for listening to the statist-minded industrialists and ignoring the Manchester liberals. There was little reason for government leaders to believe that anti-statist business leaders—like Sir Joseph Flavelle and Edward Beatty—spoke for the business community when the presidents of the two largest banks were advocating social insurance and marketing boards. Why should R.B. Bennett accept the anti-New Deal viewpoint of Beatty when he had received so much encouragement from businessmen to proceed in the direction of the New Deal programs? Why should he back down when a who's who of businessmen was congratulating him for his radical-sounding New Deal speeches even before the legislation promised had been drawn up? W. Sanford Evans could make all the speeches he wanted against marketing boards, but the fact remained that the Toronto and Montreal Boards of Trade favoured marketing boards, even if the boards could compel all producers and industrialists to participate. Opposition to public works and public housing had to compete with the cries of the construction and finance industries that government action in these areas was necessary. It would have been unseemly of the government to believe that banks and mortgage-lenders wanted to reserve for themselves the right to loan money to homeowners and farmers when banks and lenders insisted that they preferred to share this privilege with the government. Bennett indicated clearly that he believed the capitalist system was losing credibility with the working class and farmers, and finding that as a class the capitalists were not adverse to changes that might restore class harmony, Bennett acted accordingly.

The extent to which governments saw stimulation of the private sector as the primary aim of programs of government intervention was the extent to which business, especially big business, could effectively direct reform legislation. The programs of state intervention that businessmen thought might encourage investment—mortgage-lending, planned public works, full federal control over relief through unemployment insurance and other measures, orderly marketing—were adopted by governments. Socialization programs increasing the taxes of the rich and the corporations, extensive monetary inflation, support of collective bargaining, restriction of monopolies were proposals put forward by various non-business and small business groups. Because these programs offended important investors and directors of big corporations, whose investment and employment decisions were most crucial to the nation, these programs were either rejected by the government or legislated in a half-hearted window-dressing fashion.

Businessmen achieved somewhat less than the full program of state intervention that they had hoped to see instituted in the 1930s. Provincial resistance, aided by the courts, prevented the establishment of a federal agency to supervise the borrowings of municipalities and provinces. The sections of the Dominion Trade and Industry Commission Act that would allow federal sanctioning of private cartel arrangements were found *ultra vires*, though the restrictive trade practices legislation was rarely used before or after the court decision.

Role of the State

Fear of haphazard action by governments carrying out palliative programs during economic recessions caused businessmen more anxiety than the idea of government having a permanent, defined role in the economy. Municipal bankruptcies and the public funds wasted on hastily-conceived relief projects that did not stimulate the economy as a whole convinced economic leaders that a better means of coping with unemployment must be possible. Arthur Purvis, the industrialist whose National Employment Commission report in 1938 won almost unanimous support from business, had pulled together many of the ideas businessmen had been urging on governments for several years. Unemployment insurance, housing policy, manpower agencies, public works and the Bank of Canada should all be coordinated in order to insure that public policies were used to maintain high levels of employment and productivity in the private sector and to smooth out major fluctuations in the business cycle.[7]

The Montreal Board of Trade, which could count both Purvis and Beatty among its influential members, supported Purvis' view of the state's role in the economy. It told the Royal Commission on Dominion-Provincial Relations in 1938 that governments had failed to appreciate that "many of the services rendered by the state and which had their origin in certain emergency situations of the past few years have now assumed a permanent nature."[8] The board argued that governments and private citizens must come to accept the positive interventionist state as beneficial:

> In estimating the cost and the effects of public expenditures, it is necessary to distinguish between public and private economy.
>
> Both cannot be judged by the same criteria. The individual normally takes a temporary view of his economic activities and expects an early return in the form of profits measured in dollars and cents. The state, on the other hand, can take a much larger view and its return need not be pecuniary at all. Expenditures which promote social welfare and those which provide security, order and justice are productive but yield no immediate financial profit to the government.[9]

The board warned that all expenditures "are limited by the available resources of the state," but that large expenditures "are justified if they give a compensatory stimulus to the production which may be checked by the taxation necessary to meet the expenditures."[10] Echoing the conservative views of Cassidy and Macdonnell, the Montreal Board of Trade added:

> ...taxation for the purpose of social services transfers purchasing power from the richer to the poorer classes, raises the standard of living of the poor, increases their demand for commodities and thereby tends towards industrial stability and prosperity. Furthermore, in a period of economic depression, heavier government expenditures, whether paid for by taxes or by loans, are justified and necessary in order to fill the gap resulting from fear and inactivity which paralyze private enterprise.[11]

Traditionalists like Flavelle and Beatty were unconvinced. But the tenor of business thought during the 1930s had increasingly moved towards the views expressed by the Montreal board. Each year the variety of proponents and proposals for reform in the business press and at company annual meetings increased. The traditionalists had fewer followers, not because their positions within the business community had been changed but because the prosperity they said would return of its own volition did not appear to be just around the corner. Businessmen, such as Sir Charles Gordon, A.O. Dawson, Arthur Meighen and Arthur Purvis, who before the 1930s had held views that might be called traditionalist, became convinced that some reforms were needed. Support from these conservative and successful men of industry no doubt gave these reforms an aura of respectability and encouraged further business support of the various reform programs. The diehard traditionalists advocating a self-correcting business cycle were being proved wrong in practice and could not prevent their fellow businessmen from turning to governments for solutions.

Since business was not alone in favouring reforms, it might be argued that the reforms satisfied the demands of other sectors of society. Farmers and workers shared with business a desire for government planning and for programs of insurance and mortgage-lending. Even while attacking the specifics of all the reform measures of the decade, the CCF generally admitted that these reforms tended in the right direction and ended up voting for them. While the working class and farmers' struggles were a key factor in the willingness of the ruling class and the state to pursue these programs, the working class was not strong enough nor radical enough to prevent these programs from being instituted in ways that preserved the existing class structure. In order not to discourage domestic or foreign investment the Bank of Canada limited its operations and made no attempt to alter investment patterns. While raising the prices received by primary producers, marketing boards also raised the prices received by distributors. Monopolies were strengthened or created by the boards.

The reform programs left the state holding the bag in some cases. The reforms transferred to governments largely unprofitable and risky activities and left profitable activities to the private sector. For business this meant that profits would accrue to private hands and that necessary losses would be socialized. Responsibility for unemployment, for necessary but high-risk loans, for care of the casualties of the system would become for once and for all a social responsibility separated from the responsibilities of the businessmen. Funds for all this had to come from somewhere. Government largesse to the railways and the Hudson's Bay Company in the form of land grants, guaranteed loans and direct subsidies had resulted in high land costs for many Prairie immigrants. The tariff granted eastern manufacturers had been onerous enough to farmers to spawn a new political movement, the Progressive party. The new government programs would also have to be financed by someone. Since the idea of many of these programs was to encourage investment, it would have been killing the goose that laid the golden egg to depend mainly on the wealthy for revenue. The tendency of governments since the 1930s has been to raise more and more of their revenues from the lower income earners through direct taxes and social insurance premium deductions.[12]

Since the success of many of these programs was premised on an ever-growing economy, it was not necessary to worry whether income was actually being redistributed. It was enough that governments had more disposable income to use to smooth out the business cycle and to help low-income citizens make necessary purchases. If the economy should stop growing despite government spending, much of the rationale—not to mention the funds—for government activity in the economy would be removed. Heavy government spending under such circumstances might necessitate greater taxation of corporate wealth and cause a resistance of private investors to risk capital. The result would be an even lower rate of economic growth. It is also possible that government programs once favoured by business would be continued even if the business community turned against them. But this is more a subject related to the present and to the future; what happened in the 1930s offers little help in determining whether the welfare state is a permanent or a temporary feature of advanced capitalist societies.

What then can be said to be the motivations of the Canadian state of the 1930s? Did the Bennett and King governments turn to reform as a reflection of a change of strategy of the entire bourgeoisie? Or did the governments of the period, recognizing the imminent threat to the capitalist system, impose upon the capitalist class a set of agencies and policies that it did not want but whose net effect was to save the capitalist class from itself and to preserve the system?

Neither of these views is accurate. The inaccuracy of the view that the capitalist class was forced to accept reforms it did not want is apparent in the close connection between the business community and all levels of government, elected and appointed. Each of the agencies of reform had important business advocates and the forms these agencies took reflected the business community's conception of reform.

Why was the anti-reform segment of the business community unsuccessful in preventing change? It should be noted first that the opponents of reform were a minority as indicated by the extent of active support Bennett received for his New Deal. More importantly, the state, as Poulantzas observes, is charged with protecting the long-term interests of capital, and in the 1930s the Canadian state was interested in abating the heightened class struggle produced by the Depression and in rationalizing the economic order so that future depressions and class struggles would be eliminated. While the capitalist class as a whole shared these goals, many of its members were more interested in their short-term goals of maximizing profit. They would contribute very little in helping state leaders find the means to restore stability to the capitalist order.

In general it would appear that the banking and manufacturing sectors, mainly concerned with restoring the home economy, were the first converts to reform. The resource industries, importers and exporters were still largely convinced that Canada could not afford to tinker with its economy and that international markets would be upset by new state interventions. While the demands of this group could not be ignored, particularly within the Liberal party, the overall weakness of this group at the national level had been shown historically by its failure to defeat protectionism. On the other hand, the resource industry, importers and exporters dominated the provincial scene. As the strength of provincial governments grew in relation to the federal government, this group opposed not only reform but also the separate economic existence of Canada on the North American continent.[13]

How autonomous was state action in the reform process? It was autonomous in the sense that the state did not call for a direct vote on reform measures among the leading capitalists. It was not autonomous in the sense that the specific actions were taken only with the encouragement of large sectors of the bourgeoisie and that staffing of the agencies was almost exclusively in the hands of the capitalist class. The autonomy of the state might be said to exist within certain circumscribed limits, not because the economic and political leadership do not intertwine—in Canada in the 1930s they clearly did—but because the politicians must finally act, knowing that some members of the business community would be opposed to their decisions. The actions taken were those that businessmen-politicians and other pro-capitalist politicians believed would placate working-class and farmer demands while being assured at the same time that business power within the overall system would be preserved.

APPENDIX

BUSINESS AFFILIATIONS OF CABINET MINISTERS AND APPOINTEES IN THE THIRTIES

Bennett Cabinet (1930-35)

1. R.B. Bennett
   a) Prime Minister (1930-35)
   b) Vice-president of Alberta Pacific Grain Company; partner in Canada Cement; director of Imperial Tobacco and Canada Packers; chief solicitor for Canadian Pacific Railway; shareholder and lawyer in Imperial Oil; major shareholder in E.B. Eddy Match, E.B. Eddy Newsprint and Royal Bank; shareholder in Arizona Lead Mines, Coal Sellers Company, Cotton Belt Mines, International Petroleum, Monarch Lead, McLeod Oil, Oatman United Gold Mining, Okalta Oils, Vancouver Milling and Grain, and Royalite.
2. C.H. Cahan
   a) Secretary of State (1930-35)
   b) Partner in Canada Cement.
3. R.B. Hanson
   a) Minister of Trade and Commerce (1934-35)
   b) Director of New Brunswick Telephone Company and chief legal advisor for Fraser Cities Ltd.
4. J.A. Macdonald
   a) Minister without Portfolio (1930-35)
   b) President of J.A. Macdonald Company and Associated Shippers Inc.; secretary-treasurer of Cardigan Electric; director of Cardigan Silver Fox and Georgetown Fish.
5. Arthur Meighen
   a) Government leader in Senate (1930-35)

b) President of Canadian General Securities; vice-president of Canada Life; chairman of Canada General Fund, Canada General Investments Ltd. and Third Canadian Investment Trust Ltd.; director of Canadian Celanese, Northern Canada Mining and Toronto General Insurance.

6. Sir George Perley
   a) Deputy Prime Minister (1930-35)
   b) Vice-president of Reed Lumber Company and Canadian Atlantic Railway; director of Bank of Ottawa.
7. E.N. Rhodes
   a) Minister of Finance (1930-35)
   b) President of British North America Nickel Corporation.
8. E.B. Ryckman
   a) Minister of National Revenue (1930-33)
   b) President of Dunlop Tire and Rubber Goods; director of Gurney Foundry, IBM, Russell Motor Company and Addressograph Company.

Mackenzie King Cabinet (1935-

1. T.A. Crerar
   a) Minister of Mines and Resources (1935-*
   b) Director of Great West Life and Investment Foundation Ltd.
2. Charles Dunning
   a) Minister of Finance (1935-39)
   b) President of Maple Leaf Milling Corporation and Ontario Equitable Life; director of Canadian Investment Fund and Barclay's Bank (Canada); chairman of Ogilvie Mills.
3. William Euler
   a) Minister of Trade and Commerce (1935-
   b) President of Pilot Automotive and Accident Insurance Company and Kitchener News-Record Ltd.; director of Dominion Life Assurance and Economical Fire Insurance.
4. C.D. Howe
   a) Minister of Transport (1935-
   b) Chairman of Ogilvie Flour Mills; director of Bank of Mon-

*No second date indicates that the individual remained in that position after the 1940 election.

treal, National Trust, Crown Life, Rio Tinto Mining, RCA Victor and Canadian Investment Fund.

5. W.L. Mackenzie King
   a) Prime Minister (1935-
   b) Industrial relations advisor for Rockefeller Foundation.

Appointments

1. Edward Beatty
   a) Chairman of Royal Commission on Technical and Professional Services
   b) President of Canadian Pacific Railway.
2. John I. McFarland
   a) Chairman of Canadian Wheat Board (1935-36)
   b) Controlling interest in Alberta Pacific Grain Company; stockholder in Royalite and Turner Valley operations of Imperial Oil.
3. John R. Murray
   a) Chairman of Canadian Wheat Board (1936-
   b) Vice-president of Alberta Pacific Grain Company; secretary of Winnipeg Grain Exchange.
4. Arthur Purvis
   a) Chairman of National Employment Commission (1936-38)
   b) President of Canadian Industries Ltd. and Dunlop Tire.
5. Newton Rowell
   a) Chairman of Royal Commission on Dominion-Provincial Relations (1937-38)
   b) General counsel for Canadian Life Insurance Officers Association; corporation lawyer.
6. Joseph Sirois
   a) Chairman of Royal Commission on Dominion-Provincial Relations (1938-40)
   b) Director of Provincial Bank of Canada, Catelli Macaroni Products and Montreal Administration and Trust Society.
7. Graham Towers
   a) Chairman of the Bank of Canada (1934-
   b) Assistant general manager of Royal Bank; director of Royal Bank, General Motors, Bell Telephone and Hudson's Bay Company.

NOTES

I Introduction

1. Standard academic works with this kind of an interpretation include Robert A. Dahl, *Pluralist Democracy in the United States: Conflict and Consent* (Chicago: Rand, McNally, 1967); and Arnold M. Rose, *The Power Structure: Political Process in American Society* (New York: Oxford University Press, 1967). For Canada, see R. MacGregor Dawson, *The Government of Canada*, 4th ed. (Toronto: University of Toronto Press, 1963); and J.A. Corry and J.E. Hodgetts, *Democratic Government and Politics*, 3rd ed. (Toronto: University of Toronto Press, 1957).
2. On concentration of economic power see Wallace Clement, *The Canadian Corporate Elite: An Analysis of Economic Power* (Toronto: McClelland and Stewart, 1975). Studies dealing with distribution of political power include Robert Presthus, *Elite Accommodation in Canadian Politics* (Cambridge: Cambridge University Press, 1970); and Khayam Zev Paltiel, *Political Party Financing in Canada* (Toronto: McGraw-Hill Ryerson, 1970). Also useful is John Porter, *The Vertical Mosaic: An Analysis of Social Class and Power in Canada* (Toronto: University of Toronto Press, 1965).
3. See, for example, A.R.M. Lower, *Colony to Nation: A History of Canada* (Toronto: Longmans, Green and Company, 1942), pp. 515-522; D.G. Creighton, *Canada's First Century* (Toronto: Macmillan, 1970), pp. 218-219; and such secondary works as Ernest Watkins, *R.B. Bennett: A Biography* (Toronto: Kingswood House, 1963).
4. On the Canadian state and the railroads, see Gustavus Myers, *History of Canadian Wealth* (1914; repr., Toronto: James, Lewis and Samuel, 1972); and Robert Chodos, *The CPR: A Century of*

Corporate Welfare (Toronto: James, Lewis and Samuel, 1973). On the tariff, see John H. Dales, *Protective Tariff in Canadian Development* (Toronto: University of Toronto Press, 1966). The most useful account of state involvement in labour disputes is Stuart Jamieson, *Times of Trouble: Labour Unrest and Industrial Conflict in Canada, 1900-1966* (Ottawa: Queen's Printer, 1971). Other important studies of state-business relations in Canada include H.V. Nelles, *The Politics of Development: Forests, Mines and Hydro-Electric Power in Ontario, 1849-1941* (Toronto: Macmillan, 1974); and Alan F.J. Artibise, *Winnipeg: A Social History of Urban Growth, 1874-1914* (Montreal: McGill-Queen's University Press, 1975).

5. Canada, *Report of the Royal Commission on Price Spreads and Mass Buying* (Ottawa: King's Printer, 1935).

6. See Stanley Ryerson, *Unequal Union* (Toronto: Progress Books, 1968), pp. 42-53, 113-117; D.G. Creighton, *Empire of the St. Lawrence* (1936; repr., Toronto: Macmillan 1956), pp. 151-162, 314-316; Gilles Bourque, *Classes Sociales et Question Nationale au Québec, 1760-1840* (Montreal: Parti Pris, 1970), pp. 170-8; Alfred Dubuc, "Problems in the Study of the Stratification of the Canadian Society from 1760 to 1840," *Canadian Historical Association Annual Report,* 1965, pp. 13-29; Myers, *History of Canadian Wealth*, pp. 63-113.

7. Bourque, *Classes Sociales*, pp. 276-7, 310.

8. Ryerson, *Unequal Union*, pp. 273-7; G.N. Tucker, *The Canadian Commercial Revolution, 1845-1851* (Toronto: McClelland and Stewart, 1964), p. 84.

9. I use the word "manipulate" advisedly. Several authors have observed that the Québécois of the pre-1837 period were anti-statist and anti-capitalist. But their desire to avoid assimilation led them to support a program that made the state an insurance fund for railway companies. When union with Upper Canada was forced upon them, the democratic choices left open to the Québécois seemed limited. On the pre-1837 attitudes of the Québécois towards capitalism and state expenditure for commercial development, see: Creighton, *Empire*, p. 154; Fernand Ouellet, *Histoire Economique et Sociale du Québec, 1760-1850* (Montreal: Fides, 1966); "Les Insurrections de 1837-38," Michiel Horn and Ronald Sabourin,

eds., *Studies in Canadian Social History* (Toronto: McClelland and Stewart, 1974), p. 402.

The view that the Québécois had been more dynamic before the conquest and were gradually beaten into submissiveness is found in Maurice Séguin, "La Conquête et la vie économique des Canadiens," *L'Action Nationale*, December 1946, p. 309; Michel Brunet, *Canadians et Canadiens* (Montreal: Fides, 1960), pp. 109-110.

10. Myers, *History of Canadian Wealth*, pp. 218-243; and Robert Chodos, *CPR*, pp. 18-26.

11. Myers, pp. 150-217.

12. David Hall, "The Political Career of Clifford Sifton, 1896-1905" (Ph.D. thesis, University of Toronto, 1974), p. 336.

13. Hall, "Clifford Sifton," p. 432.

14. See L. Ethan Ellis, *Reciprocity, 1911* (New Haven: Yale University Press, 1939), chapter 14; and L.E. Ellis, "Canada's Rejection of Reciprocity in 1911," *Canadian Historical Association Annual Report*, 1939, pp. 99-111.

15. Stuart Jamieson, *Times of Trouble*, pp. 66-72.

16. W.L. Morton, *The Progressive Party in Canada* (Toronto: University of Toronto Press, 1950), pp. 256-7, 266.

17. Antonio Gramsci, *The Modern Prince and Other Writings* (New York: International, 1967).

II Business and Government Leaders in the Thirties

1. *Canadian Parliamentary Guide, Who's Who in Canada*, the *Financial Post Directory of Directors*, and *Prominent Men of Canada* as well as the *Financial Post, Financial Times* and *Monetary Times* were consulted for this section.

2. Bennett invested $100,000 in the venture and his profits, according to Beaverbrook, were "considerable." A.J.P. Taylor, *Beaverbrook* (London: Hamish Hamilton, 1972), pp. 15, 36-37, 86. Beaverbrook's own account of his relations with R.B. Bennett can be found in: Maxwell Aitken, *Friends: Sixty Years of Intimate Personal Relations with Richard Bedford Bennett* (London: Heinemann, 1959).

3. Evidence of Victor Ross, vice-president of Imperial Oil, before

Canada, House of Commons Select Standing Committee on Banking and Commerce, *Minutes of Proceedings and Evidence—Reference: Price of Gasoline*, 8 March 1932, p. 14; R.B. Bennett Papers, Public Archives of Canada, Ottawa, Vol. 901, pp. 563867-563900. In all, there were 52 companies in which Bennett was listed as a shareholder. His 1509 shares (of 3000) in E.B. Eddy made him the majority shareholder. His involvement with the E.B. Eddy Match Company, in and out of office, is detailed in R.B. Bennett Papers, Vols. 915, 916, 917. The labelling of Canada Packers and Imperial Tobacco as oligopolies appears in Canada, *Report of the Royal Commission on Price Spreads and Mass Buying* (Ottawa: King's Printer, 1935), pp. 53, 59. Bennett was reported as one of the largest shareholders in the Royal Bank in *Financial Post*, 5 May 1934, p. 2. According to the newspaper, Bennett held 1200 shares worth approximately $250,000 at then-depressed prices.

4. Of 3,923,000 working Canadians in the 1930s, 2,565,000 were wage earners and over one million were engaged in agriculture. Canada, *Report of the Royal Commission on Price Spreads*, p. 105.

5. There was no information on the occupations of eighteen caucus members.

6. *Financial Post*, 3 November 1934, p. 9; *Canadian Business*, November 1936, p. 22; Libby Park and Frank W. Park, *Anatomy of Big Business* (Toronto: James Lorimer, 1973), p. 57. Canada Power and Pulp, which Dunning served as a director from 1931, was alleged by the *Manitoba Free Press* to have been the victim of a massive stock-watering by Sun Life and other interests. The watering-down of these stocks in 1931 was being carried out without any public enquiry into the questionable dealings of the company. Dunning's appearance as a director of Canada Power and Pulp led the *Free Press* to comment that "his days as a western agrarian leader must look a long way off to him," *Manitoba Free Press*, August 1931. In R.B. Bennett Papers, Vol. 917, p. 577067.

7. *Financial Post*, 19 January 1935, p. 6.

8. *Journal of the Canadian Bankers Association*, October 1934, p. 15; Park, *Anatomy of Big Business*, p. 60. Although it does not appear to be an unusual move to appoint a banker to head the new central bank, it is questionable whether an agency intended in part

to supervise the banking system is best headed by someone from within the system.

9. Canada, Special Committee on the Marketing of Wheat and Other Grains under Guarantee of the Dominion of Canada, *Proceedings and Evidence*, 24 April 1936, p. 146.

10. *Who's Who* for 1936-1937 listed among Purvis's directorships the Bank of Montreal, Bell Telephone, British-American Oil, Canadian Investment Fund, Consolidated Paper Corporation, General Motors, Liverpool and London and Globe Insurance and Sun Life Assurance.

11. Christopher Armstrong, "The Politics of Federalism: Ontario's Relations with the Federal Government, 1896-1941," Volume One (Ph.D. thesis, University of Toronto, 1972), p. 88.

12. Canada, Select Standing Committee on Banking and Commerce, Hearings on Bill 18, *Proceedings and Evidence*, 1934, p. 15.

13. *Monetary Times*, 3 July 1937, p. 21. Ferguson's other directorships included Toronto General Trusts, Western Assurance Company and British American Assurance Company.

14. *Monetary Times*, 6 August 1938, p. 4.

15. Mackenzie King Diaries, 3 August 1934, Public Archives of Canada, Ottawa. Frank O'Connor was president of Laura Secord Candy Shops; Albert Matthews was head of a Toronto investment house; and E.G. Long was a Toronto lawyer and director of National Trust. See J.L. Granatstein, "Financing the Liberal Party, 1935–1945," in Michael Cross and Robert Bothwell (eds.), *Policy by Other Means* (Toronto: Clarke Irwin, 1962), pp. 179-99.

16. Khayam Zev Paltiel, *Political Party Financing in Canada*, p. 29; *Monetary Times*, 22 June 1934, pp. 7-8.

17. Ralph Miliband, *The State in Capitalist Society: The Analysis of the Western System of Power* (London: Quartet, 1973), pp. 54-55.

18. Interview by John A. Munro with Harry H. Stevens in H.H. Stevens Papers, Public Archives of Canada, Ottawa, Vol. 162A, p. 4, 28 June 1966; Stevens to Bennett, n.d., copy in King Papers, Public Archives of Canada, Ottawa, pp. 173561-2.

19. King Diaries, 13 July 1934; 9 March 1933; 10 March 1933; 25 August 1933; 26 May 1937; 13 April 1937; 24 November 1937.

20. H. Blair Neatby, *William Lyon Mackenzie King: The Lonely*

Heights (Toronto: University of Toronto Press, 1963), pp. 262, 274-75, 376-77.

21. Premier Henry held $25,000 worth of Abitibi-Ontario Power Service bonds, bonds bought out by the province in July 1932 when Abitibi was in insolvency. The government purchase tripled the value of the bonds. North American Life, for which Henry served as a director, also held some of the bonds bought by the government. So did a number of companies in which Meighen was involved, though Meighen said he had not been aware of this. William Price (Attorney-General of Ontario) to Bennett, 24 March 1933, Bennett Papers, Vol. 452, p. 602442.

22. Granatstein, "Financing the Liberal Party," pp. 195-96.

23. Research Committee of the League for Social Reconstruction, *Democracy Needs Socialism* (Toronto: Thomas Nelson and Sons, 1938), p. 9.

24. Canada, *Parliamentary Debates* (Commons), 22 January 1935, p. 114.

25. E.A. Forsey, "Concentration in Canadian Industry," *Canadian Forum* XIV, No. 157 (October 1933), pp. 9-10.

26. Canada, House of Commons, Select Standing Committee on Banking and Commerce, *Minutes of Proceedings and Evidence*, 27 March 1934, pp. 143-188.

27. League for Social Reconstruction, *Democracy Needs Socialism*, pp. 6-7; Forsey, "Canadian Industry," p. 10.

28. Forsey, "Canadian Industry," pp. 10-12. An elaboration of the Forsey article appears in Research Committee of the League for Social Reconstruction, *Social Planning for Canada* (1935; Toronto: University of Toronto Press, 1975).

29. Canada, *Report of the Royal Commission on Price Spreads and Mass Buying* (Ottawa: King's Printer, 1935), pp. 50, 55, 60, 76.

30. Canada, House of Commons, *Debates*, January 22, 1935, p. 115; Peter C. Newman, *Flame of Power: Intimate Profiles of Canada's Greatest Businessmen* (Toronto: Longmans, Green and Company, 1959), p. 22.

31. Just how did one get to be part of the economic élite—through ownership of a company or through an appointment to top management? The *Report of the Royal Commission on Price Spreads* (p. 16) stated that 42.8 per cent of the company assets represented

by the biggest 145 non-banking corporations (26 companies in all) were under effective management control—defined by the report to cover all companies in which no individual or definable group owned more than 6 percent of the shares. Another 41 companies, representing 18.5 percent of the assets of the big 145, were said to have joint control of management and the largest minority shareholder—defined by the report to cover companies in which an individual or group held 6 to 19.99 percent of all shares. Minority shareholders, with 20 to 49.99 percent of all shares, were said to control 29 companies with 15.6 percent of the total assets. Another 28 companies had a majority shareholder with 50 to 79.99 percent of all shares. These companies represented 14.2 percent of the assets of the 145 companies under study. Finally, 21 companies, representing 8.9 percent of the total assets, could be said to be privately-owned since 80 percent or more of voting shares were in the hands of one individual or group.

But the report admitted that these figures likely understated the holdings of groups in various companies:

> In classifying the schedules to arrive at the above results, numerous difficulties were encountered. The large number of brokers who appeared as the registered owners of shares in some companies was surprising. It was impossible to go behind these registered owners, and it was assumed that they represented roughly the actual division of shares among individuals; the schedules were thus classified on a strict mathematical basis. This condition doubtless obscures the real situation at times, and it is possible that, had complete data been available, the companies would be classified differently. But there is certainly no method of eliminating this difficulty. Financial institutions such as trust companies also appeared in the lists with great regularity. In some cases, the holdings were specified "in trust;" in others no such specification occurred. It is difficult to say to what extent this practice also hid the real situation. Another problem was that of detecting those individuals who, although reported as independent and separate holders, were in fact acting together. A few obvious cases could be detected and in these cases the separate holders were regarded as forming one group, but there were doubtless many

more which could not be distinguished with the information available. It would require a detailed investigation of the personal relationship in every case to settle the point.

Report of the Royal Commission on Price Spreads, p. 17. In other words, it is difficult to establish for this period to what degree ownership and control were coterminous. Only the availability of far more information would allow us to conclude whether the economic élite was a largely managerial or an owner-manager élite.

32. Roger Graham, *Arthur Meighen: Volume II: And Fortune Fled* (Toronto: Clarke Irwin, 1963), p. 152.

33. Graham, *And Fortune Fled*, p. 285.

34. R.B. Bennett Papers, Vol. 160, p. 108378, Imperial Economic Conference, 1932, Copy Number One, Secret Memorandum on American Branch Factories in Canada, prepared by the General Economic Committee of the Preparatory Organization for the Imperial Economic Conference, 1932.

35. Bennett Papers, p. 108386.

36. Financial Post, *Directory of Canadian Directors and Officials* (Toronto: Maclean Publishing, 1941), p. 231.

37. Frank A. Southard and Kenneth W. Taylor, *Canadian-American Industry* (New York: Russell and Russell, 1936), pp. 23, 56, 71, 72, 108.

38. Francis Hankin and T.W.L. McDermot, *Recovery by Control* (Toronto: Dent and Sons Ltd, 1933), pp. 169-70; *Canadian Banker*, July 1937, pp. 408-13.

39. S.D. Clark, *The Canadian Manufacturers' Association: A Study in Collective Bargaining and Political Pressure* (Toronto: University of Toronto Press, 1939).

40. None of the Canadian Manufacturers Association presidents of the 1930s listed in *Who's Who* or the *Directory of Directors* held a directorship in a finance company of any sort. None of them had a directorship in the larger-scale firms of the country. Some of the presidents and many of the subordinate officers did not merit inclusion in *Who's Who* or the *Directory of Directors*. The Canadian Chamber of Commerce, on the other hand, included among its presidents in this decade men with many directorships both in

finance and the largest non-finance companies. A.O. Dawson, president of Canadian Cottons and director of the Bank of Montreal, among many other directorships, was 1935 president. Millionaire investment banker and former cabinet minister R.C. Matthews was 1936 president. The group of Chamber of Commerce delegates who appeared before the Royal Commission on Dominion-Provincial Relations in 1938 included officials of Bell Telephone, Royal Trust and Greenshields-Hodgson-Racine (Royal Commission on Dominion-Provincial Relations, *Evidence and Proceedings*, 20 May 1938, p. 9509). Toronto Board of Trade presidents included Imperial Bank of Canada chairman Frank Rolph (1930); Goodyear Tire president C.H. Carlisle (1931); National Trust general manager J.M. Macdonnell (1934); and K.P. Marshall, president of Standard Fuel (1938). These men all held many important directorates. The Montreal Board of Trade president in 1930 was Walter Molson, president of Molson, Lobley and Company, and director of a large number of companies including National Trust, Dominion Glass, and Lake of the Woods Milling. R.J. Magor, president in 1934, was president of National Steel Car, among many other concerns.

41. Canada, Department of Labour, *Twelfth Report on Organization in Industry, Commerce and the Professions* (Ottawa: King's Printer, 1938); Royal Commission on the Textile Industry, *Proceedings and Evidence*, Brief Number One of Commission Counsel to the Commission (Ottawa: King's Printer, 1938), pp. 273-74.

42. The Trades and Labour Congress, for example, dropped from a membership of 142,000 to 122,000 between the 1931 and 1932 conventions. By the 1933 convention, membership had fallen to 105,000. Trades and Labour Congress of Canada, *Report of the Proceedings of the 47th, 48th and 49th Annual Conventions*, 1931, 1932, 1933. Estimated trade union membership in Canada was 378,000 in 1919; 310,000 in 1931; and 315,000 in 1936. Canada, Department of Labour, *Annual Report*, 1919, 1931, 1936. See also A.E. Grauer, *Labour Legislation: A Study Prepared for the Royal Commission on Dominion-Provincial Relations* (Ottawa: King's Printer, 1939), pp. 68-69.

43. See Stuart Jamieson, *Times of Trouble: Labour Unrest and Industrial Conflict in Canada, 1900-1966* (Ottawa: Queen's Printer, 1971).
44. Ivan Avakumovic, *The Communist Party in Canada: A History* (Toronto: McClelland and Stewart, 1975), pp. 71-75.
45. For example, the federal government joined in 1920 with the Western Coal Operators Association to support the United Mine Workers' attempt to hold on to the mines of the Crow's Nest Pass region. The miners had voted 90 percent to join the One Big Union and 6200 mine employees in 41 firms struck for four months to win recognition for their union. The federal government took what Martin Robin calls "an unprecedented move" and extended the tenure of the director of Coal Operations, who operated under the War Measures Act. An order-in-council was then passed on 21 July 1920, "requiring that all men who worked in and around the mines eligible to become members of the United Mine Workers must join the organization and agree to sign a check-off for all dues, assessments and fines." Martin Robin, *Radical Politics and Canadian Labour* (Kingston: Queen's University Press, 1968), pp. 190-1.

Government appointments of labour leaders to government committees and commissions went exclusively to Trades and Labour Congress representatives. Attacking the One Big Union and the All-Canadian Congress of Labour for having asked the government to include representatives from their organizations when such appointments were made, the Trades and Labour Congress newspaper accused its more radical rivals of wishing "to build up an industrial form of organization by which they could exercise a dictatorship over all other classes of the country." *Canadian Congress Journal*, February 1933, p. 7.
46. The front page of the 2 September 1932 edition congratulated Mussolini for advocating a world conference to establish a forty-hour universal work week. Gushed the *Labour Leader*:

> Like Premier Bennett, Mussolini has done many things. He is sincere and has courage. Premier Bennett also has these two sterling qualities in abundance. Let us hope that Mussolini will meet with the same success with his proposed conference as did our premier at Ottawa.

The *Labour Leader* was, in particular, an advocate of the cooperation of conservative trade unionists with employers and the state against radical labour. The 21 December 1934 edition reported:

> ...We fear that this red organization will cost Canadian industry many millions in lost time and wages unless sufficient cooperation is extended by all friends of legitimate labour organizations so that *together we may successfully combat this new menace to peaceful progress as we have done with other revolutionary groups that have gone before.* [emphasis mine].

47. Louis A. Wood, *A History of Farmers' Movements in Canada*, (Toronto: University of Toronto Press, 1974), pp. xv-xviii.
48. Anthony Downs, *An Economic Theory of Democracy*, p. 269.
49. Barry Hindess and Paul Q. Hirst, *Pre-Capitalist Modes of Production* (London: Routledge and Kegan Paul, 1975), p. 36.
50. Nicos Poulantzas, *Political Power and Social Classes* (London: New Left Books, 1973); Nicos Poulantzas, *Classes in Contemporary Society* (London: New Left Books, 1975).
51. Hugh Aitken, a conventional Canadian economic historian, posited in 1956 the central role of the Canadian state in promoting Canadian development. In partnership with private enterprise, the state had sponsored tariff, railway and immigration legislation that allowed the growth of a national economy. Aitken sees the state as the crucial motor of a national development but says that the theory that the state merely acted as an agent for private economic interests in these matters "could probably be supported." He adds that the distinction between "the state" and "private enterprise" in Canada "often seems artificial." Hugh G.J. Aitken, "Defensive Expansionism: The State and Economic Growth in Canada," in Hugh G.J. Aitken, ed., *The State and Economic Growth: Papers of A Conference Held on October 11-13 Under the Auspices of the Committee on Economic Growth* (New York: Social Science Research Council, 1959), pp. 79-114.
52. See, in particular, Tom Naylor, *History of Canadian Business*, Volumes One and Two (Toronto: James Lorimer, 1976); Wallace Clement, *Continental Corporate Power* (Toronto: McClelland and Stewart, 1977).
53. Ralph Miliband, *The State in Capitalist Society* (London:

Weidenfeld and Nicolson, 1969), pp. 56, 66-7, 75.
54. Miliband, *The State*, p. 157.
55. The American business community was deeply divided over continuing the war in Vietnam once defeat appeared likely. The confusion of the British capitalist class in the 1970s is discussed in Andrew Gamble and Paul Walton, *Capitalism in Crisis: Inflation and the State* (London: Macmillan, 1976), pp. 30-2, chapter Six.

III Combines Legislation

1. Tom Naylor, *The History of Canadian Business, 1867-1914*: Volume Two: *Industrial Development* (Toronto: James Lorimer, 1975), pp. 162-199; Michael Bliss, "An Anti-Trust Tradition: Canadian Anti-Combines Policy, 1889-1910," *Business History Review*, XLVII, No. 2 (Summer 1973), pp. 177-188.
2. Robert Simpson Company, when it began to make its shares available to the public, added an additional burden of fixed cost of $1 million per annum in creating the security structure. Some classes of public securities of Simpson's were yielding no return in the 1930s. Wood Gundy, the investment dealers responsible for the reorganization, received an excessive remuneration.

Burns overvalued its assets in order to issue new securities. The investment house involved misstated the income figures, and in the depression came the inevitable reorganization.

Each time Canadian Canners acquired a new company, it revalued the total value of the company's plants. The appreciation and other intangible assets included in the 1933 balance sheet were double the figure for actual capital expenditure. The company's president was a stock broker and his firm was the largest shareholder in Canadian Canners. *Report of the Royal Commission on Price Spreads and Mass Buying*, pp. 36-7.

Dominion Textiles resulted from the consolidation in 1905 of four textile companies. Their total shares, worth $2,594 million, were watered to $5 million. — Factum of commission counsel on Dominion Textile Company. Canada, *Royal Commission on the Textile Industry*, Factum Three (Ottawa: King's Printer, 1937).
3. Gideon Rosenbluth, *Concentration in Canadian Manufacturing*

Industries (Princeton: Princeton University Press, 1957), p.9; "Secret" Memorandum Prepared for the Imperial Economic Conference, 1932, Bennett Papers, Vol. 159, p. 107959; R.J. Manion to R.B. Bennett, 8 May 1933, Manion Papers, Vol. 4.

4. See, for example, the *Financial Times*, 19 August 1932. In a front-page editorial it called for a "dictator" in the industry with "absolute power to control output and to apportion business among the mills to the greatest advantage economically." The *Monetary Times* and *Financial Post* expressed similar attitudes.

5. Minutes of Proceedings and Evidence, Select Standing Committee on Banking and Commerce, *Hearings on Relation of Chartered Banks and Pulp and Paper Industry*, 23 May 1934, pp. 882-84. On Holt, see Park, *Anatomy*, p. 49; Newman, *Flame of Power*, pp. 22, 38, 41. See also Canada, *Parliamentary Debates* (Commons), 1935, p. 25; *Canadian Business*, September 1935, pp. 12-13, 42.

6. See comments of S.L. Willson (president of the American Pulp and Paper Association), *Pulp and Paper of Canada*, March 1934, pp. 226-7. At a time when many large employers in the United States were beginning to oppose the National Recovery Administration because of the alleged favouritism towards unions, the association president could point out that the "code" in his industry had virtually eliminated cut-throat competition, stabilized prices, increased employment and purchasing power and developed a spirit of cooperation.

General works on the pulp and paper industry include L. Ethan Ellis, *Newsprint Producers, Publishers and Political Pressures* (Rutgers, N.J.: Rutgers University Press, 1960), pp. 16-18; L. Ethan Ellis, *Print Paper Pendulum* (Rutgers: Rutgers University Press, 1948). The cartel in the 1920s is discussed in Ervin Hexner, *International Cartels* (Chapel Hill: University of North Carolina Press, 1945), pp. 376-77.

7. *Pulp and Paper of Canada*, January 1934, pp. 52-3.

8. L.J. Belnap to Robert Weir, 9 November 1934, Natural Products Marketing Act Papers, Department of Agriculture, Public Archives of Canada, Ottawa, Box 576; Canada, *Parliamentary Debates* (Commons), 25 June 1935, p. 3966.

9. C.H. Carlisle to Arthur Meighen, 1 May 1934; Meighen to R.B. Bennett, 2 May 1934, Bennett Papers, Vol. 771, pp. 43190-3.

10. Even the *Financial Post*, an avowedly free-trade journal, gave front-page editorial support to Carlisle's proposals, which it concluded were not for state control but for self-government by business: *Financial Post*, 2 June 1934, p. 1; Special Committee on Price Spreads and Mass Buying, *Proceedings and Evidence*, Vol. Two, pp. 2174-93. For details of the British plans for industrial rationalization, see *Price Spreads Report*, pp. 252-3; A.J. Youngson, *The British Economy, 1920-1957* (London: George Allen and Unwin, 1960), pp. 98-102, 105, 116, 132-134; Charles Loch Mowat, *Britain Between the Wars, 1918-1940* (London: Methuen, 1955), pp. 441-448.
11. "Address of Arthur Purvis to the Canadian Construction Association," 23 January 1935, Bennett Papers, Vol. 714, pp. 437864-5. The evolution of NRA is discussed in Ellis Hawley, *The New Deal and the Problem of Monopoly* (Princeton: Princeton University Press, 1966).
12. Canadian businessmen aside, the judgment of at least one British economic historian on the long-term effects of the flight from competition in the British economy of the 1930s is harsh. Says A.J. Youngson: "...there is no doubt that the limited, exiguous, emasculated, etiolated competition of the 1930s was too little for good economic health then and that the economy still suffered years later from the unenterprising habits acquired at that time." Youngson, *British Economy*, p. 134.
13. Major L.L. Anthes (president of Canadian Manufacturers Association) to R.B. Bennett, 20 February 1934, Bennett Papers, Vol. 138, pp. 92078-81; R.B. Bennett to L.L. Anthes, 26 February 1934, Bennett Papers, pp. 92082-3.
14. *Canadian Grocer* reported food sales of $92,150,000 by six chains in 1933. Total food sales for Canada, chain and non- chain, were $238 million. Dominion was the leading chain with sales of $20 million by 510 stores. It was followed by Loblaws with $3.8 million in sales by 110 stores; A and P with $12 million by 278 stores; and Safeway with $9 million sales by 185 stores: *Canadian Grocer,* 1 December 1933, p. 1. *Financial Post* reported that all supermarkets had suffered a drop in profits during 1934 as a result of price wars in Montreal. *Financial Post*, 7 October 1934, p. 14;

Royal Commission on Price Spreads, *Evidence*, 29 November 1934, pp. 1741-2; 10 December 1934, p. 1760; 13 December 1934, p. 2584.
15. *Monetary Times*, 23 January 1933, p. 4; *Monetary Times*, 22 June 1934, pp. 7-8.
16. Roger Graham, *Arthur Meighen, Vol. Three: No Surrender* (Toronto: Clarke Irwin, 1965), pp. 67-68.
17. George Drew to R.B. Bennett, 22 November 1933, Bennett Papers, Vol. 139, pp. 92067-9.
18. Douglas Campbell, president of St. Lawrence Flour Mills, writing in *Monetary Times*, 8 January 1932, p. 19; *Monetary Times*, 12 January 1934, p. 32; Price Spreads Commission *Evidence*, 8 January 1935, p. 3924.
19. Canada, *Parliamentary Debates* (Commons), 1923, pp. 2524-5; H.H. Stevens to Robert Borden, 24 April 1934, Stevens Papers, Vol. 14; Gray Miller (president of Imperial Tobacco) to H.H. Stevens, 16 June 1934; Stevens to Bennett, 18 June 1934.
20. H.H. Stevens interview with John A. Munro, 12 July 1966, Stevens Papers, Vol. 162A, pp. 11-12; 1957 interview with Stevens, Stevens Papers, Vol. 162A., p. 154; Retail Merchants Association of Canada to W. White (chairman of Board of Commerce), 8 July 1920, Board of Commerce Papers, Vol. 13.
21. Warren Cook to H.H. Stevens, 10 August 1933; Stevens to R.C. Matthews, 7 October 1933, Stevens Papers, Vol. 22; Stevens to R.B. Bennett, 19 January, 1934, Stevens Papers, Vol. 14; Special Committee on Price Spreads, *Evidence*, p. 291. Department store opposition to high tariffs was expressed in the brief of the Canadian Importers and Traders Association to the Royal Commission on Dominion-Provincial Relations, *Evidence and Proceedings*, 27 April 1938, p. 7026.
22. Stevens to Bennett, 26 October 1934, King Papers, p. 173552. Bennett wrote:

> My colleagues and I made it clear to you that a Minister of the crown, even though chairman of a committee or a commission, is presumed to be speaking for the government and that the principle of Cabinet solidarity may not recklessly be departed from. In dealing with questions of governmental policy, a Minister of the Crown should take care that his

public pronouncements represent the views of the Government of which he is a member.

Bennett to Stevens, n.d., King Papers, p. 173558.

23. Roosevelt's programs included the establishment of codes of fair practice for business on an industry-by-industry basis, public housing, guaranteed floor prices and quotas for farmers, and unemployment insurance. Publicists stressed that Roosevelt, by increasing the role of the national government, was redistributing wealth from the rich to the poor and power from the corporations to the government. But current revisionist American historians claim that these programs increased business power by encouraging monopoly under the guise of regulating fair practices and by providing the private sector with lucrative public contracts.

24. *Winnipeg Free Press*, 3 January, 1935, p. 1.

25. All references are from the Bennett papers. A.O. Dawson to Bennett, 5 January 1935, Vol. 713, pp. 437648-9; H.B. Henwood to Bennett, 26 January 1935, Vol. 715, p. 439241; C.H. Carlisle to Bennett, 10 September 1935, Vol. 718, p. 441952; Col. Cockshutt to Bennett, 14 January 1935, Vol. 715, p. 439311; Thomas Bradshaw to Bennett, 29 January 1935, Vol. 715, p. 439950; Ward Pitfield to Bennett, 23 January 1935, Vol. 714, p. 438181; W.W. Butler to Bennett, 10 January 1935, Vol. 714, p. 438181; J.W. McConnell to Bennett, 18 January, 1935, Vol. 949, p. 599331; Sen. C.J. Ballantyne to Bennett, 8 January 1935, Vol. 713, p. 437724 (Ballantyne also mentions the full support of Johnson and Southam); James McGroaty to Bennett, 30 January 1935, Vol. 715, p. 439311; A.C. Fraser to Bennett, 10 January 1935, Vol. 718, p. 441711; Arthur Purvis' speech to Canadian Construction Association, 23 January 1935, Vol. 714, p. 437867.

26. Senator C.J. Ballantyne to Bennett, 8 January 1935, Bennett Papers, Vol. 713, p. 437724; C.O. Knowles (editor), *Toronto Evening Telegram*, to Bennett, 9 January 1935, Bennett Papers, Vol. 715, p. 439298; F.D.L. Smith (chief editor) *Mail and Empire*, to Bennett, 15 January 1935, Bennett Papers, Vol. 715.

27. *The Globe*, 21 January 1935, p. 1.

28. Michael Bliss, "A Canadian Businessman and War: The Case of Joseph Flavelle," in J.L. Granatstein and Robert Cuff, eds.,

War and Society in North America (Toronto: Thomas Nelson and Sons, 1971), pp. 20-36.

29. Canada, *Parliamentary Debates*, (Commons) 14 June 1935, pp. 3651-4.

30. W.W. Kennedy to Bennett, 8 June 1935, Bennett Papers, Vol. 772, pp. 473948-9; Bennett to Kennedy, 11 June 1935, p. 473957. Another example is a letter from Conservative MP Onesime Gagnon in which the charge is made that most people would see the legislation as sacrificing the people to big business. Gagnon to Bennett, 14 June 1935, p. 474018.

31. Canada, *Parliamentary Debates* (Commons), 18 February 1935, pp. 951-2.

32. Interview with H.H. Stevens 28 July 1967, Stevens Papers, p. 9.

33. Canada, *Parliamentary Debates* (Commons), 28 May 1935, pp. 3098-3114. Stevens used American Federal Trade Commission reports as evidence for the misuse of patents by the electrical equipment industry.

34. *Winnipeg Free Press*, 15 September 1935, p. 1.

35. Dawson wrote in part:

> If your plans are made effective, higher wages will of course have to be collected from industry, but no objection should be taken to this if wages are made more or less uniform throughout the land and at the same time the necessary protection be given to the Canadian industries that have to compete with countries where the wages paid are much lower than those being paid by most of the industries in Canada.
>
> It seems to me that manufacturers and merchants who are trying to do the right thing by their customers should welcome regulations made by the Government to prevent unfair and unjust practices by those who have no consideration of anyone or anything but their own selfish interests.

Dawson to Bennett, 5 January 1935, Bennett Papers, Vol. 713, pp. 437648-9.

36. *Monetary Times*, 6 February, 1937, p. 3. Arthur Meighen, commenting for the Conservatives in the Senate, said rather dramatically that "this class of legislation just makes life not worthwhile at all." He was commenting on the 1937 legislation,

which provided for an expanded combines branch with greater powers of investigation and a more rigid definition of combines. The actual legislation that was passed in 1938 did little more than restore the legislation as it had existed before 1935. Canada, Senate Standing Committee on Banking and Commerce, *Proceedings*, 8 April 1937, pp. 14-15; for Canadian Chamber of Commerce reaction see *Canadian Business*, April 1937, p. 36.

King wrote of the 1937 legislation:

> I felt that the criticism of the Opposition was well directed against certain features of the measure as drafted. It goes much too far in making parties to the combine "likely to" prejudice public interest, criminals: also it builds up far too much of a bureaucracy and additional machinery for the Commissioner... The Senate, I think will throw the measure out and will be justified in doing so.

Mackenzie King Diaries, 1 April 1937, p. 190. See also L.A. Skeoch, ed., *Restrictive Trade Practices in Canada* (Toronto: McClelland and Stewart, 1966), pp. 103-7.

37. Skeoch, *Restrictive Trade Practices*, pp. 103-7.

IV Natural Products Marketing Boards

1. The laws in question are the British Columbia Produce Marketing Act of 1927 and the Dairy Products Sales Adjustment Act of 1929. The former was ruled out by the courts in 1931; the latter in 1933. The Saskatchewan legislation was ruled out in 1931. J.A. Corry, *The Growth of Government Activities Since Confederation: A Study Prepared for the Royal Commission on Dominion-Provincial Relations* (Ottawa: King's Printer, 1939), pp. 36-37.

2. *Report of the Royal Commission on Price Spreads and Mass Buying*, pp. 50-54.

3. In the 1930s the major corporations in the milk distribution industry included:

Dairy Corporation of Canada. Subsidiaries included City Dairy, Winnipeg; Purity Dairy Products Ltd; City Dairy Saskatoon; City Dairy, Edmonton; Mount Royal Dairies Ltd, Prairie Creameries, Regina; Purity Dairy, Regina; Purity Ice Cream, Winnipeg;

Canada Creameries, Toronto. Dairy Corporation also had an interest in United Dairies Ltd, with creameries and distributing centres in Alberta and in British Columbia and in Woodland Dairies.

Borden's Ltd of Jersey City controlled the following: City Dairy of Toronto; Hamilton Pure Milk Dairy Ltd; Ottawa Dairy Ltd; Chateau Cheese Co. Ltd; Laurentian Dairy Ltd, Ottawa; Walkerside Dairy, Windsor; Borden Farm Products Ltd; Halls Ltd, Montreal; Borden's Niagara Dairies Ltd, Niagara Falls. Borden's also owned concentrated milk plants at Truro, Nova Scotia; Ingersoll, Tillsonburg, Norwich and Belmont, Ontario; South Sumas, British Columbia; and receiving plants at Basford, Brownsville and Hickson, Ontario.

Eastern Dairies owned Elmhurst Dairy, Montreal; Crescent Creamery, Manitoba and Saskatchewan; Acme Dairy, Toronto, Hamilton, Napanee and Sydenham. Silverwood owned dairies in Peterborough, Woodstock and London. Highland Dairy owned Citizens' Dairy in Belleville, Whitby, Havelock and Tweed. Dri-Milk Co. Ltd had plants in Princeton, Toronto, Simcoe, Listowel and Staffordville. Carnation Company Limited had plants in Toronto, Springfield and Aylmer.

See J.E. Lattimer and Harold A. Innis, "American Tariff Policy and the Canadian Dairy Industry," in H.A. Innis, ed., *The Dairy Industry in Canada* (Toronto: Ryerson Press, 1937).

4. Imperial Tobacco's net profits after taxes and depreciation were $36,225,253 in the period from 1929 to 1934 on a company-claimed capitalization of $55,285,160. In other words, an average profit of 11 percent per annum was earned. *Price Spreads Report*, p. 52; Canada Packers average annual profits were 8.9 percent between 1929 and 1933, *Price Spreads Report*, p. 57. Canadian Canners, which suffered some losses during the Depression, nevertheless made a profit of $1,501,239 on an inflated investment claim of $7,408,812 for the year ending June 1930. *Canadian Canner and Preserver*, June 1930, p. 16.

5. John Burns, general manager of Burns and Company, to John I. Brown, manager of poultry department for Canada Packers, undated, 1933, Bennett Papers, Vol. 84, p. 55279. Burns and Co. operated dairies and creameries, packing houses, retail meat and provision markets and wholesale fruit depots. In 1929 and 1930 it

had extended its dairy and ice cream business through the acquisition of Valley Dairy, Vancouver's second largest distributor of milk; Cobourg Dairy Ltd of Moose Jaw; and ice cream and butter-making firms in Regina. *Canadian Dairy and Ice Cream Journal*, June 1930, p. 47.

6. John Burns to Robert Weir, 18 August 1934, Department of Agriculture Papers, Vol. 137, p. 357476. The resolution of the Quebec and Ontario creameries and butter distributors read in part:

> That any voluntary system of removing the exportable surplus is not possible and will not obtain the objective desired.
>
> That the Minister of Agriculture be requested to take such immediate action as will result in the compulsory removal of the exportable surplus (p. 357397).

7. The annual value at point of production of fruits and vegetables handled by the Canadian Fruits and Vegetables Association, the largest organization of wholesalers, dropped from $26 million in 1929 to $8 million in 1930 and $4 million in 1933. The volume handled, however, remained almost constant. Canada, *Parliamentary Debates* (Commons), 26 April 1934, pp. 2583-4.

8. The British Marketing Act provided that, when a majority of both the producers and the processors of an agricultural product agreed to a plan for setting prices and production quotas, the plan—if acceptable to government—would be legislated and enforced by the government and would be binding on all the producers and processors of the product.

9. J. Arthur McBride to L.F. Burrows (secretary-treasurer of Canadian Fruit and Vegetable Jobbers Association), 31 March 1934; Burrows to Weir, 4 April 1934, NPMA series, Department of Agriculture Papers, Vol. 567, pp. 348093-4.

10. *Canadian Canner and Preserver*, April 1933, p. 10; July, 1933, p. 8; April 1934, p. 8.

11. Lloyd G. Reynolds, *The Control of Competition in Canada* (Cambridge, Mass.: Harvard University Press, 1940) p. 43. Special Committee on Price Spreads, *Evidence*, 9 May 1934, pp. 1596-1614; Royal Commission on Price Spreads, *Evidence*, 11 January 1935, p. 4221.

12. *Canadian Dairy and Ice Cream Journal*, March 1934, p. 39. The journal was the official organ of the Canadian Creamerymen's

Association of Ontario; Toronto Dairymen's Bottle Association; Western Canadian Ice Cream Manufacturers Association; Canadian Association of Ice Cream Manufacturers; Manitoba Buttermakers Association; Nova Scotia Ice Cream Manufacturers Association; Ontario Milk and Cream Distributors' Association; Eastern Ontario Cheesemakers Association; Central Ontario Cheesemakers Association. The Journal and its member associations had long fought for compulsory pasteurization. See February 1930, p. 39; April 1930, p. 27; December 1931, p. 28; December 1933, p. 22.

13. C.M. Ruttan, president of City Dairy of Toronto, Borden's Ltd, testifying before the Select Standing Committee on Agriculture and Colonization, 1933, Bennett Papers, p. 60852; *Canadian Dairy and Ice Cream Journal*, December 1933, p. 22.

14. Henry's continued association with the dairy was regarded as a conflict of interest by Liberal MP J.O. Pouliott, Canada, *Parliamentary Debates* (Commons), 29 May 1931, p. 2094; Reporting the legislation the *Financial Post* noted:

> Large milk concerns in which the public has a considerable interest apparently fear no further ill effects on securities as a result of the bill now before the Ontario Legislature to establish a milk control board for Ontario. In fact, they expect the effect to be favourable insofar as the new board succeeds in bringing some order into marketing conditions for the industry.

Financial Post, 10 March 1934, p. 10.

15. J.A. Caulder to Robert Weir, 22 March 1934, Department of Agriculture Papers, Vol. 137, p. 354297.

16. Canada, *Parliamentary Debates* (Senate), 14 June 1934, pp. 532-535.

17. Regina Board of Trade to R.B. Bennett, 24 June 1931, Bennett Papers, Vol. 79, pp. 51466-8.

18. Associated Boards of Trade of the Fraser Valley to R.B. Bennett, 6 October 1933, Bennett Papers, Vol. 79, p. 52052; *Canadian Dairy and Ice Cream Journal*, March 1934, p. 22; Winnipeg Board of Trade Papers, Public Archives of Manitoba, Winnipeg, 29 January 1934.

19. Canada, *Parliamentary Debates* (Commons) 16 April 1934, pp.

2205, 2201; for the legislation, see also *Canada Year Book*, 1935, p. 1181.

20. Canada, *Parliamentary Debates* (Commons) 19 April 1934, p. 2334.

21. Montreal Board of Trade Papers, Public Archives of Canada, Ottawa, 4 April 1934, pp. 481 (1)-481 (2); J.M. Macdonnell, president of Toronto Board of Trade and F.D. Tolchard, general manager of Toronto Board of Trade, to R.B. Bennett, 12 April 1934, Bennett Papers, Vol. 776, pp. 475-92. The Toronto Board of Trade wrote Bennett:

> The Council heartily approves of the compulsory grading of natural products and the regulation, through a Dominion Marketing Board of trade, of practices including such items as packaging, etc. and that, as far as may be practical, grading be carried through to the consumer. The Council is also in favour of all possible assistance, short of the actual engaging by the Government Board in any marketing scheme, being extended to the producers in the marketing of their products, including research work relating to production and marketing. The Council of the Board is however opposed to the proposed Dominion Marketing Board having power to engage in the marketing of any product.

22. C.L. Burton to Mackenzie King, 1 May 1934, King Papers, Vol. 199, p. 169850; *Commerce of the Nation*, November 1931, pp. 8-9, 21; Burton to King, Vol. 204, pp. 174910-14.

23. *Canadian Business*, June 1934, p. 25.

24. Robert Weir to R.B. Bennett, 9 May 1934, Bennett Papers, Vol. 777, pp. 476275-83.

25. *Financial Post*, 9 February 1934, p. 3.

26. *Canada Gazette*, 31 January 1935, PC 259; NPMA Papers, Volume 569.

27. Dominion Marketing Board, *Official Report of Hearings*, Saskatchewan and Alberta Live Stock Schemes, NPMA Papers, Vols. 570, 571, 572; H.H. Stevens to R.J. Manion, 14 November 1933, H.H. Stevens Papers, Vol. 22.

28. R.H. Milliken to R.B. Bennett, Bennett Papers, p. 475893.

29. NPMA Papers, Vols. 566, 570, 572; National Dairy Council resolutions in *Canadian Dairy and Ice Cream Journal*, March 1936,

p. 32; King Diaries, 18 December 1936, p. 605. King wrote:

> The Farmers' Creditors Arrangement Act, the Criminal Code and legislation regarding restraint of trade will be declared valid. No information yet in regard to the Marketing Act, which I hope and believe will also be declared valid.

30. Reynolds, *Control of Competition*, p. 43.

V The Canadian Wheat Board

1. The most complete account of the farmers' struggle for control over marketing is Vernon Clifford Fowke, *The National Policy and the Wheat Economy* (Toronto: University of Toronto Press, 1957). See also W.L. Morton, *The Progressive Party in Canada* (Toronto: University of Toronto Press, 1950).
2. R.B. Bennett to Sidney Smith, 2 June 1933, Bennett Papers, Vol. 314, p. 210096.
3. John I. McFarland to Robert Weir, 22 May 1931, Bennett Papers, Vol. 322, pp. 216503-6.
4. McFarland to Bennett, 15 November 1933, Bennett Papers, Vol. 315, p. 211222.
5. This sequence of events with supporting documentation is found in the testimony of S.H. Logan, president of the Canadian Bankers Association before the Select Standing Committee on Banking and Commerce, *Minutes of Proceedings and Evidence*, 22 March 1934, pp. 130-35; in minutes of meetings of the three Prairie premiers with Acting Prime Minister Sir George Perley and the Hon. A.J. Ryckman, 15 November 1930, Bennett Papers, Vol. 322, pp. 216037-40; and Sir James Flavelle to Perley, 18 November 1930, Bennett Papers, Vol. 322, p. 216044.
6. R.B. Bennett to Beaudry Leman, president of the Canadian Bankers Association, 20 January 1931, Select Committee on Banking, *Proceedings*, pp. 134-35.
7. James A. Richardson, president and general manager of James A. Richardson and Sons Ltd, Commission to Inquire into Trading in Grains Futures, *Evidence and Proceedings*, 14 April 1931, p. 62; J.R. Murray, manager of Alberta Pacific Grain Company, p. 264; C.G. Shortt, president of the Canadian National Millers Association, p. 123.

8. Bennett-McFarland correspondence, Bennett Papers, Vols. 314-321.
9. *Royal Grain Report*, pp. 95-96; Canada *Parliamentary Debates* (Commons), 24 July 1931, p. 4149.
10. Evidence of J.H. McIvor, sales manager of Canadian Co-Operative Wheat Producers, Special Committee on Canada Grain Board Act (Bill 98), *Minutes of Proceedings, Evidence and Report*, 1935, p. 367; Grain Report, 1938, p. 96.
11. Grain Report, 1938, p. 98.
12. Richardson to Bennett, 30 November 1933, Bennett Papers, Vol. 314, p. 210112; Sidney Smith to R.B. Bennett, 6 November 1933, Bennett Papers, Vol. 315, pp. 210363-4; J.R. Murray to McFarland, 12 March 1934, Bennett Papers, Vol. 315, p. 210674.
13. J.A. Gilchrist to M.A. McPherson, 6 February 1934, Bennett Papers, Vol. 314, p. 209877; H.G.L. Strange to M.A. McPherson, 9 October 1933, Bennett Papers, Vol. 314, p. 209855.
14. For example, the Canadian Chamber of Commerce convention in 1934 passed a resolution declaring unemployment a national problem and endorsed land settlement as its major solution. *Industrial Canada*, October 1934, p. 56.
15. Canada, Select Committee on Banking, *Proceedings*, 22 March 1934, p. 133.
16. McFarland to Bennett, 24 January 1935, Bennett Papers, Vol. 315, pp. 211043-211044.
17. McFarland to Bennett, 28 February 1935, Bennett Papers, Vol. 315, p. 211103.
18. McFarland to Bennett, March 1, 1935, ibid., p. 211109.
19. Among opponents of the bill in its initial form were the Canadian Chamber of Commerce and the boards of trade of Winnipeg, Montreal, Saskatoon, Vancouver, Edmonton and Moose Jaw. Bennett Papers, Vol. 319, pp. 213176-80; Winnipeg Board of Trade Papers, 13 June and 18 June meetings, 1935.

Winnipeg's board was most vehement and said the bill would establish a "marketing monopoly," putting "dictatorial control...into the hands of a government agency of three men." Based on the principle of compulsion, it would mean "further unnecessary extension of government activity in the field of detailed business operation." It "would destroy an open market for grain'' which the board claimed had been the means of maintaining touch with current supply and demand throughout the world. Winnipeg Board of Trade Papers, 13 June 1935.

20. Canada, *Parliamentary Debates* (Commons), 30 March 1936, p. 1616.

21. Testimony of R.W. Milner, president of the Winnipeg Grain Exchange, Canada, Special Committee on Bill 98, *Proceedings*, pp. 23-24.

22. James Richardson to Bennett, 4 February 1935, Bennett Papers, Vol. 316, pp. 211077-9; McFarland to Bennett, 10 February 1935, Bennett Papers, Vol. 316, p. 211074; Bennett to McFarland, n.d., Bennett Papers, Vol. 316, p. 211081.

23. McGibbon, p. 36.

24. Crerar wrote to King:

> The principle embedded in the wheat board legislation is the creation of a bureaucracy in the marketing not only of wheat but in other cereal grains and as such, is opposed to every principle of liberalism. It is the application of Woodsworth's theories to one of our great industries and will inevitably lead to the regimentation of wheat producers and other farmers as well.

Crerar thought a board to liquidate the ''mess'' McFarland had created was necessary but its objective should be ''restoration of the free market operations in handling wheat.'' Crerar to King, King Papers, Vol. 205, p. 175500.

25. Testimony of J.R. Murray before Special Committee on the Marketing of Wheat and Other Grains, *Proceedings and Evidence*, 21 April 1936, pp. 37, 43; J.R. Murray to Cecil Lamont, 12 December 1935, in *Evidence*, Special Committee on the Marketing of Wheat and Other Grains, p. 145.

26. McFarland quoted in an interview 19 December 1935 in *Evidence*, Special Committee on the Marketing of Wheat and Other Grains, p. 155.

27. Murray testimony in *Evidence*, Special Committee on the Marketing of Wheat and Other Grains, 18 April 1936, pp. 158-59.

28. King Diaries, 26 August 1936.

29. *Royal Grain Report*, p. 38.

30. King Diaries, 26 July 1938.

31. *Royal Grain Inquiry Report*, 1938, pp. 83, 185, 194. See evidence of Winnipeg Grain Exchange, Royal Grain Commission, *Proceedings and Evidence*, Vol. 6, pp. 1729-1783; and Vol. 7, pp. 1888-2121.
32. King Diaries, 6 July 1938; James Gardiner to King, 10 September 1938, King Papers, Vol. 250, p. 213494.
33. *Financial Times*, 12 August 1938, p. 1.
34. *Submission of the Western Committee on Markets and Agricultural Re-Adjustment* to the Dominion Government on the Necessity of Continuing the Canadian Wheat Board and a Guaranteed Minimum Price of at Least 80¢ per Bushel for 1939 Wheat Crop (Winnipeg: Western Committee on Markets and Agricultural Re-Adjustment, 1939), pp. 3, 10, 11.
35. *Ibid.*, p. 11.
36. *Ibid.*, p. 6.
37. *Submission of the Western Committee*, 24 April 1939, pp. 11, 13.
38. T.A. Crerar to King, 13 April 1939, King Papers, Vol. 266, pp. 225731-3. Crerar's views regarding mining companies are expressed in Crerar to King, 30 April 1936, King Papers, Vol. 215, pp. 185521-4.
39. Vernon Fowke, *The National Policy and the Wheat Economy* (Toronto: University of Toronto Press, 1957), p. 274.
40. Fowke, *The National Policy*, p. 202.
41. Canada, *Parliamentary Debates* (Commons), 25 April 1939, p. 3143.
42. McGibbon, p. 118.
43. *Report of the Royal Commission on Banking and Currency* (Ottawa: King's Printer, 1933), p. 71.
44. W.T. Easterbrook, *Farm Credit in Canada* (Toronto: University of Toronto Press, 1938) p. 131; Britnell, pp. 227-230; *Canada Year Book*, 1935, p. 1111.
45. Provincial debt adjustment legislation is detailed in Easterbrook, *Farm Credit* pp. 140-145; and Britnell, pp. 83-85.
46. R.B. Bennett to George A. Cruise, Attorney-General of Saskatchewan, 6 February 1934, Bennett Papers, Vol. 87, p. 57825.
47. Bennett Papers, Vol. 87, pp. 57941-8.
48. Dominion Mortgage and Investments Association to W.C.

Clark, 29 March 1934, Bennett Papers, Vol. 87, pp. 57975-8.
49. Bennett Papers, Vol. 87, pp. 57975-6.
50. Dominion Mortgage and Investments Association to Bennett, 14 June 1934, Bennett Papers, Vol. 87, pp. 58148-9.
51. *Financial Times*, 15 June 1934, p. 8.
52. Canada, *Report of the Royal Commission on Banking and Currency* (Ottawa: King's Printer, 1933), p. 71.
53. Dominion Mortgage and Investments Association to W.C. Clark, 29 March 1934, Bennett Papers, Vol. 87, p. 57976.
54. The problems of the Prairies—and other industrially underdeveloped areas—are discussed in T.N. Brewis, "The Problem of Regional Disparities," in T.N. Brewis, ed., *Growth and The Canadian Economy* (Toronto: Macmillan, 1969) pp. 90-111. The tragicomical attempts by provincial governments in the poorer provinces to attract industry at any cost are the subject of Philip Mathias, *Forced Growth: Five Studies of Government Involvement in the Development of Canada* (Toronto: James, Lewis and Samuel, 1971). Alberta's failure to use its oil resources for more than short-term gains is convincingly argued in Larry Pratt, *The Tar Sands: Syncrude and the Politics of Oil* (Edmonton: Hurtig, 1975).
55. Although the Social Credit Party is its major focus, an excellent philosophical approach to farmers' ideology is provided in C.B. Macpherson, *Democracy in Alberta* (Toronto: University of Toronto Press, 1953).

VI Social Insurance

1. For a discussion of social welfare in Ontario during the nineteenth century, see R.B. Splane, *Social Welfare in Ontario, 1791-1893: A Study of Public Welfare Administration* (Toronto: University of Toronto Press, 1965). The early introduction of public health and free elementary education is discussed in Elisabeth Wallace, "The Origins of the Social Welfare State in Canada," *Canadian Journal of Economics and Political Science*, Vol. XVI, No. 3 (August 1950), pp. 383-93.
2. James Weinstein, *The Corporate Ideal in the Liberal State,*

1900-18 (Boston: Beacon Press, 1969); Ontario, *Commission on Laws Relating to the Liability of Employers to Make Compensation to Their Employees for Injuries Received in the Course of Their Employment. Final Report* (Toronto: King's Printer, 1912-13), in Public Archives of Ontario, Toronto; CMA interest in compensation is discussed in Michael Bliss, *A Living Profit* (Toronto: McClelland and Stewart, 1974), p. 42; CMA—and labour—reaction to the Ontario Workmen's Compensation Act, 1914, is detailed in *Canadian Annual Review of Public Affairs*, 1914, pp. 391-95. The CMA said the act was based to a considerable extent on their proposals for a system of collective insurance under state control; but they objected to several administrative features of the act and also to the level at which compensation payments were set.

3. Ontario, *Report of the Ontario Commission on Unemployment*, 1916, pp. 82-83, in Public Archives of Ontario, Toronto.

4. Dennis Trevor Guest, "The Development of Income Maintenance Programmes in Canada, 1945-1967" (Ph.D. Thesis, University of London, 1968); on mothers' allowances see John S. Morgan, "Welfare in Canada," in Michael Oliver, ed., *Social Purpose for Canada* (Toronto: University of Toronto Press, 1961).

5. Canada, Department of Labour Papers, Vol. 167, Files 612.316, vols. 1 and 2, and 612.513; Court, p. 49.

6. Kenneth McNaught, *A Prophet in Politics: A Biography of J.S. Woodsworth* (Toronto: University of Toronto Press, 1959).

7. A.E. Grauer, *Labour Legislation: A Study Prepared for the Royal Commission on Dominion-Provincial Relations* (Ottawa: King's Printer, 1939), pp. 5-6.

8. The Economic Council of Canada reported in 1972 that at least 27 percent of Canadians are living in poverty, if poverty is defined as "an insufficient access to certain goods, services and conditions of life which are available to everyone else and have come to be accepted as basic to a decent, minimum standard of living." A study prepared for the Economic Council indicated that governments, while establishing programs that transferred wealth to the lowest income group, used methods of taxation that involved "extreme regressivity. . .at the lower end of the income scale and the lack of any significant progressivity over the remainder of the income

range." *Canada Yearbook, 1972* (Ottawa: Queen's Printer), pp. 1218-19; Allan Maslove, *The Pattern of Taxation in Canada* (Ottawa: Queen's Printer, 1972), p. 64. A more critical study of the British pattern of taxtion has been prepared by Richard A. Titmuss in *Income Distribution and Social Change* (London: George Allen and Unwin, 1962).

9. Canada, *Parliamentary Debates* (Commons), 29 April 1931, pp. 1100-04; Bennett Papers, Vol. 811. The trade unions represented in sending the Communist formula resolution to Bennett were broadly representative of the rail, construction crafts and industrial unions of Canada of the time.

10. Canada, *Parliamentary Debates* (Commons), 28 April 1931, p. 1077.

11. Canada, *Parliamentary Debates* (Commons), 29 April 1931, p. 1104.

12. *Financial Times*, 5 August 1932, p. 8. For a discussion of unemployment insurance in Great Britain, see Bentley B. Gilbert, *British Social Policy, 1914-1939* (London: B.T. Batsford, 1970), pp. 52-97, 162-75. Gilbert discusses the origins of the insurance program and its decay to the point where the public treasury, rather than the insurance fund alone, paid a substantial part of the benefits.

13. Canada, *Parliamentary Debates* (Commons), 18 February 1935, p. 941; 29 January 1935, pp. 283-84; 6 May 1930, p. 1831.

14. Sir Charles Gordon to R.B. Bennett, 6 January 1934, Bennett Papers, Vol. 811, p. 503059.

15. For example, as reported in *Canadian Business*, December 1934, Gordon told the annual meeting of the Bank of Montreal, 3 December 1934:

> Never before in the history of Canada or the United States has the problem of unemployment and direct relief loomed so large as it does today. In fact, it has become the greatest problem that we have had to face since the war. In Great Britain, this problem has been dealt with in a most thorough manner. Some of us thought, when we first heard of old age pensions, unemployment insurance—misnamed the dole—and other measures that Parliament was going too far in introducing social legislation of this nature. It has taken some twenty-five

> years and many acts of Parliament to construct in Great Britain the organization which is now carrying on so effectively. It is not a haphazard way of dealing with the situation but a highly organized department of government whose function it is to distribute to those who should have it the relief to which they are entitled.
>
> Legislation to deal with this whole subject will have to be undertaken by the governments of Canada and the United States; otherwise the problem will get out of hand and it will be impossible to control the proper expenditure of the vast sums which are being voted for the purpose of unemployment relief.

16. *Monthly Review of the Bank of Nova Scotia*, August 1934, p. 4; Canada, Department of Labour Files, Vol. 167, File 612:5:3; Bennett Papers, Vol. 811.
17. *Canadian Machinery and Manufacturing News*, April 1934, p. 8; *Canadian Machinery and Manufacturing News* to R.B. Bennett, 29 May 1934, Bennett Papers, Vol. 812, p. 503182.
18. *Canadian Machinery and Manufacturing News*, June 1934, pp. 16-17; T.A. Russell, president of Massey-Harris, to R.K. Finlayson, 30 November 1933; Finlayson to Russell, 7 December 1933, Bennett Papers, Vol. 811, pp. 203038-503040.
19. *Financial Post*, 8 September 1934, p. 9.
20. Canada, *Final Report of the National Employment Commission* (Ottawa: King's Printer, 1938).
21. Canada, *Parliamentary Debates* (Commons), 27 April 1938, p. 2307.
22. On the 1929 strike, see Dorothy Kidd, "Women's Organization: Learning from Yesterday," *Women at Work: Ontario 1850-1930* (Toronto: Canadian Women's Educational Press, 1975), pp. 351-57; *Financial Times*, 21 September 1934, p. 1.
23. The Montreal Board of Trade appointed a committee of five to investigate unemployment insurance. Its members were too divided for a recommendation to be made. *Minutes of the Montreal Board of Trade*, Montreal Board of Trade Papers, 30 November 1932, p. 373 and 1 March 1933, p. 397. The *Toronto Board of Trade Journal* had supported unemployment insurance as a means of "intelligent provision against the days of unemployment" in

February 1931. But the board's committee on the subject would only propose that any unemployment insurance scheme must be contributory and compulsory and tied to an efficient system of employment bureaus; it would not recommend for or against such a scheme. *Toronto Board of Trade Journal*, February 1931, p. 17 and January-February 1933, p. 10. The Chamber of Commerce also limited itself to comment on the features it wanted to see in an insurance bill without comment on the principle itself. Canadian Chamber of Commerce to Bennett, Bennett Papers, Vol. 812, pp. 503502-4; CMA on unemployment insurance, old-age pensions, health insurance: *Industrial Canada*, June 1935, p. 47; July 1931, p. 192; May 1931, p. 140.

24. Edward Beatty to R.B. Bennett, 19 February 1935, Bennett Papers, Vol. 812, p. 503976.

25. Sir Thomas White to Bennett, Bennett Papers, 22 August 1934, p. 503201.

26. Winnipeg Board of Trade Papers, Provincial Archives of Manitoba, Winnipeg, 5 December 1932.

27. For a partial list of the businessmen who supported Bennett, see Chapter III; the speeches were printed in full in a pamphlet by the Conservative Party, Bennett Papers, Vol. 812; Pitfield in *Montreal Gazette*, 20 September 1934, in Bennett Papers, Vol. 812, p. 503215.

28. Canada, *Parliamentary Debates* (Senate), 31 January 1934, p. 19.

29. *Quebec Chronicle Telegraph*, 11 December 1934, in "Unemployment Insurance" series, Canada, Department of Labour papers, Vol. 162, file 612.01:50.

30. Canada, *Parliamentary Debates* (Senate), Canada, 31 January 1934, p. 21 and 18 April 1934, p. 269.

31. Canadian Chamber of Commerce to Bennett, 13 April 1935, Bennett Papers, Vol. 812, pp. 503502-4. For the act (c. 38, 25-26, George V), see *Canada Year Book*, 1936, p. 113.

32. Canada, *Parliamentary Debates* (Commons), 29 January 1932, p. 278; H.H. Wolfenden, one of the chief accountants drawing up the plan, also noted the British experience as having been important in drafting the plan. *Industrial Canada*, July 1934, pp. 89-94.

33. R.B. Bennett to Howard Robinson, 11 June 1935, Bennett Papers, Vol. 715.
34. *Winnipeg Free Press*, 19 September 1935, p. 1 and 10 September, 1935, p. 1.
35. Canada, *Parliamentary Debates* (Commons), 19 February 1935, p. 990; *Financial Post*, 25 May 1934, p. 1; Canadian Manufacturers Association to Bennett, Bennett Papers, Vol. 812, p. 503983.
36. Ontario Associated Boards of Trade and Chambers of Commerce to King, King Papers, Vol. 238, p. 204650. The association's resolution noted "with satisfaction and approval the announcement by the Dominion government that it has invited the provincial governments to join with it in requesting an amendment to the BNA Act to make possible the establishment by federal authority of unemployment insurance and labour employment agencies."

The association "entertains no doubt that upon this subject the national interest requires a nation-wide system of unemployment insurance, administered by the Dominion Government and believes that Canada should show on this occasion that national unity of effort among the provinces can be achieved where national interests require it."
37. J.S. Woodsworth quoting Thomas Bradshaw speech to North American Life Assurance annual general meeting, 20 January 1936, in Canada, *Parliamentary Debates* (Commons), 5 May 1936, p. 2545; *Monetary Times*, 23 January 1937, pp. 30-31.
38. Purvis had demanded and received from King the right to veto participation on the commission of anyone with whom he did not wish to work. Arthur Purvis to King, 31 March 1936, King Papers, Vol. 225, p. 193524. On the development of the role of the conservative ideology of the trade unions, see Robert H. Babcock, *Gompers in Canada* (Toronto: University of Toronto Press, 1975); H. Blair Neatby, "The Liberal Way: Fiscal and Monetary Policy in the 1930s," in Victor Hoar, ed., *The Great Depression: Essays and Memoirs from Canada and the Great Depression* (Toronto: Copp Clark, 1960), pp. 89-113. Purvis' earlier views on recovery and the importance of the British example are seen in "Address of Arthur Purvis to the Canadian Construction Association, January 23, 1935," Bennett Papers, pp. 437862-437875.

39. Canada, *Final Report of the National Employment Commission*, pp. 29-32.
40. King Diaries, 22-23 January 1938, pp. 65-66 and March 25, p. 244; D.L. Morrell, "The Canadian Chamber of Commerce," *Canadian Banker*, July 1937, p. 410; Canada, Royal Commission on Dominion-Provincial Relations, *Evidence*, Canadian Chamber of Commerce, 20 May 1938, p. 9513.
41. *Canadian Business*, December 1937, p. 10.
42. Canada, Royal Commission on Dominion-Provincial Relations, *Evidence*, Retail Merchants Association, 31 May 1938, p. 9691; Commission on Dominion-Provincial Relations, *Evidence*, Ontario Association of Real Estate Boards, 19 January 1938, p. 2739.
43. H.M. Cassidy, *Social Security and Reconstruction in Canada*(Toronto: Ryerson Press, 1951), p. 21.
44. Canada, Special Committee of the House of Commons on Bill Number 98 Respecting Unemployment Insurance, *Minutes and Evidence*, pp. 131, 134, 204, 214, in "Unemployment Insurance" Series, Department of Labour Files, Vol. 163.
45. Royal Commission on Dominion-Provincial Relations, *Evidence*, CMA, pp. 2375-76. John S. Morgan, "Welfare in Canada," in *Social Purpose for Canada*.
46. Canada, *Parliamentary Debates* (Commons), 24 January 1935, pp. 179-80. Opposition to the British Columbia bill is discussed in *Canadian Business*, May 1936, p. 17. The medicare proposal, its popular support and the withdrawal of the bill are discussed in Margaret Ormsby, "T. Dufferin Patullo and the Little New Deal," *Canadian Historical Review*, Vol. XLIII, No. 4 (December 1962), pp. 277-97.
47. *Canadian Business*, July 1938, p. 12.

VII The Construction Industry

1. The value of construction of all kinds in 1929 was $576,651,000. *Canada Year Book*, 1932, quoted in Volume One, Royal Commission on Banking and Currency, *Proceedings*, 1933, p. 2724. The twelve-month low-point for construction was from July 1932 to

June 1933. During the first half of this period, construction amounted to $58,111,200. In the last half it was $32,912,300. The $91,000,000 total for this period indicates a drop of over 600 percent from 1929. National income in this period had dropped from about $5.5 billion in 1929 to $3.3 billion in 1933. *Canadian Business*, May 1935, p. 12.

2. T.J. Crowder address to Retail Merchants Association annual convention, reported in *Canadian Grocer*, 15 August 1930, pp. 15-16.

3. *Monetary Times*, 16 January 1931, p. 18.

4. *Monetary Times*, 8 January 1931, p. 32.

5. Members of the NCCC included the Canadian Construction Association; the Canadian Manufacturers Association; Canadian Lumbermen's Association; Trades and Labour Congress; Royal Architectural Institute of Canada; Engineering Institute of Canada; Brick Manufacturers Association; Canadian Ceramic Society; Asphalt Roofing Manufacturers Association; Structural Clay Tile Association of Canada; Canadian Founders and Metal Trades Association. *Canadian Machinery*, August 1933, p. 24.

6. Banking and Currency, *Proceedings*, p. 2716.

7. Canada, Special Committee of the House of Commons on Housing, *Evidence and Proceedings* (Ottawa: King's Printer, 1935), p. 100.

8. Banking and Currency Commission, *Evidence*, p. 2715; J.B. Carswell to Bennett, Bennett Papers, 4 October 1933; Volume 777, p. 476712.

9. *Financial Post*, 28 April 1934, p. 7.

10. W.H. Yates, Jr., president of Canadian Construction Association, *Monetary Times*, 11 January 1936, p. 50; J.B. Carswell, chairman of Survey Committee of National Construction Council of Canada, to R.B. Bennett, 20 September 1935; Bennett to Carswell, 25 September 1935, Bennett Papers, Volume 94; W.H. Yates to Bennett, 26 January 1935, Bennett Papers, Volume 714, p. 438201; Carswell to Bennett, 4 October 1933, Bennett Papers, Volume 777, p. 476712.

11. Canada, Department of Finance Papers, Volume 705, File 203-1, Memo to James Coyne, 7 June 1939; Ward Pitfield speech to Canadian Chamber of Commerce, sent by Pitfield to Bennett, 16

October 1933, Bennett Papers, Volume 776, p. 475677. Companies representing over 80 percent of corporate loans for mortgage purposes were in the Dominion Mortgage and Investments Association, according to T. D'Arcy Leonard, solicitor for the organization. Standing Committee on Banking and Commerce, 1939, *Proceedings and Evidence Respecting Bill 132*, p. 7.

12. Canada, *Parliamentary Debates* (Commons), 25 June 1935, p. 3948.

13.*Loc. cit.*

14. For example, an editorial in *Canadian Lumberman,* 1 July 1934, p. 16, called for the government to guarantee repayment of all or part of the principal on private loans of 80 percent of property value. See also *Canadian Lumberman*, 15 January 1934, p. 9.

15. *Canadian Business*, April 1936, p. 23. Morgan wrote that "private capital is apparently unable to provide adequate funds and Government assistance has not yet been proved sufficiently attractive to have been called in to any great degree." He recommended government facilitation of cheap money, long-term payments and less onerous municipal burdens on real estate. A start in this direction—but only a start as yet—had been made by the Dominion Housing Act.

16. Canada, *Parliamentary Debates*, (Commons) 24 June 1935, p. 3910.

17. Canada, Department of Finance Papers, Volume 705, File 203-1A; Canada, *Parliamentary Debates* (Commons), 29 January 1937, p. 388. An example of business encouraging King to keep the Dominion Housing Act was this resolution by the Ontario Associated Boards of Trade and Chambers of Commerce:

> The Ontario Associated Boards of Trade and Chambers of Commerce, recognizing the desirability of stimulating employment in the construction industries throughout Canada, urge the Government to support and encourage the plan of the Dominion Housing Act for the aid of house construction throughout the Dominion with special consideration of the smaller centers of population; and we respectfully urge that any real amendments to the existing Act be made as quickly as possible in order to stimulate the effective use of all available lending and building agencies, and to release credits now avail-

> able for this purpose from private sources. But this resolution is not to be construed as advocating public lending in competition with private agencies.

Ontario Associated Boards of Trade and Chambers of Commerce to King, 6 January 1936, King Papers, Vol. 219, p. 188325.

18. *Canadian Banker*, October 1936, p. 17.

19. Canada, *Parliamentary Debates* (Commons), 8 June 1938, p. 3653.

20. Ontario Associated Boards of Trade and Chambers of Commerce to King, 6 January 1936, King Papers, Volume 219, p. 188325; Canada, *Parliamentary Debates* (Commons), 8 June 1938, pp. 3658-60; Charles Dunning to King, 10 December 1937, King Papers, Vol. 234, p. 200726. Details of the Montreal plan are in Canada, Department of Labour Papers, Vol. 59.

21. *Financial Times*, 24 January 1938, p. 1; *Monthly Review, Bank of Nova Scotia*, June 1939, p. 4; King Diaries, 20 May 1938. The Bank of Nova Scotia stated in the *Monthly Review*:

> ...The reasons for emphasis on stimulating construction and particularly residential building, both in the [National Employment] Commission's Report and in recent Dominion legislation are sufficiently apparent. Since the unemployed are concentrated in this field, it is highly desirable that new opportunities should be of a kind that they are capable of grasping and it is because so much of the continued unemployment is attributable to depression in construction and associated heavy industries that a broad improvement in this group would do more to reduce unemployment and thus to promote the national welfare than a corresponding improvement in any other branch of Canadian industry.

22. Canada, House of Commons, Standing Committee on Banking and Commerce, *Minutes of Proceedings and Evidence Respecting Bill 132, an Act to Incorporate the Central Mortgage Bank*, 27 May 1939, pp. 7-9.

23. Standing Committee on Banking and Commerce, 30 May, 1939, p. 88.

24. Standing Committee on Banking and Commerce, 31 May, p.

iv; 30 May, p. 91; 31 May, p. 119; J.L. Ralston to T.A. Crerar, 10 October 1939, Canada, Department of Finance Papers, Volume 2675.

25. Canada, *Final Report of the National Employment Commission* (Ottawa: King's Printer, 1938); Canada, Department of Labour Papers, National Employment Commission Series, Volume 72.

26. Canada, Parliamentary Debates (Commons), 8 June 1938, pp. 3657-58; and 17 June, p. 3787.

27. *Timber of Canada*, April 1942, p. 16, lists organizations supporting NHA; S.E. Briard, manager, mortgage department, Sun Life, to J.L. Ilsley, Finance Minister, 25 April 1942, Canada, Department of Finance Papers, Volume 704; Hamilton Pressed Brick to King, 12 May 1942; Interprovincial Brick to King, 11 May 1942; Galt Board of Trade to Karl Homuth, MP, 19 March 1942; Moncton Board of Trade to Ilsley, 23 March 1942; Fort William Chamber of Commerce to Ilsley, 25 March 1942; Montreal Lumber Dealers Association to Ilsley, 18 March 1942; M.J. Smith, general manager, Equitable Life, to Ilsley, 6 July 1942; CCA to Ilsley (undated); R.W. Gould, general secretary, Canadian Builders Supply Association to Ilsley, 4 November 1942; all in Canada, Department of Finance Papers, Volume 706; *Building in Canada*, 31 March 1942, p. 3.

28. Brief on CMA to Canada, Royal Commission on Dominion-Provincial Relations, *Evidence*, pp. 6823-4, 8153; *National Employment Commission Report*, p. 34.

29. Chamber of Commerce support is elaborated in an editorial in *Commerce of the Nation*, January 1930, p. 1. Maritime financial difficulties resulting from highway-building are discussed in *Report of the Royal Commission on Dominion- Provincial Relations*; Ontario Associated Boards of Trade support in George Henry Papers, "OABOT" file, Public Archives of Ontario, Toronto.

30. Toronto District Construction Council to Croll, 20 May 1935; Deputy Minister Louis Fine to Croll, 26 June 1935; Home Builders Association to Croll, 11 March 1936; Harold Perkins, secretary of Toronto Building and Construction Association, to Croll, 2 March 1936; Builders Exchange Association to Croll, 4 May 1936; *Ontario*

Gazette, 28 November 1936; all in Industrial Standards Act Files, Department of Labour, Public Archives of Ontario, Toronto.
31. Quebec industry reaction is described by the president of the Canadian Construction Association, *Monetary Times*, 11 January 1936, p. 52.

VIII The Bank of Canada

1. See, for example, R.T. Naylor, "The Rise and Fall of the Third Commercial Empire of the St. Lawrence," in Gary Teeple, ed., *Capitalism and the National Question in Canada* (Toronto: University of Toronto Press, 1973), pp. 1-41. See also Kari Levitt, *Silent Surrender: The Multinational Corporation in Canada* (Toronto: Macmillan, 1970); and Daniel Drache, "Canadian Capitalism: Sticking with Staples," *This Magazine*, Vol. IX, No. 4 (July-August 1975), pp. 7-10.
2. The monetary debate of the inter-war period is best treated in Irving Brecher, *Monetary and Fiscal Thought and Policy in Canada, 1914-1939* (Toronto: University of Toronto Press, 1957). The central bank discussion of the post-war period is also treated in R. Craig McIvor, *Canadian Monetary, Banking and Fiscal Development* (Toronto: Macmillan of Canada, 1961), pp. 101-103, 109-111; and L.M. Grayson, "The Formation of the Bank of Canada, 1913-1938" (Ph.D. Thesis, University of Toronto, 1974), pp. 20-44. The extent of the Bank of Montreal's role as government banker is treated in Merrill Denison's sycophantic *Canada's First Bank: A History of the Bank of Montreal*, Volume Two (Toronto: McClelland and Stewart, 1967), p. 388.
3. Social Credit monetary and political theories are discussed in C.B. Macpherson, *Democracy in Alberta: Social Credit and the Party System* (Toronto: University of Toronto Press, 1953), pp. 93-119.
4. Canada, Royal Commission on Banking and Currency, *Proceedings*, Vol. I (Ottawa: King's Printer, 1933), p. 2727.
5. Canada, *Parliamentary Debates* (Commons), 17 April 1931, p. 710.
6. Canada, *Parliamentary Debates* (Commons), 14 November 1932, p. 1125.

7. Evidence of R.T. Evans, Northwestern Grain Dealers Association, Royal Commission on Banking and Currency, *Proceedings*, p. 1864.
8. Royal Commission on Banking and Currency, *Proceedings*, p. 1864.
9. *Ibid.*, p. 1714.
10. Evidence of John Ross, president, Canadian Chamber of Commerce, Royal Commission on Banking and Currency, *Proceedings*, p. 195.
11. Burton's support is noted by Mackenzie King in King Diaries, 28 November 1933; Beatty's support is mentioned in Beatty to King, 29 August 1933, King Papers, Vol. 195, p. 165189.
12. Ward Pitfield to R.B. Bennett, 16 October 1933, Bennett Papers, Vol. 776, pp. 475689-475690; E.A. Pickering to King, 29 November 1933, King Papers, Vol. 149, p. 108497.
13. Evidence of L.G. Beaubien, president, Montreal Stock Exchange, 7 September 1933, Royal Commission on Banking and Currency, *Proceedings*, pp. 2538-41.
14. Evidence of J.A. Macleod, president, Canadian Bankers Association, Royal Commission on Banking and Currency, *Proceedings*, 11 September 1933, p. 3359.
15. Royal Commission on Banking and Currency, *Proceedings*, pp. 3350-73, 3377-80.
16. Bank of Nova Scotia, *Monthly Review*, May 1933, Vol. VII, No. 5, p. 2.
17. King Papers, Vol. 149, p.108496.
18. Canada, *Report of the Royal Commission on Banking and Currency in Canada*, (Ottawa: King's Printer, 1933), p. 63.
19. Sir Charles Gordon in *Canadian Business*, December 1934, p. 29. Sir Thomas White to R.B. Bennett, 6 November 1933, Bennett Papers, Vol. 94, p. 63067; Bennett to White, 10 November 1933, Bennett Papers, Vol. 94, p. 63068.
20. Canadian Bankers Association to Bennett, 25 January 1934, Bennett Papers, Vol. 94, pp. 63365-6.
21. Bennett angrily wrote F.D.L. Smith, chief editor of the *Toronto Mail and Empire*, who had written Bennett that leading officials of the Imperial Bank opposed a central bank:

If the people must engage in conflict with those who worship

> profits as their god and who regard the welfare of the nation as being of secondary importance, then I know in which camp I will be enlisted. It is not too much to say that Rolph knows nothing at all about a central bank; and Phipps, who used to be a manager at Calgary, is concerned only about one thing and that is his balance sheet.

F.W.L. Smith to R.B. Bennett, 28 November 1933, Bennett Papers, Vol. 94, p. 62870; Bennett to Smith, 24 November 1933, Bennett Papers, Vol. 94, p. 62871.

22. Canada, *Parliamentary Debates* (Commons), 29 February 1932, p. 649. R. Craig McIvor notes that most bankers in the 1930s were disdainful of academic criticism of their operations. They claimed banks only lend the amount of savings which the public has seen fit to deposit with them or that banks only created credit in response to the needs of business. McIvor, *Canadian Monetary, Banking and Fiscal Development*, p. 127.

23. *Winnipeg Free Press*, 21 November 1933, p. 1.

24. *Loc. cit.*

25. Sir Thomas White to R.B. Bennett, 27 March 1934, Bennett Papers, Vol. 95, pp. 63551-3; Beaudry Leman to R.B. Bennett, 20 March 1934, Bennett Papers, Vol. 95, 63538-40 and 7 June 1934, Bennett Papers, Vol. 95, p. 63833.

26. *Journal of the Canadian Bankers Association*, October 1934, Vol. XLII, No. 1; W.C. Clark to Bennett, 27 June 1934, Bennett Papers, Vol. 95, p. 63597.

27. D.L. Morrell, "The Canadian Chamber of Commerce," *Canadian Banker*, July 1937, p. 410.

28. King Diaries, 28 March 1938.

29. Banking and Commerce Committee, 1939, *Proceedings*, pp. 149-50.

30. *Ibid.*, p. 151.

31. Canada, *Parliamentary Debates* (Commons), 8 March 1938, p. 1154.

32. *Loc. cit.*

33. Canada, *Parliamentary Debates* (Commons), 25 February 1937, p. 1215.

34. Canada, *Report of the National Employment Commission* (Ottawa: King's Printer, 1938), p. 25.

35. *Monetary Times*, 23 October 1937, p. 25.
36. These proposals were, for example, rejected by the Montreal Board of Trade in a communication by its secretary to the Select Standing Committee on Banking and Commerce, *Minutes of Proceedings and Evidence*, 27 March 1934, p. 210.
37. D.H. Miller-Barstow, *Beatty of the CPR: A Biography* (Toronto: McClelland and Stewart, 1950).
38. E.P. Neufeld, *The Financial System of Canada: Its Growth and Development* (New York: St. Martin's Press, 1972), pp. 137-38.
39. *Report of the Royal Commission on Banking*, p. 71.
40. Canada, *Parliamentary Debates* (Commons), 14 March 1932, pp. 1090-94.
41. *Ibid.*, pp. 1100, 1102.
42. King Diaries, 21 October 1932; 23 October 1932; E.P. Neufeld writes that the effect of the stock market collapse on Sun Life "has never to our knowledge been revealed in detail." Neufeld, *The Financial System of Canada*, p. 241.
43. Christopher Armstrong, "The Politics of Federalism: Ontario's Relations with the Federal Government, 1896-1941," Vol. 1 (Ph.D. Thesis, University of Toronto, 1972).
44. E.P. Neufeld, *The Financial System of Canada*, p. 241.
45. *Year Book of the Canadian Life Insurance Officers Association*, 16 November 1934, p. 13.
46. Canada, *Parliamentary Debates* (Commons), 7 June 1935, pp. 3422-23.
47. *Financial Post*, 17 February 1934, p. 8.
48. Thomas Bradshaw speech at the North American Life Insurance Company general meeting, 20 January 1936, quoted by J.S. Woodsworth, Canada, *Parliamentary Debates* (Commons), 5 May 1936, p. 2545.
49. *Financial Post*, 6 January 1934, p. 6.
50. *Financial Times*, 15 June 1934, p. 8.

IX Dominion-Provincial Relations

1. See, for example, H.V. Nelles, *The Politics of Development: Forests, Mines and Hydro-Electric Power in Ontario, 1849-1941*

(Toronto: Macmillan, 1974); and H.F. Quinn, *The Union Nationale: A Study in Quebec Nationalism* (Toronto: University of Toronto Press, 1949).

2. Rulings of the Judicial Committee are detailed in R.A. Olmstead, *Canadian Constitutional Decisions of the Judicial Committee*, Vol. I-III (Ottawa: Queen's Printer, 1950); rulings from the 1930s are listed in C.P. Plaxton, ed., *Canadian Constitutional Decisions of the Judicial Committee of the Privy Council, 1930 to 1939* (Ottawa: King's Printer, 1939).

3. Evidence of Canadian Chamber of Commerce, Royal Commission on Dominion-Provincial Relations, *Report of Hearings*, Ottawa, 20 May 1938, p. 9504. The journal of the Chamber called the appointment of the commission a "signal victory" for "Canadian business," which it said had conducted a "persistent and well-directed campaign" for the commission. *Canadian Business*, March 1937, p. 36.

4. *Report of Hearings*, 20 May 1938, pp. 9504-11.

5. *Ibid.*, p. 9513.

6. *Loc. cit.*

7. *Report of the National Employment Commission* (Ottawa: King's Printer, 1938), p. 34.

8. *Report of Hearings*, 12 May 1938, pp. 9513-14.

9. *Ibid.*, pp. 9524-26.

10. Evidence of Montreal Board of Trade, *Report of Hearings*, 12 May 1938, pp. 8141, 8152.

11. *Ibid.*, p. 8153.

12. *Ibid.*, p. 8146.

13. Evidence of Canadian Life Insurance Officers Association, *Report of Hearings*, 18 January 1938, pp. 2527-29.

14. *Ibid.*, 18 January 1938, p. 2526.

15. Christopher Armstrong, "The Politics of Federalism: Ontario's Relations with the Federal Government, 1896-1941, Vol. I," (Ph.D. Thesis, University of Toronto, 1972), pp. 88, 92-94.

16. J.C. Johnston and Morley Smith, Canadian Chain Store Association, *Report of Hearings*, 27 April 1938, pp. 7003-4, 7009-22.

17. *Report of Hearings*, 18 January 1938, pp. 2513, 2501.

18. Evidence of All-Canada Insurance Federation, *Report of Hearings*, 18 January 1938, pp. 2555, 2581.

19. Evidence of Associated Boards of Trade of British Columbia,

Report of Hearings, 23 March 1938, p. 5403.

20. Evidence of Investment Dealers Association of Canada, *Report of Hearings*, 24 January 1938, p. 3205.

21. *Financial Post*, 20 April 1935, p. 1.

22. *Record of Proceedings, Dominion-Provincial Conference, 1935, Ottawa, December 9-13, 1935* (Ottawa: King's Printer, 1936), pp. 44, 46 in C.H. Cahan Papers, Vol. 9, Public Archives of Canada, Ottawa.

23. D.L. Morrell, "The Canadian Chamber of Commerce," *Canadian Banker, July 1937, pp. 409-10.*

24. Financial Post, 6 April 1935, p. 1; King Diaries, 24 November 1937; Neil McKenty, *Mitch Hepburn* (Toronto: McClelland and Stewart, 1967), pp. 65-9, 155; E.N. Rhodes to Morris Wilson, president of the Royal Bank, 5 April 1935; Armstrong, "Politics of Federalism," p. 339.

25. Charles Dunning to C. Cockcroft, provincial treasurer of Alberta, 17 March 1936, King Papers, Vol. 215, p. 185284; Dunning to William Aberhart, 30 March 1936, King Papers, Vol. 215, p. 185295.

26. Henry Morgan, president, Canadian Chamber of Commerce, to King, 23 October 1937, King Papers, Vol. 239, p. 205606; E.W. Beatty, president of CPR, to King, 27 May 1938, King Papers, Vol. 245, p. 210250; King Diaries, 19 May 1938, p. 374; Donald V. Smiley, ed., *The Rowell-Sirois Report* (Toronto: McClelland and Stewart, 1963); an in-depth study of Edmonton-Ottawa relations in this period is J.R. Mallory, *Social Credit and the Federal Power in Canada* (Toronto: University of Toronto Press, 1954).

27. S.G. Dobson, president, Canadian Bankers Association, *Report of Hearings*, 24 January 1938, pp. 3135-67, 3180.

28. Evidence of W.D. Black, first vice-president, Canadian Manufacturers Association, *Report of Hearings*, 17 January 1938, pp. 2329-30.

29. *Report of Hearings*, 26 April 1938, pp. 6823-27, 6839.

30. *Report of Hearings*, 17 January 1938, pp. 2373, 2388-92.

31. *Ibid.*, pp. 2340, 2366.

32. *Report of Hearings*, p. 2431; Evidence of John Imrie, Edmonton Chamber of Commerce, *Report of Hearings*, 3 March 1938, p. 6035.

33. F. Kent Hamilton, general counsel, Ontario Association of

Real Estate Boards, *Report of Hearings*, 19 January 1938, p. 2730.
34. Brief of Vancouver Real Estate Exchange, *Report of Hearings*, 23 March 1938, p. 5523.
35. T. D'Arcy Leonard for Dominion Mortgage and Loans Association, *Report of Hearings*, 27 April 1938, pp. 6921, 6970, 6980.
36. King Diaries, 9 February 1938.
37. Primary Products Publishing Company brief, *Report of Hearings*, 23 March 1938, p. 5765.
38. *Report of Hearings*, 23 March 1938, p. 5769.
39. H.R. MacMillan for Associated Boards of Trade of British Columbia, *Report of Hearings*, 23 March 1938, pp. 5393-5408.
40. Rene Morin for Montreal District Chamber of Commerce, *Report of Hearings*, 12 May 1938, pp. 8224, 8228.
41. *Ibid.*, p. 8228.
42. *Ibid.*, p. 8230.
43. Hughes also mentions that the Montreal Board of Trade represented largely English-speaking business with large capital investments while the Montreal District Chamber of Commerce represented largely small French-speaking operations. Everett Cherrington Hughes, *French Canada in Transition* (Chicago: University of Chicago Press, 1945), p. 203. The Dun and Bradstreet analysis used by Hughes is based on 10,964 Montreal firms rated in the *Dun and Bradstreet Directory* of 1935. Hughes also mentions that of the directorates of 83 of the largest corporations with headquarters in Montreal, 768 were held by English-speaking people and only 93 by French-speaking.
44. Gerald Fortin, "Le Nationalisme Canadien-Francais et les Classes Sociales," *Revue Historique de l'Amerique Française,* XXXII, No. 4 (March 1969), pp. 523-37.
45. Robert Rumilly, *Premier Gouvernement Duplessis: Histoire de la Province de Quebec*, XXVII (Ottawa: Fides, 1968), p. 88.
46. Canada, *Report of the Royal Commission on Dominion-Provincial Relations*, Book Two: *Recommendations* (Ottawa: King's Printer, 1940).
47. *Recommendations*.
48. *Recommendations,* pp. 151, 157, 270-74.
49. J.H. Stewart Reid, Kenneth McNaught, Harry S. Crowe, *A Source-Book of Canadian History* (Toronto: Longmans, 1959).

The CCF's Regina Manifesto, with its concentration on a series of central planning boards to plan the economy and redistribute wealth, indicates the lack of concern of 1930s socialists with the question of citizens' participation. Current social democratic attempts to effect a compromise between the demands of central planning and local participation are discussed in Charles Taylor, *The Pattern of Politics* (Toronto: McClelland and Stewart, 1971).

50. Frank Underhill, "Nationalism and Provincialism," in Violet Anderson, ed., *Problems in Canadian Unity: Lectures Given at the Canadian Institute on Economics and Politics*, August 6 to 19, 1938 (Toronto: Thomas Nelson and Sons, 1938), pp. 67-78.

51. J.W. Pickersgill, ed., *The Mackenzie King Record*, Vol. I (Toronto: University of Toronto Press, 1960), pp. 145, 161-62. The Liberal Government of Quebec (1939-1944) led by Premier Adelard Godbout was beholden to the federal Liberals for its existence. Federal Liberal cabinet ministers from Quebec had threatened to resign should the nationalist Duplessis government with its recalcitrant opposition to the War Measures Act be returned as the provincial government. *King Record*, pp. 35-36.

52. Alexander Brady, "Contradictory Post-War Trends in Canadian Federalism," in Paul Fox, ed., *Politics Canada: Problems in Canadian Government*, 2nd ed. (Toronto: McGraw-Hill, 1966); J. Stefan Dupre, "Contracting Out: A Funny Thing Happened on the Way to the Centennial," *Politics Canada*, pp. 168-76.

53. H.V. Nelles and Christopher Armstrong, "Private Property in Peril: Ontario Businessmen and the Federal System, 1898-1911," *Business History Review*, Vol XLVII, No. 2, Summer, 1973, pp. 158-60.

54. Underhill, "Nationalism and Provincialism," p. 74. Though Underhill had observed that business had used nationalism in its own self-interest in earlier periods, he believed business interests were opposing centralization in 1938:

> There are interests in this country who do not want effective government action at all. They do not want to have their opportunities for making profit as they see fit regulated by any government. They know that the provincial governments are not big enough to regulate or control them. And so they are advocates of "provincial rights." It is not an accidental coin-

cidence that the politicians and newspapers who are most vehement in shouting about provincial rights are those of Ontario and Quebec where our big business interests are concentrated.

X The Radical Alternatives

1. Part of the philosophy of the British Labour party was that the interests of workers and capitalists could be harmonized by the election of a government that was sympathetic to labour's cause and that was willing to use the legislative process to improve labour's position within the capitalist system.
2. *Canadian Unionist*, September 1935, p. 102.
3. J.H. Stewart Reid, Kenneth S. McNaught, Harry Crowe, *A Source-Book of Canadian History* (Toronto: Longmans, Green, 1960), pp. 419-423.
4. The most complete account of the League for Social Reconstruction is Michiel Horn, "League for Social Reconstruction: Socialism and Nationalism in Canada, 1931-45" (Ph.D Thesis, University of Toronto, 1969).
5. Frank Underhill, "Bentham and Benthamism," *Queen's Quarterly*, November 1932, p. 663; see also Frank Underhill, "Fabians and Fabianism," *Canadian Forum*, March 1946, pp. 277-80; April, 1946, pp. 8-12. See also Walter Young, *Anatomy of a Party: The National CCF, 1932-1961* (Toronto: University of Toronto Press, 1969), pp. 48, 49.
6. Reid, McNaught, Crowe, *Source-Book*.
7. See Young, *Anatomy of a Party*, pp. 50-3.
8. *Canadian Congress Journal*, February 1933, p. 7. The ACCL included unions among workers in the building trades, the railways, marine transport, general transport, clothing, communication, distributive trades, electrical trades, entertainment, lumbering and woodworking, metal trades, municipal services, power engineering and food processing.
9. *Canadian Unionist*, June 1935, pp. 26-8.
10. *Ibid.*, p. 6.
11. *Ibid.*, p. 7.

12. Colin McKay, "Wage Policy and Recovery," *Canadian Unionist*, June 1935, pp. 239-40, 251-2.
13. *Canadian Unionist*, June 1935, p. 6.
14. Gad Horowitz, *Canadian Labour in Politics* (Toronto: University of Toronto Press, 1968), pp. 234-241, 255.
15. *Canadian Congress Journal*, February 1932, p. 11.
16. *Canadian Congress Journal*, October 1933, p. 10; Trades and Labour Congress of Canada, *Report of the Proceedings of the 51st Annual Convention*, 1935, pp. 101-02; *Report of the Proceedings of the 55th Annual Convention*, p. 101.
17. Trades and Labour Congress, *Proceedings of the 52nd Annual Convention*, 1936, p. 198.
18. Trades and Labour Congress, *Report of the Proceedings of the 48th Annual Convention*, 1932, pp. 132-4.
19. Ivan Avakumovic, *The Communist Party in Canada: A History* (Toronto: McClelland and Stewart, 1975), pp. 71-75.
20. This is the general assumption of the standard trade union history of Canada, *Trade Unions in Canada: Their Development and Functioning* (Toronto: Macmillan, 1948). The opposite point of view is suggested in Stuart Jamieson, *Times of Trouble: Labour Unrest and Industrial Conflict in Canada, 1900-1966* (Ottawa: Queen's Printer, 1971).
21. Robertson said workers would enjoy trade union membership rights "only so long as the organization to which they belong is not one which has for its purpose the destruction of industry and of existing institutions." His government passed an order- in-council on 21 July, 1920, requiring striking miners in Alberta's Crow's Nest Pass region to become members of the United Mine Workers. The strikers wanted recognition of the One Big Union as their bargaining agent. Martin Robin, *Radical Politics and Canadian Labour, 1880-1930* (Kingston: Industrial Relations Centre, Queen's University, 1930), p. 191.
22. *Labour Leader*, 21 December 1934, p. 2.
23. *Canadian Labour Defender*, 1932, 1933, 1934.
24. C.B. Macpherson, *Democracy in Alberta* (Toronto: University of Toronto Press, 1953).
25. It is interesting to speculate whether socialist farmers in Alberta would not have done better to establish a separate party outside the

UFA rather than to take over the party only to find that the government using the party's name refused to be dictated to by the annual conventions. The Saskatchewan membership of the United Farmers of Canada, free from any association with past or present governments in Saskatchewan, was to enjoy great success while the UFA-CCF was stillborn.
26. *UFA*, 1 February 1930, p. 7.
27. *UFA*, 1 February 1932, p. 7.
28. *UFA*, 1 March 1932, p. 24.
29. C.H. Douglas, *Social Credit* (Hawthorn, Calif.: Omni Publications, 1966).
30. Louis Even, *Salvation Island* (1938, Ottawa: Regards, 1975).

XI Business and the Reform Process

1. H.M. Cassidy, "An Unemployment Policy: Some Proposals," in J.R.H. Wilbur, ed., *The Bennett New Deal: Fraud or Portent?* (Toronto: Copp Clark, 1968), p. 33.
2. "Remarks on the History of Inflation: An Address Given before the Liberal-Conservative Summer School at Newmarket, September 1933 by J.M. Macdonnell," p. 15. J.M. Macdonnell Papers, Vol. 52, Queen's University Archives, Kingston.
3. "The Canadian Institute of Economics and Politics, Report of the Addresses and Editorial Comment from the *Orillia Packet and Times*, Verbatim Address by J.M. Macdonnell," p. 7, J.M. Macdonnell Papers, Vol. 52, Queen's University Archives, Kingston.
4. *Orillia Packet and Times*, p. 14.
5. *Loc. cit.*
6. J.L. Granatstein, *The Politics of Survival: The Conservative Party of Canada, 1939-1945* (Toronto: University of Toronto Press, 1967), pp. 209-10.
7. Canada, *Final Report of the National Employment Commission* (Ottawa: King's Printer, 1938), pp. 6, 39-40.
8. Owen Libby, Montreal Board of Trade, Royal Commission on Dominion-Provincial Relations, *Report of Hearings*, 12 May 1938, p. 8141.
9. *Report of Hearings*, 12 May 1938, p. 8151.
10. *Ibid.*, p. 8152.
11. *Ibid.*, p. 8153.

12. In 1930 only 129,663 of ten million Canadians paid income taxes. An income of $3000 was required before taxes were assessed. By the 1970s most income-earners in Canada were required to pay income taxes. Personal exemptions had been reduced and, in any event, inflation and increases in productivity combined to make an income of $3000 a poverty income, whereas in the 1930s it had been a comfortable income. As observed in Chapter VI, taxes by the 1970s were considered to be regressive at the lower end of the income scale. R.B. Bennett, Canada, *Parliamentary Debates* (Commons), 6 May 1930, p. 1831; Allan Maslove, *The Pattern of Taxation in Canada* (Ottawa: Queen's Printer, 1972).
13. See Garth Stevenson, "Federalism and the Political Economy of the Canadian State," in Leo Panitch (ed.), *The Canadian State* (Toronto: University of Toronto Press, 1977).

BIBLIOGRAPHY

1. Theories of Business-State Relations

There is abundant literature on the role of the state in capitalist societies. Among the best general works from a Marxist perspective are Ralph Miliband, *The State in Capitalist Society: An Analysis of the Western System of Power* (London: Weidenfeld and Nicholson, 1969) and Nicos Poulantzas, *Political Power and Social Classes* (London: New Left Books, 1973). A standard liberal interpretation is provided by Robert A. Dahl in *Pluralist Democracy in the United States: Conflict and Consent* (Chicago: Rand, McNally, 1967); a more critical view of liberal democracy, from a liberal perspective, is offered by Anthony Downs in *An Economic Theory of Democracy* (New York: Harper and Row, 1957).

There are several important historical works on the evolution of state-business relations in the United States. These include Gabriel Kolko's study of reform in the Progressive era, *The Triumph of Conservatism: A Reinterpretation of American History, 1900-16* (New York: Free Press of Glencoe, 1963) and Robert H. Wiebe's more conservative assessment of the same period, *The Search for Order, 1877-1920* (Boston: Hill and Wang, 1967). An excellent bibliographic essay on the reform question in the United States is Thomas K. McCraw's "Regulation in America: A Review Article," *Business History Review,* XLIX, No. 2, Summer 1975, pp. 165-183.

An interesting study of the backlash by American business in the 1970s against reforms it had previously endorsed is James O'Connor's *The Fiscal Crisis of the State* (New York: St. Martin's Press, 1973), which deals with the business attack against state social programs and public service salaries. On the evolution of the government's role in the British economy see Samuel H. Beer's *British Politics in the Collectivist Age* (New York: Alfred A. Knopf, 1965); the confusion of the British capitalist class in the 1970s over the question of state intervention is detailed in Andrew Gamble and Paul Walton's *Capitalism in Crisis: Inflation and the State* (London: Macmillan, 1976).

The inability of welfare state policies to redistribute wealth or power is discussed by Gabriel Kolko in *Wealth and Power in America: An Analysis of Social Class and Income Distribution* (New York: F.A. Praeger, 1962); and, for Britain, by Richard A. Titmuss in *Income Distribution and Social Change* (London: George Allen and Unwin, 1962).

2. Business and Government in Canada

There are no general texts with a critical analysis of the Canadian state. But important monographs and essay collections on various aspects of Canadian government have appeared in recent years. The best collection of essays is Leo Panitch's *The Canadian State: Political Economy and Political Power* (Toronto: University of Toronto Press, 1977), which includes theoretical and historical material on the nature of the Canadian state, the decision-making process in Canada and business-government relations. A number of interesting essays appear in a collection from the Marxist Institute of Toronto, *Imperialism, Nationalism and Canada* (New Hogtown Press/Between the Lines, 1977).

The most thorough study of the Canadian ruling class and its power in government is Wallace Clement's *The Canadian Corporate Elite: An Analysis of Economic Power* (Toronto: McClelland and Stewart, 1975). Robert Presthus provides abundant statistical data (though few specific examples) of business control of government decision-making in *Elite Accommodation in Canadian Politics* (Cambridge: Cambridge University Press, 1970). Control of Canada's political parties is analyzed by Khayam Zev Paltiel in *Political Party Financing in Canada* (Toronto: McGraw-Hill Ryerson, 1970); and by Reginald Whitaker in *The Government Party: Organizing and Financing the Liberal Party of Canada, 1930-1958* (Toronto: University of Toronto Press, 1977). Though there is no critical study of the Conservative party to complement Whitaker's masterful study of the Liberals, there is useful information in J.L.

Granatstein's *The Politics of Survival: The Conservative Party of Canada, 1939-1945* (Toronto: University of Toronto Press, 1967). Granatstein also supplements Whitaker's study in "Financing the Liberal Party, 1935-1949," Michael Cross and Robert Bothwell (eds.), *Policy by Other Means: Essays in Honour of C.P. Stacey* (Toronto: Clarke Irwin, 1972), pp. 179-199.

Important historical works dealing with the evolution of government involvement in the Canadian economy include J.A. Corry's *The Growth of Government Activities Since Confederation: A Study Prepared for the Royal Commission on Dominion-Provincial Relations* (Ottawa: King's Printer, 1939); and Hugh G.J. Aitken's "Defensive Expansionism: The State and Economic Growth in Canada," in Hugh G.J. Aitken (ed.), *The State and Economic Growth: Papers of a Conference Held on October 11-13 under the Auspices of the Committee on Economic Growth* (New York: Social Science Research Council, 1959), pp. 79-114. An interesting study from a conservative point of view of the harmful effect to the public purse of close business-government cooperation on large projects is Philip Mathias' *Forced Growth: Five Studies of Government Involvement in the Development of Canada* (Toronto: James, Lewis and Samuel, 1971). Two historical studies, one dealing with a provincial government, the other a municipal government, carefully demonstrate the extent of business control of government decisions: H.V. Nelles' *The Politics of Development: Forest, Mines and Hydro-Electric Power in Ontario, 1849-1941* (Toronto: Macmillan, 1974); and Alan F.J. Artibise's *Winnipeg: A Social History of Urban Growth, 1874-1919* (Montreal: McGill-Queen's University Press, 1975).

Useful historical works dealing with specific areas of government policy include Chester Martin's *Dominion Lands Policy* (Toronto: Macmillan, 1938), which deals with government involvement in the development of Western Canada; and John H. Dales' *Hydroelectricity and Industrial Development: Quebec, 1898-1940* (Cambridge, Mass.: Harvard University Press, 1957). There are two excellent histories of labour legislation in Canada. While obviously dated, A.E. Grauer's *Labour Legislation: A Study Prepared for the Royal Commission on Dominion-Provincial Relations* (Ottawa: King's Printer, 1939) is a thorough account of labour legislation and its enforcement at federal and provincial levels of government to the end of the thirties. A more up-to-date work is Stuart Jamieson's *Industrial Relations in Canada* (Toronto: Macmillan, 1973, 2nd ed.). Jamieson is also the author of the most thorough and insightful account of twentieth-century labour strife and the role of governments in this strife, *Times of Trouble: Labour Unrest and Industrial Conflict in Canada, 1900-66* (Ottawa: Queen's Printer, 1968).

There are no worthwhile historical accounts of social legislation in Canada. However, some descriptive materials are available. They include R.B. Splane's *Social Welfare in Ontario, 1791-1893: A Study of Public Welfare Administration* (Toronto: University of Toronto Press, 1965); and Dennis Trevor Guest's "The Development of Income Maintenance Programmes in Canada, 1945-1967" (unpublished Ph.D. thesis, University of London, 1968). A perceptive statistical study of the rather slight redistributive impact of social welfare programs in Canada is Allan Maslove's *The Pattern of Taxation in Canada* (Ottawa: Queen's Printer, 1972).

The attitudes of the state towards combines have received much critical attention. Though somewhat dated, Lloyd G. Reynolds' *The Control of Competition in Canada* (Cambridge, Mass.: Harvard University Press, 1940) provides the best historical account of the extent to which governments in Canada have promoted combines in industry. A more recent but less perceptive account is L.A. Skeoch's *Restrictive Trade Practices in Canada* (Toronto: McClelland and Stewart, 1966). Two articles with useful historical information on anti-combines policy are Michael Bliss' "Another Anti-Trust Tradition: Canadian Anti-Combines Policy, 1889-1910," *Business History Review* XLVII, No. 2, Summer, 1973, pp. 177-189; and H.G. Thorburn's "Pressure Groups in Canadian Politics: Recent Revisions of the Anti-Combines Legislation," *Canadian Journal of Economics and Political Science,* XXX, No. 2, May, 1964, pp. 157-74. Among important empirical studies on this question, the best are: Thomas D. Traves "The Board of Commerce and the Canadian Sugar Refining Industry: A Speculation on the Role of the State in Canada," *Canadian Historical Review*, LV, No. 2, June, 1974, pp. 159-175; and J.C.H. Jones "Mergers and Competition: The Brewing Case," *Canadian Jour-*

nal of Economics and Political Science, XXXIII, No. 4, November, 1967, pp. 551-568.

There are several studies that contain significant information on the relations between the various levels of government in Canada. Although it deals with only one province, the most analytical study is Christopher Armstrong's "The Politics of Federalism: Ontario's Relations with the Federal Government, 1896-1941" (unpublished Ph.D. thesis, University of Toronto, 1972). Helpful standard references include W.A. Mackintosh's *The Economic Background of Dominion-Provincial Relations*, (Ottawa: King's Printer, 1939); J.A. Maxwell's *Federal Subsidies to the Provincial Governments in Canada,* Harvard Economic Studies, Vol. LVI (Cambridge, Mass.: Harvard University Press, 1937); and Donald V. Smiley's (ed.) *The Rowell-Sirois Report*, Book One, (Toronto: McClelland and Stewart, 1963).

3. Histories of Canadian Business

There are a number of excellent histories of Canadian business. From a Marxist perspective, the most complete of these is Tom Naylor's two-volume *The History of Canadian Business* (Toronto: James Lorimer, 1975), which documents the historical preference of Canada's businessmen for commercial activities over manufacturing activities. Naylor argues that this entrepreneurial conservatism allowed American investors to take over the industrial sector of the Canadian economy. The myth of social mobility within Canadian business is presented in T.W. Acheson's unpublished University of Toronto dissertation, "The Social Origins of Canadian Industrialism: A Study in the Structure of Entrepreneurship, 1880-1910." The best collection of essays on Canadian business history is Glenn Porter and Robert Cuff's *Enterprise and National Development: Essays in Canadian Business and Economic History* (Toronto: Hakkert, 1973); more uneven is David S. Macmillan (ed.), *Canadian Business History: Selected Studies, 1497-1971* (Toronto: McClelland and Stewart, 1971).

Business ideology is skilfully presented in Michael Bliss' *A Living Profit: Studies in the Social History of Canadian Business, 1883-1911* (Toronto: McClelland and Stewart, 1974). Bliss' account, while it is well-written and covers a wide range of topics, is generally uncritical of business rhetoric.

A useful study of government-business links is Libby C. Park and Frank W. Park's *Anatomy of Big Business* (Toronto: Lorimer, 1973). A muck-raking history of the development of capitalism in Canada until the late nineteenth century is covered in Gustavus Myers' *History of Canadian Wealth* (Toronto: Lorimer, 1972).

Although most of the standard economic histories are dry reading, Kenneth Buckley's *Capital Formation in Canada, 1896-1930*, which relates the growth of western Canada to the expansion of business activity in the nation as a whole, is well worth reading.

Among the better histories of particular Canadian industries are O.W. Main's *The Canadian Nickel Industry: A Study in Market Control and Public Policy* (Toronto: University of Toronto Press, 1955); L. Ethan Ellis' *Newsprint Producers, Publishers and Political Pressures* (Rutgers, New Jersey: Rutgers University Press, 1960); and H.A. Innis (ed)., *The Dairy Industry in Canada* (Toronto: Ryerson: 1937). Sources on the development of Canadian banking include E.P. Neufeld's *The Financial System of Canada: Its Growth and Development* (Toronto: Macmillan, 1972); and R. Craig McIvor's *Canadian Monetary, Banking and Fiscal Development* (Toronto: Macmillan, 1961).

Business organizations have received little attention since the now dated study by S.D. Clark, *The Canadian Manufacturers' Association: A Study in Collective Bargaining and Political Pressure* (Toronto: University of Toronto Press, 1939). There are also few revealing biographies of Canadian businessmen.

4. The Depression

There are monographs of varying quality on most aspects of the Depression of the 1930s. Michiel Horn's collection, *The Dirty Thirties: Canadians in the Great Depression* (Toronto: Copp Clark, 1972), deals with the views of political and business leaders, as well as ordinary people, and summarizes major events of the period. The best overview of the Canadian economy in the period is A.E. Safarian's *The Canadian Economy in the Great Depression* (Toronto: McClelland and Stewart, 1970). Canada's poor economic performance is related to the economic downturn in all capitalist countries in the 1930s in Edward Marcus' *Canada and the International Business Cycle, 1927-1939* (New York: Bookman

Associates, 1954). Economic attitudes in the decade are assessed in Irving Brecher's *Monetary and Fiscal Thought and Policy in Canada, 1919-1939* (Toronto: University of Toronto Press, 1957). Sources on unemployment and the relief programs provided for the unemployed include H.M. Cassidy's *Unemployment and Relief in Ontario, 1929-1932* (Toronto: Dent, 1932); and Lother Richter (ed.), *Canada's Unemployment Problems* (Toronto: Macmillan, 1939).

The problems of the wheat economy and the government response are most critically examined by Vernon C. Fowke in *The National Policy and the Wheat Economy* (Toronto: University of Toronto Press, 1957); other good accounts are G.E. Britnell's *The Wheat Economy* (Toronto: University of Toronto Press, 1939) and D.A. McGibbon's *The Canadian Grain Trade 1931-1951* (Toronto: University of Toronto Press, 1952).

Labour unrest in the period and the resulting push for industrial unions are examined in Stuart Jamieson's *Times of Trouble* and Irving M. Abella's *Nationalism, Communism and Canadian Labour: The CIO, the Communist Party and the Canadian Congress of Labour, 1935-1956* (Toronto: University of Toronto Press, 1973).

The available political biographies of the major political figures of the period, R.B. Bennett and Mackenzie King, are shallow. But Kenneth McNaught's *A Prophet in Politics: A Biography of J.S. Woodsworth* (Toronto: University of Toronto Press, 1959) is an illuminating study of the first leader of the Co-operative Commonwealth Federation. *Social Planning for Canada*, written by the Research Committee of the League for Social Reconstruction, the CCF brain trust, (reprinted by University of Toronto Press, 1975), was the major theoretical work by the Left of the period. It provides a detailed analysis of political and economic life from a social democratic point of view. While the Communist party produced no equivalent work, it also played a large role in organizing opposition to unemployment and particularly in organizing trade unions. Oscar Ryan's hagiography of Tim Buck, *Tim Buck: A Conscience for Canada* (Toronto: Progress Books, 1975), documents the party's contribution. On the political right, the Social Credit party was the outstanding new protest movement of the period. The ideology and the rise of this movement is brilliantly examined in C.B. Macpherson's *Democracy in Alberta: Social Credit and the Party System* (Toronto: University of Toronto Press, 1953).

Good works on daily life and suffering in the unemployment decade include Barry Broadfoot's *Ten Lost Years, 1929-1939: Memories of Canadians Who Survived the Depression* (Toronto: Doubleday, 1973); James Gray's *The Winter Years: The Depression and the Prairies* (Toronto: Macmillan, 1966); L.M. Grayson and Michael Bliss' *The Wretched of Canada: Letters to R.B. Bennett, 1930-35* (Toronto: University of Toronto Press, 1971); and Victor Hoar (ed.), *Recollections of the On-to-Ottawa Trek by Ronald Liversedge* (Toronto: McClelland and Stewart, 1973).

5. Histories of the Thirties

A good general history of the 1930s in Canada remains to be written, but there are many primary sources available to a researcher. The Public Archives of Canada includes the extensive papers of R.B. Bennett and Mackenzie King, as well as King's strange but lengthy diaries, and the papers of lesser politicians of the period, such as Harry Stevens and C.H. Cahan. The Public Archives of Ontario has the papers of premiers George Henry and Mitchell Hepburn.

Businessmen, unlike politicians, have left little to the public record and most of what is in manuscript collections appears to have been well-sifted. But careful readings—particularly between the lines—of business periodicals and annual reports of business organizations reveal much about the thoughts and actions of the country's economic leaders. For the 1930s the *Financial Post* and the *Monetary Times* are the most useful sources. *Canadian Business* and *Industrial Canada* provide respectively the official opinions of the Canadian Chamber of Commerce and the Canadian Manufacturers Association.

Of inestimable value are the statements of business leaders and organizations, as well as other groups, before the large number of royal commissions and special committees of the House of Commons set up in the decade. Some of the hearings worth reading include the Special Committee and the Royal Commission on Price Spreads and Mass Buying; the Royal Grain Inquiry Commission; the Royal Commission on the Textile Industry; the Special Committee of the House of Commons on Housing; the Royal Commission on Banking and Currency; and the Royal Commission on Dominion-Provincial Relations. The reports of these commissions and committees are a wealth of information about the period. Other important reports include the 1938 report of the National Employment Commission and the large number of reports on combines made by the Combines Registrar during the decade.

INDEX